Leadership and Command
The Anglo-American Military Experience
Since 1861

LEADERSHIP AND COMMAND

The Anglo-American Military Experience since 1861

EDITED BY
G. D. SHEFFIELD

BRASSEY'S

First English Edition 1997
This revised paperback edition 2002

Brassey's

A member of **Chrysalis** Books plc

64 Brewery Road
London N7 9NT

Library of Congress Cataloging in Publication Data
available

British Library Cataloguing in Publication Data
A catalogue record for this book is available
from the British Library

ISBN 1 85753 366 6

Printed & bound by Creative Print & Design
Ebbw Vale, Wales

Dedicated to the members of the
British Commission for Military History

CONTENTS

ACKNOWLEDGEMENTS

The editor and contributors are grateful to the following publishers for permission to quote from copyrighted material:

Excerpt from H.N. Schwarzkopf and P. Petre, *It Doesn't Take a Hero*, courtesy Bantam Doubleday Dell

Excerpt from *Three Years With Grant* by Sylvanus Cadwallader, ed. Benjamin P. Thomas. Copyright 1955 Benjamin P. Thomas. Reprinted by permission of Alfred A. Knopf Inc.

Excerpt from B. Fergusson, *Beyond the Chindwin*, courtesy of HarperCollins *Publishers*.

Excerpt from B. Bond (ed.) *Fallen Stars*, courtesy Brassey's (UK) Ltd

Excerpts from interviews with Brigadier Sir Alexander Stanier and General Fox-Pitt courtesy Imperial War Museum Sound Archive.

Excerpt from the Haig Papers, courtesy Trustees of the National Library of Scotland

Crown copyright material in the Public Records Office and the Imperial War Museum appears by permission of the Controller of Her Majesty's Stationary Office.

To anyone whose copyright we have unwittingly infringed, in spite of our best efforts to contact copyright holders, we offer our sincere apologies.

PREFACE

This book has its origins in a series of British Commission for Military History (BCMH) conferences on command and leadership. Command, in particular, is a subject that has yet to receive the attention it deserves, and the success of the first conference encouraged the officers of the BCMH to move towards publication. While these conferences covered more than just the experiences of the United States and British armies, at the suggestion of Brassey's Major General Tony Trythall, we limited this book to that theme in order to give some shape to what threatened to be an unmanageably large project. For the same reason, we have not attempted to cover all aspects of the subject, which is clearly in need of further research. More comparative studies would be especially useful, along the lines of Robert O'Neill's chapter in this volume, in which he provides a partial exception to our rule by examining the Australian and New Zealand experience alongside that of the British and American.

The BCMH is an organisation that brings together working historians to advance knowledge of military history, broadly defined. Many of Britain's leading academic historians are members, but the BCMH's membership is not drawn solely from 'professional' historians from universities, the armed forces, military academies and museums. Lay people such as civil servants, journalists and lawyers who share a commitment to scholarly research in the field of military history make up a significant proportion of the membership. A BCMH conference serves as a valuable forum for lively and informed debate on a particular theme. Subjects as diverse as colonial warfare, the First World War, military biographies, naval warfare, air power and the use of literature for the military historian have been discussed over the last few years, with papers being presented on aspects of the military history of many countries in many different periods.

One of the most pleasurable aspects of writing or editing a book is that it puts one in a position to thank one's friends and colleagues. The BCMH has thrived under the leadership of its current president, Professor Brian Bond of the Department of War Studies, King's College London. I am very grateful for the support he has given me during my time as BCMH Secretary-General, and especially in playing a key role in gathering such a distinguished team of contributors to this present volume. I would also like to thank John Lee, Treasurer of the BCMH, for his outstanding contribution to the Commission over the last seven years; Chris McCarthy and Kate Mazur for their invaluable assistance with numerous mundane but important administrative tasks; Martine and Nigel de Lee for their work on BCMH battlefield tours; and Ray Sibbald and Will Coster, our new partners at ISWAS, De Montfort University Bedford, for their enthusiastic support of the BCMH. The present officers have built on the pioneering work of our predecessors, especially Christopher Duffy, David Chandler and Peter Simkins.

It is particularly fitting that Brassey's are publishing this book, as their sponsorship of the BCMH in the early 1990s helped the Commission to expand its activities. Our thanks are due to Major General Tony Trythall and Jenny Shaw for their staunch support over the years, and to Robert Zealley, my editor at Brassey's, for his forbearance.

Finally, I would like to thank my many friends here at the University of Southern Mississippi for making my all-too-short time as a Visiting Professor such a rewarding experience, and for providing such a pleasant and intellectually stimulating atmosphere in which to complete this book.

G.D. SHEFFIELD
Hattiesburg, MS
January 1997

BIOGRAPHICAL NOTES

(Postitions of contributors are those held at time of first publication)

The Editor:

G.D. Sheffield is Senior Lecturer in War Studies, Royal Military Academy Sandhurst, Senior Research Fellow, De Montfort University Bedford, and Secretary-General of the British Commission for Military History. He is the author of *The Redcaps: A History of the Royal Military Police and its Antecedents From the Middle Ages to the Gulf War* (1994).

Contributors:

Stephen Badsey is Senior Lecturer in War Studies, Royal Military Academy Sandhurst, and Senior Research Fellow, De Montfort University Bedford. He is the joint editor of *The Gulf War Assessed* (1992).

Ronald J. Barr is Lecturer in History at University College Chester. He is writing a book on the US Army of the late 19th Century.

Ian F. W. Beckett is Professor of History at the University of Luton. He is the author of *The Amateur Military Tradition* (1992).

J. M. Bourne is Lecturer in Modern History at the University of Birmingham. He is the author of *Britain and the Great War 1914–18* (1989).

Nigel de Lee is Senior Lecturer in War Studies, Royal Military Academy Sandhurst. His most recent publication was an article on postmodernism and military history.

Brian Holden Reid is Senior Lecturer in War Studies, King's College, and Resident Historian at the (Army) Staff College, Camberley. He is the author of *J. F. C. Fuller: Military Thinker* (1987).

Sir Michael Howard was until recently Robert A. Lovell Professor of Military and Naval History at Yale University. He is the author of *The Lessons of History* (1991).

Robert O'Neill was Chichele Professor of the History of War at the University of Oxford. He is the joint editor of *The West and the Third World: Essays in Honour of J. D. B. Miller* (1980).

David Rooney was formerly Senior Lecturer at the Royal Military Academy Sandhurst. He is the author of *Burma Victory* (1992).

Major General Julian Thompson commanded 3 Commando Brigade in the 1982 Falklands War. He is the author of *No Picnic* (1985) and *Lifeblood of War* (1993).

Andrew Wiest is Assistant Professor of History at the University of Southern Mississippi. He is the author of *Passchendaele and the Royal Navy* (1995).

INTRODUCTION TO THE PAPERBACK EDITION

Since 1991, the strategic landscape has changed beyond recognition. The Cold War has ended and the United States has emerged as the world's sole superpower. In 2002, while the possibility of major inter-state conflict remains a possibility, albeit an increasingly remote one, intra-state conflict is a living reality. Over the last decade fighting has broken out in a number of failed states in the Third World, and, closer to home, in the Former Republic of Yugoslavia (FRY).

The response of the USA and Britain has been to take on the role of global policing, an endeavour which is closer in spirit to the 1880s than the 1980s. This Age of Kipling Revisited has resulted in a steady diet of operations. Generally, these have taken the form of what the British call Peace Support Operations (PSOs), that range from traditional peacekeeping and humanitarian efforts through to peace enforcement, which involves a measure of lethal force. PSOs often involve co-operation with Non Governmental Organisations such as aid agencies, which is a further complicating factor. Thus in Sierra Leone in 2000, Britain conducted counter-insurgency operations in support of the legitimate government; British, American and troops from many other nations participated in the PSO in Bosnia in the mid-1990s; and the Kosovo crisis of 1999 saw NATO fight its first war in its fifty-year existence. The terrorist attacks on New York and Washington on 11 September 2001 opened a new era of asymmetric conflict, which led directly to the American-led campaign in Afghanistan. This new era of warfare has important challenges for leaders and commanders.

COALITION WARFARE

Coalition operations have become the norm. States can bring military capability and/or political legitimacy to an enterprise. Both are important. A major factor in Britain's role as the *de facto* primary ally of the USA is the military effectiveness of the British armed forces, and the willingness of successive governments to use them. A state's forces might lack effectiveness, or even constitute a military liability. Nonetheless, their presence in a coalition can be politically vital, especially if such a coalition is assembled under the aegis of an international body such as the United Nations or NATO.

Having to take account of domestic political realities in a number of states enormously complicates matters for commanders, as US General Wesley Clark's account of his command during Kosovo makes clear. At the beginning of the air campaign he informed the Netherlands Chief of Defence (CHOD) that a Dutch aircraft had shot down a Yugoslav MiG-29. The CHOD's immediate reaction was ask that the news of Dutch involvement should be suppressed, such was the fragility of domestic opinion in his nation.[1] General Sir Mike Jackson has likewise written memorably of the challenges involved in commanding a multinational peacekeeping force in the FRY, where national contingents might consist of a mere handful of personnel. Nevertheless, their concerns still had to be considered less the dreaded 'red card' was played.[2] Going it completely alone is likely to be unrealistic, but it is possible that in future the USA will be very selective in its choice of coalition partners.

TECHNOLOGY

According to some commentators, we are experiencing an IT-based 'Revolution in Military Affairs'. This has already made significant changes to the practice of command. Video teleconferencing (VTC) has become commonplace, a development welcomed by some commanders and loathed by others. 'Digitisation' of the battlespace, the use of technology to '[link] units together to provide the best possible communications and systems for the sharing of information', is a reality.[3] Other more extreme and futuristic visions, such as 'Network Centric Warfare' suggest that technology will indeed transform the conduct of war by allowing 'geographically dispersed forces to create a high level of shared battlespace awareness that can be exploited via self-synchronisation and other network-centric operations to achieve commanders' intent'.[4] Some suggest that it will dispel the fog of war, giving the 21st century commander a god-like view of the battlespace.

These visions beg several questions. Can any state apart from the USA afford such systems, and if not, what are the implications for coalition operations? Will the technology actually work, or can it be countered by an enemy? If it does work, to what extent will it change command, which remains the province of imperfect human beings? Improving technology will undoubtedly have an impact on command. It will make it easier for a commander to communicate with subordinates, but also for politicians to apply the 'long screwdriver' by meddling at the operational and even tactical levels. It will provide vast amounts of data. But ultimately, the commander will stand or fall by the very human attributes such as judgement, decisiveness and character, for which technology cannot be a substitute.

EXPEDITIONARY WARFARE, 'JOINTERY' AND DOCTRINE

The strategic environment of the 1990s saw the rebirth of expeditionary warfare or 'operations launched from the sea',[5] which are invariably complex and demanding. This coincided with the emergency of 'jointery', which is far more than simply the army, navy, air force and marines co-operating with each other in an effective fashion. Rather, it reflects the creation of synergy by the establishment of integrated structures, organisations and doctrine, and the growth of joint culture that breaks down the barriers between the services while retaining single-service ethos – a difficult trick to pull off.

The defining moment in the American experience of jointery was the 1986 Goldwater-Nichols Act, which enforced it by law. Since then, joint organisations and doctrine have proliferated in the United States. In the 1990s, the UK went along the same path. The most significant developments have been the creation of the Permanent Joint Headquarters (PJHQ), the amalgamation of the service staff colleges into the Joint Services Command and Staff College, and the rationalisation of operational command arrangements into workable joint structures, such as Joint Task Forces. The British forces also espoused formal doctrine, some joint, arguably for the first time in their history.

However, as an Australian Chief of the Defence Force has observed, 'You do not achieve jointery by edict. You achieve jointery by thorough practice and refinement until you have full confidence in the other contributors'.[6] The US drew some important practical lessons about joint command from the operations in Somalia[7] and critics have suggested that American forces still have a long way to go before a truly joint approach is achieved.[8] One of the problems is that 'joint' campaigns have tended to be dominated by one service. The 1999 Kosovo campaign was conducted almost entirely from the air, leading to co-ordination problems with the land component. For all that, the jointery has been a qualified success for both US and UK forces. Both are more sensibly configured for joint operations than was the case in the 1980s.

CHALLENGES FOR LEADERSHIP

In recent years, Western armed forces have faced radical societal changes. These have ranged from integration of women into combat units, generally judged a success, to the rather less satisfactory situation in the USA regarding the treatment of homosexuals. Service personnel have been increasingly inclined to seek compensation for hurts sustained with the colours, thus undermining the concept that they have 'unlimited liability'. Moreover, armed forces have been increasingly affected by legal concerns. The British government changed its policy on homosexuals in the military following a ruling of the European Court of Human Rights in 1999. Participants in the Kosovo campaign came under the temporary jurisdiction of the International Criminal

Tribunal Yugoslavia, and the establishment of the International Criminal Court, has brought the threat of individual Britons being prosecuted as war criminals a step closer (the USA has yet to ratify the treaty). As the use of airpower has become the Western weapon of choice, lawyers now have an important role in headquarters when selecting targets. Against a background of the questioning of traditional authority, and the rise of the cult of the individual,[9] it is debatable whether established methods of leadership retain their relevance. There are no easy answers. To change things too radically risks undermining operational effectiveness. But then, so does doing nothing.

Notes

1   Wesley K. Clark, *Waging Modern War*, p. 196, Public Affairs, New York (2001)

2   Sir Mike Jackson, 'The Realities of Multi-national Command', in Gary Sheffield and Geoffrey Till, *Challenges of High Command in the Twentieth Century* pp. 86-91, Strategic and Combat Studies Institute 'Occasional' No. 38, Camberley (2000).

3   Mungo Melvin and Stuart Peach, 'Reaching for the End of the Rainbow: Command and the RMA' p. 116 in Sheffield and Till, *Challenges*. This article is a sensible corrective to the more extreme claims for technology.

4   'Network Centric Warfare', *www.dodccrp.org/NCW*, accessed 2 May 2002.

5   Christian Goulter, 'Airpower and Expeditionary Warfare', in Peter W. Gray (ed.) *Airpower 21: Challenges for the New Century*, The Stationary Office, London (2000) p.183.

6   Gen. J.S. Baker, 'Command of the ADF', in *Journal of the Royal United Services Institution of Australia*, p. 27, vol.17 (Nov. 1996).

7   Kenneth Allard, *Somalia Operations: Lessons Learned* pp. 92-3, National Defense University, Washington DC (1995).

8   David T. Fauta, 'The Paradox of Joint Culture', in *Joint Forces Quarterly*, pp. 81-86, (Autumn 1986).

9   Iain Torrance, *Ethics and the Military Community* pp. 6-13, Strategic and Combat Studies Institute 'Occasional' No. 34, Camberley (1998).

INTRODUCTION: COMMAND, LEADERSHIP AND THE ANGLO-AMERICAN EXPERIENCE

G.D. Sheffield

Generalship – the study of Great and not so great Captains – has been a staple of military writers down the ages, but the mechanics of command have proved a much less popular subject for historians. In an attempt to help redress the balance, in recent years the British Commission for Military History (BCMH) held a series of meetings that considered the nature of leadership and command, with the primary focus on land, rather than sea or air, operations. This collection consists of a number of papers delivered at these conferences by BCMH members, together with others written especially for this volume.

COMMAND

While many people regard 'command' and 'leadership' as much the same thing, it is more helpful to treat them as two separate but related functions. In his chapter in this volume Michael Howard argues that successful leaders 'persuade people willingly to endure hardships, usually prolonged, and incur dangers, usually acute, that if left to themselves they would do their utmost to avoid'. Leadership is, therefore, concerned with inspiration and motivation. Command, by contrast, is a managerial function, which John Pimlott has defined as 'the direction, co-ordination and effective use of military force'. Since the end of the Second World War the phrase 'command and control' (abbreviated as C2) has come into frequent use. In this sense, Pimlott defines control as 'the management of command: the assessment and dissemination of information needed to direct military force'.[1] Modern armed forces often use the acronym C3I (command, control, communications and intelligence) and the addition of 'computers' to the list of 'Cs' has produced 'C4'. These definitions apply to command at every level: grand strategic, military strategic, operational and tactical. Command, as defined here, is a relatively unexplored subject, for academic and popular historians tend to

1

discuss senior soldiers' leadership styles and strategic and tactical ability rather than command systems. However, as Eliot A. Cohen and John Gooch have argued, while one should not underrate the importance of skilful generalship, command is 'a collaborative activity'.[2]

Joel S. Lawson has proposed a simple but helpful five-stage model of command. The first function, *sense*, involves the collection

> of data on the environment, including friendly and enemy forces, allied forces, terrain, weather, and so on. The *process* function draws together and correlates the data to give the commander information about the environment. The *compare* function juxtaposes the existing state of the environment – the relative strengths, weaknesses, positions, etc. – with the desired state, the commander's view of what the state of the environment should be. The *decide* function chooses among available courses of action for reconciling the existing state of the environment with the desired state. The *act* function translates the decision into action.[3]

To ensure that effective decisions are reached, the commander needs to have an effective organisation to provide him with information, to process that information, and to translate orders into reality. One authority has stated that the existence of such a command system is a factor that distinguishes 'true' from 'primitive' war.[4] As many commentators have noted, command and control systems are analogous to the human body. The brain sends messages to the muscles via the nervous system. In military terms, the 'brain' of an army comprises the commander and his staff, while the 'muscles' are the fighting troops, who are connected to the 'brain' (the command function) by the system of control, which equates to the 'nervous system'. Another analogy can be drawn with a complex machine. Just as the pilot of an aeroplane sometimes makes decisions based solely on the information relayed by his instruments, modern higher commanders often have to exercise their judgement based on information provided by subordinates. In his brilliant but neglected study of command systems, Shelford Bidwell graphically describes the commander as fighting actions 'mentally and in the dark', for the whole picture will never be clear to him. The effectiveness of the decisions the commander takes will be very largely dependent on the accuracy and quality and timeliness of the intelligence (that is, information that has been processed and analysed) that reaches him. The enemy, of course, will be doing its best to ensure that such information does not arrive.[5]

The subject of the influence of intelligence on command is beyond the scope of this Introduction. In recent years, historians have reassessed the performance of Anglo-American commanders in light of the revelation of the Ultra secret, a process that has produced something of a revolution in the historiography of the Second World War. Moreover, scholars are investigating the impact of intelligence on other wars.[6] While our understanding of commanders' decisions is being transformed by the study of the previously missing element of intelligence, it is worth recalling Thomas P. Coakley's warning that to provide a commander with accurate information does not necessarily mean that he will make effective use of it.[7]

At the risk of oversimplification, it is possible to identify three basic elements of effective command that are applicable to any level of warfare: a clear plan; good communications; and flexibility. First, commanders at all levels must be operating within the confines of an unambiguous overall concept of operations. Everyone involved in the operation must understand their part in it and the general intentions of the commander; in a phrase that has gained currency in political circles, everyone must be singing from the same hymn sheet. However, such a plan should not be prescriptive but should leave subordinate commanders room for manoeuvre, both literally and metaphorically. Second, good communications are all important. There must be a smooth and rapid transfer of information up and down the command chain, to ensure that commanders take decisions on the basis of the most accurate information. Third, commanders must have the flexibility to cope with what Carl von Clausewitz called 'friction' – things ranging from enemy action to accidents or incompetence that prevent operations from going exactly as planned. As Edward N. Luttwak has pointed out, while the mastering of friction is a principal role of a C3I system, the system itself is vulnerable to friction.[8] Thus a command and control system must have sufficient flexibility built into it to allow it to sustain damage without bringing about the collapse of the army.

In the last two decades, both the United States and British armies, and the United States Marine Corps, have broken with their traditional, broadly attritional, approaches to conventional warfare. Instead, they have adopted doctrines of manoeuvre warfare designed to break the cohesion of the adversary's forces rather than wear down their strength and morale. At the centre of this warfighting philosophy is the notion of getting inside the enemy's 'decision cycle' or 'OODA loop'. This term comes from the need to *O*bserve, *O*rientate, *D*ecide and *A*ct more swiftly than one's opponent. A related concept is 'Command and Control Warfare (C2W)'. This involves the use of everything ranging from electronic warfare and psychological operations to physical force to wreck the enemy's command system. Although the terminology may be new, the idea of defeating an enemy force by destroying the 'brain' and/or 'nervous system', physically or otherwise, thus depriving the 'muscles' of direction, is not. The British theorist J.F.C. Fuller's concept of 'strategic paralysis' is in this tradition and the French Army of 1940 is a classic example of an army defeated in this fashion.

A decentralised system of command and control is vital to the successful prosecution of manoeuvre warfare. Broadly speaking, there are two styles of command. *Befehlstaktik* is an inflexible, authoritarian form of 'top-down' command in which subordinates receive rigid orders that leave little or no scope to exercise low-level initiative. By contrast, *Auftragstaktik* emphasises mission-type orders; the superior commander sets broad objectives but then allows subordinates to use their initiative to achieve their part of the plan in the way they think best. The British Army's version of *Auftragstaktik* is known as 'mission command'. Put crudely, a mission-type order would be 'take that hill', while a *Befehlstaktik* order would be 'take that hill, going around the left flank'. The latter dictates not just what is to be done, but how it is to be done.[9]

Perhaps the key to the issue of command is trust and mutual understanding between the commander, his staff, and his subordinates. Ideally, such trust is founded on personal and working relationships built over a period of time, as in the case of Ulysses S. Grant and his Chief of Staff, John A. Rawlins, whose teamwork Brian Holden Reid examines in this book. General Sir Martin Farndale analysed the relationship of the commander and the chief of staff in these terms:

> The two must respect and understand each other fully. They must also have full confidence in each other and know instinctively and accurately how to act in the absence of the other. The chief of staff must know how far to go in the absence of the commander and feel confident in doing so. The commander must feel that, once he has given his orders, they will be carried out within acceptable parameters and that the chief of staff will conduct the battle in accordance with them. The chief of staff must, however, be quick to appreciate new situations developing and modify his plans accordingly or, if necessary, approach his commander with recommendations. Montgomery and de Guingand and Balck and von Mellenthin in World War II are examples of the system working well.[10]

In real life such a happy coincidence of personal and command relationships does not always occur but a military culture that creates a common philosophy of decentralised command (and provides appropriate training) is the next best thing. Unfortunately, the creation of such a culture in a hierarchical and tradition-bound organisation like an army is no easy matter.

The effectiveness of a command system may mean the difference between victory and defeat. As several historians have noted, the inadequacies of Eighth Army's command and control system were an important factor in the British defeat at the Battle of Gazala (May-June 1942). The British chain of command was certainly unwieldy, bureaucratic and inflexible, and poorly suited for the type of mobile warfare Eighth Army was trying to fight. At Gazala five levels of operational command, ranging from the Commander-in-Chief Middle East (Auchinleck) to brigade group commanders, controlled a force of only six divisions. At one stage the Army commander, Ritchie, by-passed a corps commander and issued tactical orders directly to a division, resulting in the corps commander requesting to be relieved of his command. Yet despite this plethora of command levels, the supervision exercised over the battle by higher headquarters was severely limited. In contrast to the top-heavy command structure in the desert, in Burma the headquarters of 14th Indian Division attempted to control more sub-units than was within its capabilities during the First Battle of the Arakan (1942-43), with predictably dire results.

A new command team in the shape of Montgomery and Alexander arrived in Egypt in August 1942. Among the many changes made was a fundamental shift in command arrangements. Alexander assumed responsibility for overall strategy, leaving Montgomery with operational command of the forces facing Rommel. Within Eighth Army Montgomery carried out a reorganisation that ensured that its next offensive battle, Second Alamein, was tightly controlled from the centre. While this may not have been the ideal command and control system for carrying out manoeuvre warfare, it was appropriate for the type of set-piece, attritional battle Montgomery intended to fight. It was certainly the most effective approach given the state of training and combat proficiency of the Eighth Army at that time, which was roughly similar to that of the British Expeditionary Force in France in the spring of 1917.

Perhaps the 20th century's most notorious failure of command systems occurred on the Western Front during the First World War. While some ascribe the deadlock to sheer stupidity on the part of the generals, a less emotive approach, of which J.M. Bourne's chapter in this volume is an admirable example, recognises that commanders of 1914-18 had to contend with a number of problems outside their control. While by 1914 armies had grown too large to be commanded by a general in person, in the manner of Wellington or Napoleon, radio communications had not yet evolved to the extent that command of an army in battle from a rear headquarters was a practical proposition. A network of field telephones provided commanders with a sophisticated communications system that stopped at the front line trench, that is, just where it would start to become useful in battle. Higher commanders of units larger than a battalion were powerless to influence the battle once the soldiers had gone 'over the top'. Indeed, an important reason for the inability of armies to break the trench deadlock between the end of 1914 and the beginning of 1918 was the inherent advantage bestowed upon the defender. They could use their telephones, their wires buried deep beneath the ground, to summon up reserves far more quickly than the attacker could bring its reserves forward. The experience of all armies, not just the British, illustrates the difficulties faced by commanders fighting a battle without a smooth and rapid transfer of information up and down the command chain.

In his book *Command in War*, Martin van Creveld highlights the failures of the British command system on the first day of the Battle of the Somme (1 July 1916).[11] In fact, that day marked the real beginning of the British Army's apprenticeship in large-scale modern warfare. At the end of the 142-day battle of the Somme, and the subsequent battles of Arras and Third Ypres (Passchendaele) in 1917, the British Army was a very different creature to the semi-trained body of July 1916. Command and control, like almost every other aspect of the British Army's performance, had improved dramatically by the end of the war. Improvements ranged from Haig's use in 1917 of a mobile forward headquarters based on a railway train to development of what was, by the autumn of 1918, 'a very sophisticated signals service' capable of coping with mobile warfare.[12] While Andrew Wiest's chapter on the planning of Passchendaele reminds us of the problems of command experienced in 1917, clearly the British command system was robust and flexible enough to withstand the massive German onslaught in the spring of 1918 and then to launch a counter-offensive in the autumn of that year.

This is not to suggest that incompetence played no part in the problems faced by commanders in the First World War. This was demonstrated all too clearly at Gallipoli in 1915. The ineptitude displayed in the strategic planning of the campaign illustrated the defects of Allied high command at this stage of the conflict. Sir Ian Hamilton was dispatched to the eastern Mediterranean with a hastily assembled force, wholly inadequate information on the intended area of operations and the enemy, and the minimum of time to plan his campaign. Hamilton was not consulted on the appointment of his chief of staff, and one junior staff officer had only 24 hours to calculate the establishment of the Mediterranean Expeditionary Force's headquarters and the MEF's logistic requirements. Hamilton had the dubious honour of conducting the world's first opposed amphibious landing against a determined enemy equipped with modern weapons. Moreover, the failed naval attack of 18 March 1915 had sacrificed any hope of achieving strategic surprise. It is instructive to compare command and control of the amphibious assault on

Gallipoli with that on the coast of Normandy in 1944. Apart from the obvious but vitally significant advantage of possessing good radio communications, in 1944 Eisenhower and Montgomery had a relatively experienced staff that was used to working together. Even more importantly, detailed planning for the Normandy landings occurred over a period of years.

The operational and tactical command of the assault landings on 25 April 1915 offer further stark evidence of the problems and failures of command. On three out of the five landing beaches on the southern tip of the Gallipoli Peninsula, the assaulting troops were unopposed. On Y Beach there was an opportunity for an advance into the rear of the Turkish forces that were opposing the landings at V and W beaches. This opportunity was squandered, and vague initial orders, the local commander's unwillingness to use his initiative and the neglect of the operation by higher command contributed to the failure. The commander of 29th Division, Hunter-Weston, became obsessed with the battle for W Beach and virtually ignored the rest of his area of responsibility. Hamilton had a wider view of the battle and suggested that reserves be diverted to Y Beach; he did not, however, insist that this sensible course be taken. Over three months later, in August 1915, Hamilton again failed to impose his will, this time on a weak and timid subordinate during the landings at Suvla Bay. In both April and August, Hamilton fell foul of the unofficial command doctrine, that the superior commander must set broad aims, leaving the operational commander to actually fight the battle. Although this was admirable in principle, in practice the British Army of 1915 was a rigid and hierarchical organisation that did not encourage the cultivation of initiative. Hamilton did not exercise the superior commander's ultimate prerogative: to intervene if things are obviously going wrong.

In summary, there were grave faults in the British command system at Gallipoli. There was confusion as to the precise nature of the plan at various levels. The army was too widely dispersed for a general to exercise personal command. It is a moot point whether the British Army of early 1915 was capable of operating a system of devolved command, for the command culture was highly inflexible, and it left little room for commanders below the level of division to exercise their initiative.[13]

Technological developments – most notably the widespread use of radios – had changed the ways commanders controlled their forces by the time of the Second World War, but organisational advances were also important. In 1918 the future Field Marshal Montgomery streamlined the command chain of 47th (London) Division, in which he was serving as GSO 1. Later, in the Second World War, Montgomery drew upon his earlier experiences to develop his own distinctive style of command. In Normandy in 1944 this included the splitting of his headquarters into three parts, Tactical, Main and Rear. Montgomery placed himself at 'Tac HQ', close to the fighting troops. Montgomery made good use of liaison officers who acted as his 'eyes and ears', travelling to units to find out exactly what was going on, and 'Phantom', a signal service that listened in to the radio traffic of formations under his command. These innovations enabled Montgomery to keep his finger on the pulse of the battle.[14]

The introduction of more sophisticated communications equipment can solve some problems but create others. In the American Civil War, the existence of the electric telegraph greatly enhanced the ability of military and political high command to exercise control over armies – which, depending on the circumstances, could be a blessing or a curse for local commanders. One hundred years later, advanced communications once again created both opportunities and problems for American commanders. In an echo of the British experience at Gallipoli, American forces in Vietnam discovered that organisational deficiencies and inappropriate command practices compounded existing communication problems.

Communications in the Vietnam War were superior to those in any previous conflict, and so were the possibilities for superiors to meddle in the affairs of their subordinates. Not only commanders 'in theatre' had this facility, but so did senior military and political personnel in the United States; it was possible for a White House official to call a Special Forces officer located 'in a remote camp in the Central Highlands' at 'a critical moment'.[15] Such occurrences led one soldier to comment: 'Johnson may be a great president, but he's a piss poor squad leader'.[16] A confused command and control system, which failed to curb such interference, exacerbated the communications problem.

The ideal military command structure can be represented as a chain. The top link of the chain is the Commander-in-Chief, who commands all the forces involved in an operation; below him is a well defined hierarchy of subordinates. Information from the lowliest link in the chain passes up in a direct line to the Commander-in-Chief via intermediate commanders and headquarters, while the C-in-C's orders flow down the same chain. In reality, compromises have to be made with this ideal. As Nigel de Lee's study of a British assault brigade on D-Day makes clear, triservice ('joint') operations place additional demands on commanders and staffs, while 'combined' operations involving allied forces add yet further layers of complexity. On occasions, something approaching our ideal command structure has been achieved within the context of a combined operation – the Anglo-American Combined Chiefs of Staff in the Second World War and the command organisation for Operation OVERLORD in 1944 are cases in point. However, it is more usual for a 'unified' (as opposed to 'united') structure to be created in such situations. This involves the co-ordination of different national chains of command. In Vietnam, the Americans made life difficult for themselves by failing to ensure unity of command among their own armed forces, let alone achieving unity with their allies.

While General William C. Westmoreland, head of US Military Assistance Command Vietnam (MACV) from 1964 to 1968, was generally regarded as the US commander in Vietnam, his authority was in reality severely limited. Admiral U.S. Grant Sharp, Commander-in-Chief, Pacific (CINCPAC), and the Commander-in-Chief, US Army, Pacific, were both sandwiched between Westmoreland and the Joint Chiefs of Staff in the hierarchy of command. In addition, Strategic Air Command and Seventh Fleet units fell outside Westmoreland's authority, while his control of the US Marine Corps was limited by USMC headquarters in Washington DC. CINCPAC and Washington, not MACV, ran the air war against North Vietnam. Civil Operations and Revolutionary Development Support (CORDS), the agency created in 1967 to manage the Pacification programme in the countryside of South Vietnam, was placed under MACV, but the head of CORDS sometimes went over Westmoreland's head to Washington. The US command structure in Vietnam resembled a particularly confusing wiring diagram rather than a chain. The command structure at the level of grand strategy was equally confused.[17] America's allies also had their own command structures. Westmoreland resisted the idea of a combined approach that would have encompassed the South Vietnamese Army (ARVN), officially because it would have appeared to compromise South Vietnamese independence but also, as one historian has suggested, because he feared the security implications of allowing ARVN officers access to American plans.[18]

As Robert O'Neill points out in his chapter in this book, limited war demands its own particular style of command and leadership. Much the same could be said of the various types of low intensity conflict (or Operations Other than War), such as counter-insurgency and peacekeeping, where a very high level of responsibility can be placed on the shoulders of relatively junior commanders. Command in such operations needs to strike a fine balance. Just as in other types of military operations, commanders should be allowed to exercise their initiative, but there is also the need to keep fairly tight control from above, for the military actions of a junior commander can have a disproportionate political effect. Problems of commanding and co-ordinating multi-national forces speaking different languages, using different equipment and subscribing to different doctrines further complicated recent operations in former Yugoslavia. These problems are far from unique in military history, and are liable to resurface, for this type of multi-national, peacekeeping/peacemaking operation is likely to be the staple fare of Western armies in the foreseeable future.

LEADERSHIP

Natural, inspirational leaders do not necessarily have the ability to become good commanders. According to his biographer, on promotion in 1862, Confederate officer John Bell Hood had difficulties in adjusting to the wider managerial role required of a major general.[19] At least in theory, it is possible for commanders to be bereft of leadership qualities. A case could be made that since the mid 19th century, what John Keegan has described as 'heroic' leadership[20] has become obsolete as far as senior commanders are concerned because they have controlled ever-larger armies by means of the telegraph, telephone or radio, often many miles from the fighting troops. Yet commanders from Grant and Lee onwards have continued to see themselves as having a leadership role. Even Douglas Haig, supposedly the archetypal, remote 'château general', rode up to the front line at a moment of crisis during the First Battle of Ypres in 1914. The growth of mass armies in the 19th and early 20th centuries made personal leadership by generals increasingly difficult. Since 1918 the development of advanced communications and transport – especially, in latter years, the helicopter – has once again made it feasible, as a senior officer can leave his headquarters and move rapidly around his command, while remaining in contact with his staff.

At any level the leader has two main functions: to create and sustain unit cohesion, and to ensure that the goals of the group are congruent with those of the larger organisation, the army: in short he must lead them, whether literally or not, into battle.[21] As the US Army discovered in Vietnam, these aims may conflict – staying alive may be seen by individuals and the small group as more important than fighting – and the leader has to reconcile these two contradictory impulses. The qualities required of the effective leader have been an endless source of fascination, and many senior commanders have produced lists of them. Omar Bradley's list was not untypical and included 'knowledge of the job', 'mental and physical energy', 'human understanding and consideration for others', 'confidence', 'imagination' and 'character'.[22] While such lists are useful guides to the type of leader desired by the British and United States armed forces, it should be born in mind that the third of Bradley's criteria were not much evident in the careers of a number of demonstrably effective leaders, Hitler and Stalin among them.

Even within the Anglo-American democratic tradition leaders have had very different approaches. In the Second World War both Slim and Montgomery succeeded in restoring the morale of a British Commonwealth army, yet their personal styles were markedly different. Slim's nickname among the men of Fourteenth Army was 'Uncle Bill', which neatly captures his avuncular personality, but Montgomery's character was rather more abrasive. As far back as 1927 F.C. Bartlett identified three distinct types of leaders: 'institutional' leaders, who rely on their hierarchical status; 'dominant' leaders with forceful personalities; and those 'persuasive' leaders who trust in their ability to influence others.[23] Slim was perhaps, a persuasive leader, while Montgomery was a dominant one.

In his chapter in this book, Michael Howard refers to 'command recognition'; that is, the degree to which the ordinary soldier knew his senior officers. As John Bourne makes clear in his chapter, some senior British commanders of the First World War stamped their personalities on their formations and one could add to his selection other generals, such as Brigadier General R.O. Kellett, commander of 99 Brigade from 1915-18. Yet the senior commander as personal leader is more generally associated with the Second rather than First World War. In 1939-45 the leadership styles of men such as Slim, Montgomery, Patton, and Eisenhower tended towards informality, as befitted leaders of the armies of democratic states in a people's war – not that either the British or US armed forces in the Second World War were short of their quota of remote, institutional leaders. At least as far as the British were concerned, this change reflected a fundamental shift of attitudes from the belief that leadership was largely a question of social status and education, that leaders were born, to the functional approach in which leadership is seen as something that can be taught to suitable candidates.

COMMAND AND LEADERSHIP:
THE ANGLO-AMERICAN EXPERIENCE

The Revolutionary and Napoleonic era was a period in which command underwent truly radical changes. Building on developments of the 18th century and earlier, the French developed a decentralised corps system, by which the Army was organised into a number of self-contained, balanced forces with their own staffs. Napoleon's *Grand Armée* was controlled by a sophisticated staff system, in which Napoleon's chief of staff, Marshal Berthier, played a key role. For all its efficiency, the command of the *Grand Armée* was a personalised affair that revolved around Berthier's administrative ability and the military genius of Napoleon himself. By contrast, the Prussian Army, spurred on by its crushing defeat at the hands of Napoleon's army in 1806, developed a genuinely modern, professional system of command. In 1810 Prussia created the world's first staff college. Graduates of the *Kriegsakademie* were an elite band, rigorously trained in staff work, and the excellence of their general staff gave the Prussians a decisive advantage in the wars against Austria (1866) and France (1870-1). Victories in the Wars of Unification gave Prussia – and later Germany – the reputation of the premier military power in Europe, and its innovations were widely emulated.

The British Army, largely concerned with small colonial wars rather than continental-scale warfare, lagged behind in this respect. Although the Staff College was established at Camberley in 1858, in 1870 it had only 40 students. Although the prestige and the numbers attending Staff College had increased by the end of the century, it was not until 1906 that a general staff was established. This followed the salutory experience of the Second Boer War (1899-1902), a conflict that cruelly underlined the British Army's deficiencies in command and staff work. As Ian Beckett's chapter makes clear, the late Victorian army operated a highly personalised command system. While this often worked well enough during colonial campaigns, 'improvisation was no substitute for a proper general staff structure and Wolseley's capacity to manage affairs decreased in proportion to the growth in the scale of operations'.

From 1861 to 1865 American soldiers gained experience in large-scale military operations. Since the pre-war US Army of 1860 had consisted of just 16,000 men, commanders had to learn how to command large armies while the war was in progress. As Brian Holden Reid demonstrates, an outstanding command team eventually emerged in the Union Army: Ulysses S. Grant and John A. Rawlins. Rawlins, Grant's chief of staff, has appeared hitherto as a somewhat 'shadowy and indistinct figure', but Dr Holden Reid demonstrates that the two men had 'an interdependent relationship' and that Rawlins played a significant role in Grant's success as a commander.

The post-Civil War US Army resembled its British counterpart in two ways: it lacked a Prussian-style general staff system, and was primarily concerned with fighting small wars. Ronald J. Barr's chapter charts the tortuous path of the US Army towards a greater degree of professionalism. This culminated in the early years of the 20th century with reforms associated with Secretary of War Elihu Root, especially the creation of a general staff in 1903. Despite their incomplete nature, Dr Barr argues, 'the legacy of Root's army reforms' formed 'the basis for the modern professional American army'.

Andrew Wiest's chapter on the planning of the Passchendaele offensive demonstrates the importance of the human element in command. Haig, he argues, was wrong to choose Gough as the operational commander and then compounded his mistake by offering advice, which Gough 'failed to heed', rather than giving 'clear and easily understood orders' for the assault on 31 July 1917. The initial phase of the Third Battle of Ypres, in Dr Wiest's view, 'represents the nadir of British command'.

J.M. Bourne examines the leadership qualities of that much disparaged group of men, British generals of the First World War. While recognizing the weaknesses in the BEF's command system, Dr Bourne reaches beyond the hackneyed stereotypes of château generals. He argues that 'The British Army was the passive victim neither of the German Army nor of its own High Command' and that by 1918 highly competent, meritocratic, 'front-line' generals were emerging at divisional level, men who were leaders as well as commanders.

The subject of leadership in the Second World War is discussed by Michael Howard, who writes with the dual authority of a distinguished military historian and a veteran of the Italian campaign, where he served as an officer in the Coldstream Guards. He sets the experience of 1939-45 into the broader context of military leadership, and draws some interesting comparisons with 1914-18. In his view the most important attribute of the leader is calmness, and this was reflected in the 'urbane normality' that characterised the leadership style of British officers.

Nigel de Lee provides a case study of one Second World War officer who was both a leader and a commander. Brigadier Sir Alexander Stanier commanded 231 Brigade in the North-West European campaign of 1944-45. This chapter is largely based on a series of interviews with Sir Alexander, which explored exactly how he spent 'his time in the performance of his duties'. The result is a thorough examination of the 'middle management of command'. Stanier eschewed formalised principles in making operational decisions, relying instead on 'his own experience and judgment'. During battle he successfully operated a 'hands-off' approach to command, 'go[ing] forward to give encouragement without interference' with his subordinates.

In his chapter, David Rooney examines British command and leadership in the jungles of Burma during the Chindit campaigns of 1943 and 1944. These operations, in which widely separated columns struck deep behind Japanese lines, placed peculiar demands on commanders. Much of the debate inevitably centres on the performance of Major General Orde Wingate, and David Rooney provides a favourable assessment of one of the most controversial commanders of the Second World War. Rooney points out that after Wingate's death, which occurred at the very beginning of Operation THURSDAY, many of the key command positions in the Chindits were held by men who did not believe in Wingate's concept of Long Range Penetration.

Like Michael Howard, Julian Thompson is doubly qualified to tackle his subject. Major General Thompson commanded 3 Commando Brigade during the 1982 Falklands campaign and has made a detailed study of the Anzio operation of 1944; hence his comparison of command during the two operations is of particular interest. He is particularly frank and objective when writing about his own role in the Falklands campaign, and brings his experience as a commander to bear on a discussion of the shortcomings of the Allied command at Anzio.

Another soldier-historian, Robert O'Neill, considers the very special problems of leadership and command in 'limited' wars, although, as he points out, the Korean and Vietnam Wars were total wars for the service personnel who actually had to fight in them. Professor O'Neill illustrates the problems of motivating US, British, Australian and New Zealand troops in post-1945 limited conflicts. He makes some interesting comparisons between the response of the US to the challenges posed by Korea and Vietnam, and those of their allies to their experiences of these wars. The Americans learned from the 'painful and frustrating experience' of the Korean and Vietnam Wars, he argues, and the US conduct of the Gulf War of 1991 reflected these hard-won lessons.

Finally, Stephen Badsey's chapter examines the way in which the United States responded to the challenges of leading a multi-national coalition force to victory in the Gulf War of 1991. His conclusion is that following the invasion of Kuwait, US commanders' 'greatest challenge... was not the Iraqi enemy'; rather, the fighting and winning of bureaucratic battles 'within the coalition itself'. Dr Badsey's study of the Gulf War admirably illustrates the widely held opinion that coalition operations pose extraordinarily difficult problems for the commander.

Notes

NB: I would like to thank Dr Geoffrey Jensen, Kathy Barbier and Eric Bobo for their comments on an earlier draft of this introduction.

1   My thanks are due to Dr Pimlott for allowing me to make use of his unpublished work.

2   Eliot A. Cohen and John Gooch, *Military Misfortunes*, pp. 231-232, 241-242, Free Press, New York (1990).

3   Thomas P. Coakley, *Command and Control for War and Peace*, pp. 32-33, National Defense University Press, Washington DC (1992).

4   H.H. Turney High, *Primitive War*, p. 30, 2nd edn, University of South Carolina Press, Columbia, SC (1971).

5   Shelford Bidwell, *Modern Warfare*, pp. 76-78. Allen Lane, London (1973).

6   For Ultra, see for example Harold C. Deutsch, *Commanding Generals and the Uses of Intelligence* in Michael Handel (ed.) *Leaders and Intelligence*, Cass, London (1985). For other wars, see Edwin C. Fishel, *The Secret War for the Union: The Untold Story of Military Intelligence in the Civil War*, Houghton Mifflin, New York (1995); and John Ferris, *The British Army and Signals Intelligence during the First World War*, Alan Sutton for Army Records Society, Stroud (1992).

7   Coakley, *Command and Control*, p. 22.

8   Edward N. Luttwak, *Strategy*, p. 13, Belknapp Press, Cambridge, Mass. and London (1987).

9   Faris R. Kirkland, 'Combat Leadership Styles: Empowerment versus Authoritarianism', *Parameters*, vol. XX, 6, p. 670 (1990); Ronald J. Bashista, '*Auftragstaktik*: It's More Than Just a Word', *Armor*, November-December 1994, p. 19. I owe the latter reference to Lieutenant Kyle Head USA.

10   General Sir Martin Farndale, 'Command and Control of the Joint Army Group/Tactical Air Force Battle at the Operational Level' in Brian Holden Reid and Michael Dewar (eds) *Military Strategy in a Changing Europe: Towards the Twenty-First Century*, p. 188, Brassey's, London (1991).

11   Martin Van Creveld, *Command in War*, Harvard UP, Cambridge, Mass., (1985). See also Martin Samuels, *Command or Control? Command, Training and Tactics in the British and German Armies*, 1888-1918, Cass, Portland, Oreg. (1995).

12   John Terraine, *The Smoke and the Fire: Myths and Anti-Myths of War 1861-1945*, pp. 117, 173-175, Sidgwick and Jackson, London (1980); Paddy Griffith, *Battle Tactics of the Western Front*, pp. 169-175, Yale UP, New Haven and London (1994).

13   This discussion of command at Gallipoli has been informed by reading John Lee, 'Sir Ian Hamilton and the Dardanelles, 1915' in B. Bond (ed.) *Fallen Stars*, Brassey's, London (1991), and Cohen and Gooch, *Military Misfortunes*, pp. 133-63.

14   Ronald Lewin, *Montgomery as Military Commander*, pp. 52-53, Stein and Day, New York (1971).

15 Peter M. Dunn, 'The American Army: The Vietnam War, 1965-1973' in Ian F.W. Beckett and John Pimlott, *Armed Forces and Modern Counter-Insurgency*, p. 84, Croom Helm, London (1985).

16 M.E. Morris, *H. Norman Schwarzkopf: Road to Triumph*, pp. 15-16, Pan, London (1991).

17 Harry G. Summers, Jr, *On Strategy*, pp. 200-203, Dell, New York (1984); Dunn, 'The American Army' p. 84.

18 Guenter Lewy, *America in Vietnam*, p. 122, Oxford UP, New York (1978).

19 Richard M. McMurray, *John Bell Hood and the War for Southern Independence*, p. 6, University of Nebraska Press, Lincoln and London (1992).

20 John Keegan, *The Mask of Command*, Viking, New York (1987).

21 For a discussion of this and other issues related to leadership see G.D. Sheffield, *Officer-Man Relations, Morale and Discipline in the British Army in the Era of the Great War*, Macmillan, London (forthcoming).

22 Omar N. Bradley, 'On Leadership', in Lloyd J. Matthews and Dale E. Brown, *The Challenge of Military Leadership*, pp. 5-8, Pergamon-Brassey's, Washington DC (1989).

23 F.C. Bartlett, *Psychology and the Soldier*, pp. 138-139, Cambridge UP, Cambridge (1927).

THE COMMANDER
AND HIS CHIEF
OF STAFF:
ULYSSES S.
GRANT AND JOHN
A. RAWLINS,
1861-1865

by Brian Holden Reid

W e are frequently reminded that behind every successful man there stands an ambitious and forceful woman. Whether this generalisation is true in every case is very doubtful. An equally attractive proposition is that behind every successful commander stands an able chief of staff: intuitive, energetic, gifted with foresight and tact; but above all, devoted to his chief. Lieutenant General Ulysses S. Grant was fortunate in his Chief of Staff, Colonel (later Brigadier General) John A. Rawlins. Unlike a number of other Civil War commanders, Grant did not start the war at the top. His generalship matured slowly and he was promoted from regimental command to that of higher formations with sufficient time to learn the profession of arms and the multifarious demands made upon the general's talents at various levels. And with every step up the ladder of promotion, he took with him a young man who was able to expand his horizons to match those of his commanding general, always undertook those tasks he was bidden and frequently supplied talents in which Grant was sadly lacking. Yet if a review of the books written about Grant is undertaken, Rawlins emerges as a very shadowy and indistinct figure.[1] His life was cut short by tuberculosis in 1869 just as he took up the portfolio of the Secretary of War in Grant's cabinet. His reputation therefore remained unsullied by the shabby corruption and undistinguished tenure of the Grant presidency; and yet, as he never commanded troops in the field, his career has been sadly neglected.

It is perhaps the unhappy lot of chiefs of staff, no matter how able, to be overshadowed by field commanders, no matter how mediocre. Only one biography of Rawlins has appeared, The *Life of John A. Rawlins* (1916) by another member of Grant's staff, James Harrison Wilson.[2] Yet contemporaries attested to Rawlin's importance. Sylvanus Cadwallader wrote:

> It is due to General Rawlins, Chief of Staff, to state that upon this occasion [Chattanooga], as upon that of all Grant's great campaigns, he is unquestionably entitled to one half the praise, for the strategy. Tactical successes were due to others, but no general or broad plan of command, or pitched battle was ever adopted by General Grant without the unqualified assent and approval of Rawlins. The latter was his only military confidant and adviser, and often originated many of the most successful operations. [3]

As a journalist Cadwallader was too prone to listen to gossip and to think that any man who was articulate and forceful in speech, like Rawlins, would inevitably exert a magnetic sway over a man like Grant, who certainly was not. C.F. Adams saw Grant after the Battle of the Wilderness in May 1864 and thought him 'a very ordinary looking man'. So the voluble Rawlins was in command, and the gruff, shambling figure of Grant was simply a puppet in his hands. In short, Grant was a figurehead who had surrendered all real power into the hands of his Chief of Staff. General Wilson, who knew Rawlins best, soon realised what nonsense this was. He writes nearly half a century after Rawlins's death, that 'While Rawlins was a man of extraordinary qualities and character it cannot be claimed that he was to General Grant what Berthier was to Napoleon, or even what Gneisenau and Müffling were to Blücher.' He goes on:

> Rawlins was but a country lawyer who had had no military training whatever when he entered the volunteer army, and never, even to his dying day, made the slightest pretensions to technical education in the profession of arms. [4]

So what can we make of this elusive figure? His early career bore a remarkable resemblance to that of Grant. Rawlins was born on 13 February 1831 in East Galena, Illinois, into a large family of children, with eight brothers and one sister. The family (of Ulster stock) were poor and the young Rawlins worked either on the farm or in the forests charcoal burning; this back-breaking work left him strong, fit and with a robust constitution. General Wilson, with Victorian discretion, reports that his father was of a 'roving disposition' not adverse to the bottle. His mother, by comparison, was a strong personality, sweet tempered, supportive of her son's desire to better himself, and imbued with deep religious convictions. It was she who instilled him with a somewhat self-righteous and priggish tone and a lifelong aversion to drink.

Rawlins's education was patchy. Like Grant, who loathed his vulgar, pushy and crude father's tannery business, Rawlins soon tired of charcoal burning.

Rawlins took up reading and developed an interest in history. He had attended the local neighbourhood school for eight terms (including only one at the high school). He entered the Rock River Seminary in 1852 which gave him a grounding in political economy and the classics, and an enthusiasm for rhetoric and public speaking, though not much more. A year later his money ran out, and in the best traditions of the frontier he returned to charcoal burning until he could afford to pay the fees. Determined never to return to this grimy lot, Rawlins then began to study law – the prime vehicle for social mobility on the frontier. He was admitted to the bar in October 1854, and was taken into partnership by his preceptor, whose practice he inherited in August 1855. Not a highly educated lawyer, he relied on his natural eloquence and knowledge of human nature. In March 1857 Rawlins was elected City Attorney, and, active in the local Democratic Party, was nominated to be a presidential elector on the ticket of Senator Stephen A. Douglas in the first Congressional district of Illinois. [5]

Throughout the Presidential Election of 1860, Rawlins developed his skills as a public speaker, and this was to have a profound but unwitting influence on his military career. After the firing of the first shots at Fort Sumter in April 1861 he addressed a public convention on secession. Rawlins's deep sonorous voice had a major impact on the expectant and rather rowdy audience. 'We will stand by the flag of our country and appeal to the God of Battles!' he declared. This resolute cry appealed to one very particular member of the audience, Captain Ulysses S. Grant. Grant and Rawlins were not strangers to one another, but nor were they friends. Rawlins was Jesse Grant's attorney and they had met on a number of occasions. U.S. Grant was not held in high esteem by the Galena community, and by all accounts nobody would have guessed that Rawlins would be the handservant of Grant's future renown. Nonetheless, when war was certain, shortly after the meeting addressed by Rawlins, Grant rejoined the Army. Trained officers were a rare species, and Grant was first offered a colonelcy by the Governor of Illinois and then a brigadier general's commission of volunteers by President Lincoln dating from 17 May 1861. Because of the seniority conferred by his state commission he was very soon commanding a brigade in the Department of Missouri. [6]

Grant immediately turned to the question of his staff. He was entitled to three ADCs and an Assistant Adjutant General. He was so impressed with Rawlins that on 10 August 1861 he wrote to his wife Julia, 'I have invited Mr Rollins of Galena to accept a place on my staff. I wish you would tell Orvil [Grant's brother] to say to him that I would like to have him come as soon as possible if he accepts the position.' The degree of intimacy between them is measured by Grant's misspelling of Rawlins's name. Eleven days later he asked Major General John C. Frémont to confirm Rawlins's elevation from an ADC to Assistant Adjutant General. As Grant observed to his father of his staff,

'They are all able men, from five to ten years younger than myself. Without military experience but very capable of learning.' And to the influential Congressman Elihu B. Washburne he explained, 'Mr Rawlins was the first one I decided upon for a place with me...' Grant's position was a challenging one both for him and his staff. Grant pointed out to his wife proudly that, 'I have quite an extensive and important command. It is third in importance in the country...There are so many officers of higher rank, with less commands, however, that I do not see how I am to retain it long.' It was to this problem – of Grant's comparative weakness in the patronage stakes – that Rawlins was to address his formidable energies in the year ahead.[7]

Rawlins was a young man – just 30 – and military matters had been conspicuously absent from his somewhat incomplete course of self-education. Rawlins was a handsome man of powerful physical presence. His early labours had left him very strong, lean and muscular. His character endowed that frame with vigour. His was a powerful personality, ambitious, self-confident, articulate. He could express himself forcefully in the spoken word though less well on paper. He could be zealous, and when the occasion demanded it, ruthless; yet he was essentially kind and generous, and could be approached quite freely by even the most junior and inexperienced members of the staff. But Rawlins had a mercurial temperament and lived on his nerves, he could be self-righteous and priggish, impulsive and bad-tempered. Charles A. Dana, Assistant Secretary of War, later wrote that, 'Rawlins was essentially a good man, though he was one of the most profane men I ever knew; there was no guile in him – he was as upright and as genuine a character as I ever came across.' But all agreed that Rawlins had one overwhelming loyalty which transcended all others, except love of country – a love of Grant. By December 1862, after only a close working relationship of something less than six months, he wrote to Washburne of Grant, 'All that concerns his reputation concerns me; I love him as a father; I respect him because I have studied him well, and the more I know him the more I respect and love him.' The characters of Grant and Rawlins complemented one another perfectly.[8]

The manner in which this relationship developed is conveyed in Cadwallader's memoir. He recalled during the Vicksburg Campaign that

> Rawlins quietly but relentlessly exercised his personal and official influence and authority. It came to be well understood that any staff officer who furnished General Grant a single drink; or drank with him when away from headquarters or in any way whatever connived at, or concealed, the general's drinking, would be summarily ordered to his proper command, or be disgraced, broken in rank, or run out of the service, if in his power to accomplish it. His authority was unquestioned. His control over Grant was fully recognised. More than

one staff officer was barely given the option of resigning, or of being crushed by the iron hand of the great Chief of Staff.

The manner in which Rawlins exerted this kind of influence – as Grant's moral guardian, or 'minder' – reflects on a number of important issues far transcending simply the moral (and rather trivial) issue of whether Grant was a drunkard. It had an urgent bearing on the peer struggle within the command structure. Clearly, this touched upon the political networks that were struggling for influence within the Lincoln Administration. These reflected diverging views over the most appropriate strategy to be employed during the war and which generals should implement it. Related to this dispute were relations with the newspapers. They were the medium through which the discussion was continued and acted as lightning rods which tested the popularity and reputation of field commanders. Finally, Rawlins was skilled in dealing with patronage questions. Enjoying the support of powerful patrons facilitated the manipulation of both strategic discussion and newspaper coverage, as well as the correct and economical direction of Grant's plans in the field. Rawlins's role was much broader than that of a military bureaucrat in the field; it was more akin to the lynch-pin in the coach wheel of Grant's staff. But his role would be modified over time.[9]

Rawlins was first and foremost a staff officer. At the outset Grant's staff comprised, as Rawlins realised, a very mixed bag of ability. The initial Chief of Staff, Colonel Webster, was conscientious but not a strong personality. As the Assistant Adjutant General, Rawlins soon imposed his will on the remainder of the staff. His initial duties were to ensure the rapid delivery of returns, collate reports and despatch correspondence. By the Battle of Shiloh in April 1862 Rawlins had already made himself indispensable and had to all intents and purposes by-passed the Chief of Staff. He had established himself as the man to approach to gain access to Grant. It was to Rawlins that Grant turned when vital orders were needed to be given to Lew Wallace's division at Crumps Landing, ensuring that he marched to join the rest of the Army. Rawlins blamed the slowness of this march on Wallace, and no doubt the vigour of his denunciation did much to confirm Grant in his low opinion of Wallace's generalship. Wilson, Rawlins's later biographer, joined Grant's staff before the crossing of the Tallahatchie and the Yazoo in November 1862. He recalls of his first meeting with Rawlins:

He was seated at his desk with his back to the door, with no one else in the room. As I entered he swung around with a look of inquiry upon his dark and serious face. I told him who I was, and, handing him a copy of my orders, said I had come to report to General Grant for duty. He replied at once that the general was absent at Memphis, but would be back shortly.

He then referred to a pledge made by Grant not to drink during the war. 'He dwelt upon the danger which this pledge was intended to guard against, and marked his apprehensions in a most dramatic manner by referring to the sword of Damocles.' Wilson continues with reference to the more impressive aspects of Grant's achievements, that

> [Rawlins] regarded Grant as a good man, an experienced and courageous officer, who did his duty loyally and well, and always told about it plainly and truthfully; that he was cool, level-headed and sensible, of sound judgement, singular modesty, loyalty and patriotism, and could certainly lead us to victory, if his friends could 'stay him from falling'. Rawlins then added that there were some good officers on the staff, but more bad ones, and that he wanted me to help clean them out.

Rawlins actually disliked paperwork and was happy to enlarge his sphere of activity. Grant had been criticised by his superior, Major General Henry W. Halleck, Commander of the Military Division of the Mississippi, for failing to make rapid returns and present reports. Although there were mitigating circumstances and Halleck was a fussy office general, the responsibility for this rested with Grant's staff. Rawlins was perhaps a rather awkward writer, and inclined towards involved grammatical constructions – although he could write fluently when aroused. Charles A. Dana perhaps exaggerated when he reported in July 1863 that

> Grant thinks Rawlins a first-rate adjutant, but I think this is a mistake. He is too slow, and can't write the English language correctly without a great deal of careful consideration. Indeed, illiterateness is a general characteristic of Grant's staff, and in fact of Grant's general and regimental officers of all ranks.[10]

It was Grant's habit to write out all of his own reports and orders in his own hand. In short, he did all the work of a commander himself. He had a good memory and could synthesise powerfully all the conflicting issues and draw them together into one compelling overview or concept. The documents were then handed over to Rawlins, who, assisted by Major (later Lieutenant Colonel) Theodore S. Bowers (bringing the combined talents of a lawyer and a reporter to their task), extended, developed and actually tested the assumptions and assertions, on which Grant's plans rested. It was this combination of Grant's broad intellect, his lucid writing, and Rawlins's exegesis of them, which make his documents and military papers among the most impressive and complete of the war. Horace Porter had watched this process at the beginning of the Chattanooga campaign. Faced with a crisis at every turn, Grant took calm but firm control.

> He soon after began to write despatches, and I rose to go, but resumed my seat as he said 'Sit still'. My attention was soon attracted to the manner in which he went to work at his correspondence…he wrote nearly all his documents with his own hand, and seldom dictated to anyone even the most unimportant despatch. His work was performed swiftly and uninterruptedly, but without any marked display of nervous energy. His thoughts flowed as freely from his mind as the ink from his pen; he was never at a loss for an expression, and seldom interlined a word or made a material correction. He sat with his head bent low over the table, and when he had occasion to step to another table or desk to get a paper he wanted, he would glide rapidly across the room without straightening himself, and return to his seat with his body still bent over at about the same angle at which he had been sitting when he left his chair.[11]

This evidence of Grant's astonishing calmness and power of decision even under the most vexing circumstances, raises another issue emerging from Wilson's biography. It is striking that in this account, which has many virtues, the source of all the correct paths to follow – notably at Vicksburg and Chattanooga – seems to be, Grant's staff. This is so notwithstanding Wilson's disclaimer that Rawlins was not a Berthier. Anybody who has ever watched at first hand commanders and their staff work together will be aware of two main characteristics. First, how the character of the staff, whatever the personalities of the individuals involved, as an aggregate will reflect the character of the man they serve (even if he is weak and ineffectual). Secondly, that the number of actual ideas concerning various alternatives confronting a commander at any given stage during a campaign is usually small. These are often discussed by even the most junior of staff officers with great confidence and elaboration; indeed the more junior the officer concerned, the greater his confidence that his preferred alternative is the right course.

On two occasions, during the informal 'council of war' convened by Grant in February 1863, after the failure to seize the Yazoo Pass during the First Vicksburg campaign; and later, throughout the anxious moments at Chattanooga in November 1863 as to whether General Thomas should order the advance of the Army of the Cumberland towards the Confederate rifle pits on Missionary Ridge, after the comparative failure of the assaults of Sherman and Hooker on the flanks, Wilson in *The Life of John A. Rawlins* simply gives the impression that Grant carried out the blandishments of his staff. Other sources (and Wilson himself during his account of the Vicksburg deliberation) indicate that Grant was so deep in thought that he was not only seemingly deaf but said nothing. General O.O. Howard observed the day before Thomas's attack that Rawlins's importunities seemed to have no effect as Grant smoked his cigar contemplating the position, 'looking steadily toward the troops just engaged and beyond …When General Grant spoke at last, and without turning to look at anybody, he said, "Intrench them and send up support".' From this laconic instruction led a chain of events culminating in a great victory. It is the duty of the commander *to take decisions*, and employ the appropriate expedient at just the right moment; he may be blessed with luck, as was Grant at Chattanooga when Missionary Ridge fell virtually without a fight. Nevertheless, the choice and the responsibility is no less onerous merely because it is advocated by others who do not carry the commanding general's burdens. In Grant's remorseless, ruminative dissection of the circumstances attendant to each decision that he took, we may conclude that Rawlins's entreaties were just one, though probably not an unimportant factor, in the process by which a final judgment on what measure to take was reached. Wilson's book was a reaction against the unjust neglect of Rawlins's contribution to Grant's campaigns, and it simply claims too much for him. This is not confined to the military sphere. Wilson tends to give the impression, for instance, that Rawlins did the great bulk of the work on writing Grant's final report on the Vicksburg campaign in July 1864. Grant wrote this himself; Rawlins edited it and filled in some factual detail and dates.[12]

The other area, mentioned earlier, in which Rawlins did play an important role in advising the commanding general, had more to do with political affairs. Here Grant's very strengths, his simplicity, moral courage, and modesty, were more evident as limitations. This was especially true of his dealings with the press. Grant was not a particularly experienced officer in 1861 and had no more dealings with newspapermen than any other citizen. Grant had a great deal to complain about. Vicious camp rumours led Whitelaw Reid, a journalist, to erroneously suppose that Grant was drunk at the beginning of the Battle of Shiloh. This was the source of a long-running discussion as to the extent of Grant's inability to attend to his duties because of the influence of drink.[13]

There can be no doubt that it took Grant a long time to live down his reputation as a drinker who had been forced out of the service because of an addiction to the bottle. It seems important to note that heavy drinking was the norm among the leaders of the United States at this time. General Joseph Hooker was only the most famous heavy drinker. Consequently, this whole problem is riddled with ambivalence. Heavy drinking was the norm yet everybody was of the opinion that such behaviour was disgraceful. Much of the incompetence displayed in the first months of the war could be put down to the evils of drink; it became a scapegoat, any sign of wayward conduct was due to inebriation. Yet many of the politicians who were concerned with rooting this out were themselves heavy drinkers. Grant's problem was complicated because he had very few influential supporters in the highest circles to protect him from wild accusations. This had become very evident after Grant's debut as a battlefield commander at the Battle of Belmont in November 1861. Grant's conduct during this small-scale action was less than professional – but then this is hardly surprising since Grant had never commanded anything larger than a company previously. Nonetheless, in the byzantine atmosphere of press rumour and jostling for position, rumours grew that his errors were due to incapacity induced by an alcoholic haze. Rawlins immediately sat down and wrote a long letter of explanation to Washburne. He argued 'that the statement that General Grant is drinking very hard is utterly untrue and could have originated only in malice'. He went on to make a revealing admission about Grant's methods: 'There is not an officer in the Army who discharges the duties of his command so nearly without the intervention of aides, or assistants as does General Grant.' Wilson's account tends to downgrade this feature of Grant's command, but Rawlins himself accentuated it. But the happy result of Rawlins's intervention was that it secured Washburne's undying support for Grant. He was the kind of powerful friend at Lincoln's court which Grant needed badly.[14]

As the newspapers were the vehicle through which Grant's position could be undermined, Rawlins devoted his time to winning over newspapermen. His main target was Sylvanus Cadwallader, correspondent for the *Chicago Times*, and therefore an important voice in shaping opinion in Grant's home state of Illinois. Initially, most newspaper correspondents were *persona non grata*; in Cadwallader's words 'official hostility was openly expressed and hindrance put in their way as to collecting and transmitting any news.' General Stephen A. Hurlbut, an old political ally of the President, had gone so far as to ban the *Chicago Times* from his lines, 'to the extent of seizing and destroying the papers found in the hands of the newsboys and dragging the innocent vendors to the Provost Marshal for punishment, before they knew of the orders'. Whatever the source of Hurlbut's grievance, and Cadwallader was inclined to blame the proprietors of rival newspapers for inflaming options against the *Times*, this newspaper was not only influential within Illinois but had the largest circulation of a Midwest newspaper on the eastern seaboard; it could not be alienated. There was also the issue that newspapers could be banned inconsistently on the whim of district commanders when policy on such matters should be co-ordinated by departmental commanders. Rawlins agreed with Cadwallader's complaints. They had already become close friends (and Cadwallader enjoyed messing privileges denied other civilians). The final decision rested with Grant (and Rawlins could not predict how he would react). Grant agreed with his Chief of Staff's views, observing in his clipped way that though he disagreed with the views sometimes advanced by the *Times*, 'he nevertheless admitted the right of anyone to pay for it and read it'.[15]

The other area in which Rawlins played a crucial role was in advancing Grant's political position with the Lincoln administration and ensuring that further promotion was open to him. The best example of this was dealing with the mission of Charles A. Dana, sent as emissary by the President to look over Grant and his army in April 1863. After the failure of Grant's first advance on Vicksburg and the destruction of the Federal base at Holly Springs, rumours that Grant had been incapacitated by drink circulated once more. Lincoln had despatched Dana to surreptitiously observe proceedings in Grant's army. He was regarded as a political 'spy' by Grant's staff even before he arrived. Rawlins briefed them all stressing that the paramount object was to keep Dana quiescent until Grant could work out the next phase of the campaign and then present it as a *fait accompli*. Cadwallader's account of this meeting relates that 'he [Dana] was denounced by the chief of artillery, Colonel William S. Duff, that he was a government spy and should be thrown in the river'. Rawlins took a very firm line with this kind of injudicious remark, and replied coldly:

> I am surprised, Col[onel] Duff, at your discourteous and unmilitary remarks, Mr Dana is…an official representative of the government. He should not be left in a moment's doubt as to the cordiality of his reception. He is entitled to as much official recognition as Mr Stanton…I shall expect you to see that a tent is always pitched alongside Gen[eral] Grant's, for Mr Dana's use as long as he remains at headquarters – that sentries are placed in front of it – that orderlies are detailed for his service – and a place at mess-table specially reserved for him.[16]

As a result of Rawlins's many personal kindnesses, Dana was not only mollified but became a warm admirer of Grant: another powerful ally gained in the administration.

Perhaps some further reflections on Grant's drinking are in order. John Y. Simon has emphasised that Grant was peculiarly susceptible to alcohol; that he could not really drink very much without being greatly affected – his fair complexion would become very flushed and his slow, gruff speech slurred. Thus he gave the impression of having drunk more than was actually the case. But if drinking was so much more widespread than earlier writers were prepared to admit, then Grant's occasional binges strike the twentieth-century observer as being wholly human and do not deserve the self-righteous denunciation they have occasionally received. This remark applies equally to the defensive tone of his sympathetic biographers, such as Bruce Catton, who treated descriptions of Grant's drinking as malign attempts to besmirch his reputation.[17] Even writers like Wilson who emphasised Rawlins's part in Grant's triumphs tend to treat the whole issue – including Rawlins's decisive and godly intervention – as something resembling a Samuel Smiles dissertation on the righteous virtues. If we adopt a cooler, less self-righteous approach, then neither Grant's drinking need be taken so seriously, nor Rawlins's self-appointed role as his moral guardian. Nevertheless, we should be aware of the proviso that Rawlins shrewdly undercut the political damage that rumours about drink would have inflicted on Grant's chances of further advancement. 'It did not take Grant and Rawlins to make Grant, as some have said who knew neither intimately', wrote Adam Badeau, formerly Grant's military secretary, and the author of what amounts to his official biography, 'Rawlins himself would have been the first to repel the pretension. He was simply an earnest, able man who devoted himself absolutely to serving his country, and for him this was synonymous with serving Grant.'[18]

The political pattern of Rawlins's influence was to grow in importance with Grant's increasing seniority and public standing. The military operations of the Civil War cannot be understood correctly unless they are related to the political tumult which surrounded and directed them. The major political challenge that Grant faced in 1862-63 came from Major General John A. McClernand, an important War Democrat and former Illinois congressman. His contribution was obviously important to the Lincoln Administration, especially as the southern counties of that state had exhibited latent secessionist tendencies.[19] McClernand was an opinionated and ambitious man whose military schemes and dreams outran his ability to put them into practice. He continually importuned the President for an independent command along the lines of that achieved later by Benjamin F. Butler in Virginia and Nathaniel P. Banks during the Red River Campaign. McClernand had always resented serving under Grant and in January 1862 he exploited Grant's brief absence to submit a report after the Battle of Belmont describing himself, with some effrontery, as 'Commanding District of Cairo'.[20] In September 1862 Lincoln finally agreed to a sweeping plan he proposed for him to raise 'legion' from among Illinois Democrats, sweep down the Mississippi and seize Vicksburg. The aim was hazy, the organisation sloppy, and communication poor. Grant learnt about the plan from the newspapers. It was typical of political interference in the conduct of military operations at its worst.[21]

Grant dealt with McClernand quietly – without bombastic and histrionic protests – and effectively. McClernand did not handle himself with a similar measure of skill or self-assurance. Grant, of course, remained the departmental commander, and was given permission by the General-in-Chief, Henry W. Halleck, to use all the troops in his department, including those that McClernand regarded as 'his'. McClernand lost his temper when he found that Sherman had already departed with them in Grant's preliminary moves in the campaign.

It was this intemperate behaviour that allowed Rawlins to move against McClernand's superficially strong, but organisationally weak position. The staff were irritated by McClernand's venom and wished to see him ousted. During the controversy that followed, Rawlins ensured that Dana was fully briefed on the merits of Grant's case thus ensuring that the Secretary of War, Edwin M. Stanton (also a Democrat), would not intervene on McClernand's behalf.

If anything Rawlins's impetuosity got the better of him in his desire to finish McClernand off; but Grant, always calculating and self-controlled, would not be hurried. He sensed that McClernand would hang himself with a length of his own rope. Vanity sealed McClernand's doom when, after a humiliating repulse before Vicksburg he issued a congratulatory order to the press attempting to shroud his failure in sham glory. On 17 June 1863 Grant issued an order relieving McClernand of command of XIII Corps. Rawlins remained anxious until he received confirmation that McClernand understood the order and obeyed it. It is perhaps characteristic of those that offer advice rather than carry the responsibility for it that they should urge action and then show something less than equanimity when the order is finally carried out. Grant, however, remained phlegmatic, and all of McClernand's bluster could not move Lincoln or Stanton to interfere in the chain of command and remove Grant and Haelleck, because he had been personally affronted. Of course, the eventual successful development of operations on the Vicksburg front, especially by June 1863, fortified Grant's position, but Rawlins's dexterity was of great help to him. Rawlins's position was strengthened, in turn, because he, too, was a War Democrat. Thus he was despatched to Washington on a mission to explain affairs to the President face to face, on Grant's behalf, and though Rawlins worried that the relief of McClernand might have vexed Lincoln, the issue was not raised again. Lincoln must also have been aware that McClernand would use a successful seizure of Vicksburg as a basis for a campaign to gain the Democratic nomination in the 1864 Presidential Election.[22]

A chief of staff, however forcefully or urgently he argues a particular course, gives voice to an essentially corporate view. The commanding general is invariably in a more exposed position because he, and he alone, takes responsibility for the decisions, whatever their source. Grant, unlike George B. McClellan, could take a decision and stick to it, and not agonise for weeks over its ramifications. After Grant's promotion to lieutenant general in 1864, and Rawlins's rise to the rank of brigadier general,[23] the latter enjoyed a broadening of his sphere of influence. As General-in-Chief Grant sagely decided not to combine his important strategic duties with command of the Army of the Potomac, which would undoubtedly have involved him in intricate and time-consuming detail that would have worn him down, as it had McClellan, from November 1861-March 1862.[24] Rawlins thus became Chief of Staff to the

General-in-Chief of the armies of the United States. He was therefore responsible for the issue of orders to the Commander of the Army of the Potomac, George G. Meade, the Commander of the Army of the James, Benjamin F. Butler, the Commander of the IX Corps, Ambrose E. Burnside (which remained an independent force until 24 May 1864), and all the multifarious forces operating in Virginia, Tennessee, northern Georgia and parts of the deep South and far West. Thus, although Rawlins's functions would undoubtedly have become as muddled as Grant's had the latter decided to command the Army of the Potomac in May 1864, Rawlins's new position resulted in a waning of his operational influence during the Virginia campaign.[25]

Why did this occur, while Rawlins's political importance continued unrivalled? In the first place, Rawlins (and Grant's entire staff) were overwhelmed with work, co-ordinating the movements of so many forces, led by independent-minded and prickly men; as the war drew to an end, the load on the staff – which never exceeded 15 officers – grew even heavier. Rawlins was an awkward writer and the sheer level of correspondence kept him busy.[26] Secondly, a lot of time was also spent by Rawlins in following Grant's example in trying to improve morale in the Army of the Potomac and reduce the naked feelings of inferiority in that army after its many defeats at Lee's hands. Grant realised quickly that this had to be done without humiliating those who had not served with him in the West. In pursuit of this objective Rawlins came to admire Meade immensely.[27] The third reason must also be that Grant had grown immeasurably in confidence since the failure of his first Vicksburg campaign, and simply did not require the advice of another. For example, during the series of audacious and brilliantly conceived operations culminating in the crossing of the James River in June 1864, Rawlins played a very minor and subordinate part (perhaps trying to persuade Grant to change his mind and cross the James at City Point rather than at Wilcox's Landing, advice that Grant ignored). Indeed, it could be argued that Grant tried to do too much himself during the campaign – in carrying out so many difficult functions at various levels virtually unaided.[28] The exaggeration of Rawlins's part in his earlier triumphs which had appeared in the newspapers may also have irked him – and led him to accord Rawlins's military advice less weight than he was once disposed to grant it.

A factor of not inconsiderable influence, which had little to do with the conduct of the campaign, was the drastic decline of Rawlins's health. The onset of fatal tuberculosis had begun at Chattanooga in November 1863. On 25 July 1864 Rawlins left the Army via Washington to give the President and Secretary of War despatches, not returning for three months; but by then he had delegated most of his staff work. Theodore S. Bowers kept him informed of most significant developments. But his political influence still remained formidable, as William S. Rosecrans found to his cost. In October 1864 Rawlins urged

29

Grant to relieve him on the grounds of insubordination and inefficiency, and Rawlins was also sent to St Louis to 'enforce' Grant's orders.[29]

Because of his poor health, Rawlins had offered to resign before Grant moved to Washington in March 1864. Grant did not desire this, for as Wilson avers, after he had moved east (contrary to Sherman's advice), 'He was surrounded...by strangers who were more or less incredulous as to his real capacity as a general', and he needed his friends. Yet a new environment brought new allies for a general as well as new enemies, and Grant soon grasped who had capacity and who had not among the staff officers whose acquaintance he now made, and this, too, diminished Rawlins's hold over those around him. Needless to say, Rawlins believed that this contributed to a decline in the quality of the staff and its work.[30] This generalisation may be doubted, otherwise Grant could not have organised the crossing of the James at such short notice in a highly improvised operation. What was blameworthy in the 1864 campaign was the squandering of opportunities in the forests of northern Virginia and after crossing the James, as the Union forces advanced on the important rail centre at Petersburg. This was the fault of field commanders, and not the staff.[31]

The 1864 campaign provides ample evidence that Rawlins's contributions were not fundamental to Grant's operational success, though he could certainly express, communicate and occasionally embroider Grant's thinking for his gruff and inarticulate chief. Nonetheless Grant could (and did) manage perfectly well without him, and indeed, during the James River Crossing demonstrated the acme of his skill as a commander without Rawlins's assistance. That Grant was content with this state of affairs may be put down to the undoubted fact that operationally Rawlins had reached his ceiling by May 1864. Although still adept in the political and patronage stakes, Rawlins's military thoughts could no longer rise to meet the challenges of the great battles of 1864. Grant must have found this irritating because in the strategic discussions of April 1864, Rawlins had been an unrestrained and powerful advocate of an overland campaign across northern Virginia towards Richmond, rather than making use of the Union command of the sea to mount a variant of McClellan's 'indirect approach', via Chesapeake Bay and the Peninsula. Grant's initial instincts were to make greater use of Union seapower, but he quickly abandoned this notion. Although Grant's account of his first interview with Lincoln is rather inadequate, he must have come away impressed by the determination of the President and his cabinet not to expose Washington DC to any Confederate riposte, and its vulnerability would be increased by diverting the Army of the Potomac to the Virginia coastline. Grant was always sensitive to political anxieties, and needed no tutoring in this area. In short, Rawlins's entreaties on the need for a Virginian advance merely confirmed conclusions that Grant had already reached himself.[32]

But what Grant must have found annoying was Rawlins's failure to understand that both the terrain and the dispositions of the enemy rendered it difficult for the Army of the Potomac to manoeuvre. Grant certainly hoped to bring Lee to battle on his terms decisively and destroy his army before it could retire into the Richmond defences, but this was not easy. All of Grant's battles in May 1864, Wilderness, Spotsylvania and Cold Harbor, degenerated unexpectedly into attritional encounters, whose cumulative effect weakened Lee's offensive power. This was a side effect of the prolonged struggle which pleased Grant. Rawlins denounced frontal assaults on Confederate entrench-ments ferociously, and blamed Colonel C.B. Comstock, a former member of McClellan's staff. Rawlins resented Comstock's increasing influence over Grant. That Rawlins was then expressing fawning admiration for General Meade, who was primarily responsible for the tactical combinations of the Army of the Potomac, indicated a measure of inconsistency in these criticisms. Grant did not have the freedom of action that Rawlins supposed. Though he might be criticised for some complacency in coping with trench warfare, he was not blind to the need for novel methods, as shown by the encouragement given to Emory Upton's experiments with modified offensive formations. Perhaps it was with some relief that Grant, from July 1864 onwards, granted Rawlins leave of absence and sent him on missions beyond Virginia. [33]

But Rawlins was not utterly discredited. He was still useful to Grant. Rawlins rallied around to help support his chief at the height of the crisis during the second day of the Battle of the Wilderness. Wilson, in his account, was told by Rawlins and Bowers that though outwardly always calm, imperturbable and pugnacious, on the night of 7 May, Grant retired to his tent, and 'gave vent to his feelings…he was deeply moved'. But as Grant did not allow these private doubts for a second to influence his professional judgement, such an anecdote not only gives us a human glimpse of him, but increases our admiration for this self-contained, determined and courageous general, who was determined to act and not be paralysed by the indecision that had plagued all those who had commanded before him. But Grant himself was not one for galvanising, histrionic gestures. Here Rawlins was valuable. Major General Marsena R. Patrick, the somewhat bad-tempered Provost Marshal of the Army of the Potomac, commented in his diary: 'I do not see that Grant does anything but sit quietly about, whittle, smoke and let Gen[era]l Rawlins talk big.' [34]

We may therefore conclude that General Wilson's *Life of John A. Rawlins* exaggerates Rawlins's achievements by stressing that he played a major part in Grant's operational inspiration – though his role was far from insignificant. Towards the end of the book Wilson attempts to reveal that Rawlins had an important role in ensuring that Philip H. Sheridan's cavalry was not sent to serve with Sherman, but would remain with the Army of the Potomac, provide a substantial augmentation of its strength, and be available for the strongest possible pursuit should Lee evacuate Richmond. But Wilson, although he quotes from Sheridan's *Personal Memoirs*, does not point out that Rawlins was not even present when Grant took the decision to keep Sheridan with him. Rawlins was the spokesman for a corporate view; it was Grant that was responsible for the decision, and his decision was undoubtedly the right one, as the success of the concluding operations showed. Rawlins, of course, until the end performed many signal services as a staff officer. For example, he perceptively noted during the final correspondence between Grant and Lee, prior to the surrender at Appomattox, that Lee was attempting to meet Grant to negotiate a general peace rather than unconditionally surrender his army. [35]

Apart from the odd absence, Rawlins was Grant's indefatigable companion; a cheerleader to Grant's indomitable spirit. By providing an agreeable and supportive atmosphere for the general, without which Grant would have succumbed to depression and loneliness, Rawlins made an essential contribution to his victorious career. Whatever the details of Grant's drinking, James M. McPherson is surely correct in arguing that if he had alcoholic tendencies, Grant 'should have felt pride rather than shame, because he overcame his illness to achieve success and fame without the support system of modern medicine…But…he could not see it that way'. The almost complete expunging of Rawlins from his own memoirs, and the histories of his admirers, may be attributed to Grant's discomfort over his conquest of alcoholism. Thus 'to give Rawlins his due…would perhaps have seemed a public confession of weakness and shame.' [36] Grant and Rawlins formed an interdependent relationship which was unusual among commanders and chiefs of staff. Rawlins may not have been a never-ending source of inspiration for Grant, but we can be sure that without Rawlins Grant's career would not have advanced so rapidly, and so assuredly, towards the rank of General-in-Chief.

Notes

1.   *The Personal Memoirs of U.S. Grant* I, pp. 255-256, Sampson, Low, London (1886) devotes one paragraph to Rawlins without detailing his prime contributions to Grant's success.

2.   James Harrison Wilson, *The Life of John A. Rawlins*, Neale, New York (1916).

3.   Sylvanus Cadwallader, (Benjamin P. Thomas, ed.) *Three Years with Grant*, p. 140, Alfred A. Knopf, New York (1956).

4. C.F. Adams, *An Autobiography, 1835-1915*, p. 157, Chelsea House, New York (1983 paperback edition); Wilson, *Rawlins*, pp. 17,18.

5. Wilson, *Rawlins*, pp. 23-35, 38.

6. Ibid., pp. 47-50; Grant, *Memoirs*, I, pp. 24-31; John A. Carpenter, *Ulysses S. Grant*, p. 2, Twayne, New York (1970); Maj Gen J.F.C. Fuller, *The Generalship of Ulysses S. Grant*, pp. 72-73, John Murray, London (1929), Second Edition, Indiana University Press (1957).

7. Grant to Julia Grant, 10 August, 8 September 1861; Grant to Frémont, 21 August 1861; Grant to J.R. Grant, 27 August 1861; Grant to Elihu B. Washburne, 3 September 1861, *The Papers of Ulysses S. Grant*, II, pp. 96, 125, 145, 182, 213. Southern Illinois U.P, Carbondale and Edwardsville (1969) [hereafter *Grant Papers*]. In the Cadwallader Papers there is a paper headed: 'I believe the following list embraces the names of all who ever served on the staff of General U.S. Grant.' It includes a total of 42 names excluding Cadwallader who was an honorary member. Library of Congress.

8. Wilson, *Rawlins*, pp. 71, 124.

9. Cadwallader, *Three Years with Grant*, p. 118.

10. Wilson, *Rawlins*, pp. 60-63, 72, 99-101, 124.

11. Ibid., p. 56; Horace Porter, *Campaigning with Grant*, pp. 6-7, Century, New York (1890); William S. McFeely, *Grant: A Biography*, p. 146, Norton, New York (1981); John Keegan, *The Mask of Command*, pp. 198-200, Jonathan Cape, London (1987).

12. Wilson, *Rawlins*, pp. 110-120; McFeely, *Grant*, pp. 147-8; Bruce Catton, *Grant Takes Command*, pp. 79-85, Little Brown, Boston (1968); *Grant Papers*, VIII, pp. 508-509.

13. Catton, *Grant Moves South*, pp. 252-257, 301-303, Little Brown, Boston (1960); John F. Marszalek, *Sherman: A Soldier's Passion for Order*, Free Press, New York (1993), pp., 198, 210-213. In February 1863, Sherman had Thomas W. Knox of the *New York Herald* court-martialled as a spy, and sought the death penalty.

14. The question of the influence of drink is raised in Roy F. Nichols, *The Disruption of American Democracy*, pp. 140-142, 164, 166, 310, 312. Macmillan, New York (1948); Carpenter, *Grant*, pp. 17-18; Wilson, *Rawlins*, pp. 68-69. Washburne was lobbying for Grant's promotion to Major General in October. See Grant to Julia Grant, 6 October 1861, *Grant Papers*, III, p. 23; for Washburne's unwavering support (his influence with the President) and the 'very flattering interest you have taken in my personal welfare and advancement' and Grant's determination to repay it 'that you may not be disappointed in your appreciation', see Grant to Washburne, 20 November 1861, Ibid., III, pp. 204-5, 206nl-3.

15. Cadwallader, *Three Years with Grant*, pp. 10-11, 54,57.

16. Ibid., pp. 61-62; Wilson, *Rawlins*, p. 193. Dana helped Grant increase the numbers of his staff and acquire the rank of lieutenant general. See Samuel Carter III, *The Final Fortress: The Campaign for Vicksburg, 1862-1863*, p. 306, St Martin's Press, New York (1980).

17. See for example, Catton, *Grant Takes Command*, pp. 65-67.

18. Catton, *Grant Moves South,* pp. 393-397; Adam Badeau, *Military History of U.S. Grant*, II, p. 191n, Appleton, New York (1881). There is a very fair assessment of the Grant-Rawlins relationship in McFeely, *Grant*, pp. 147-148.

19. As evidenced by cheering of Southern prisoners of war after the fall of Fort Donelson in February 1862. See Flavel C. Barber (Robert H. Ferrell, ed.), *Holding the Line: The Third Tennessee Infantry, 1861-1864*, pp. 37, 39, 62, 64-65, Kent State U.P. (1994).

20. Kenneth P. Williams, *Lincoln Finds a General*, III, p. 187, Macmillan, New York (1952).

21. T. Harry Williams, *Lincoln and his Generals*, pp. 190-194, Alfred A. Knopf, New York (1952).

22. Ibid., pp. 218-27; Wilson, *Rawlins*, pp. 130-135; Williams, *Lincoln Finds a General*, IV, pp. 433-439; Grant, *Personal Memoirs,* I, pp. 546-547; Carpenter, *Grant,* p. 38.

23. Wilson, *Rawlins*, p. 396; on Grant's irritation that Rawlins's spokesmen were justifying his promotion on the grounds that he was 'one-half Grant' and 'provided brains', see Catton, *Grant Takes Command*, pp. 136-137.

24. Brian Holden Reid, 'Rationality and Irrationality in Union Strategy, April 1861-March 1862', *War and History*, I, p. 37, (1994).

25. Grant, *Memoirs*, II, p. 116-118.

26. Wilson, *Rawlins*, p. 317; William D. Matter, *If It Takes All Summer: The Battle of Spotsylvania*, p. 130, University of North Carolina Press, Chapel Hill (1988), includes an example.

27. Michael C.C. Adams, *Fighting for Defeat: Union Military Failure in the East, 1861-1865*, pp. 152-156, University of Nebraska Press, Lincoln (1978, 1992 reprint); Gordon C. Rhea, *The Battle of the Wilderness, May 5-6, 1864*, pp. 42-45, Louisiana State UP, Baton Rouge (1994); Wilson, *Rawlins*, pp. 222, 229; Edward Steere, *The Wilderness Campaign*, pp. 182-183, Stackpole, Mechanicsburg PA (1960, 1988).

28. Brian Holden Reid, 'Another Look at Grant's Crossing of the James, 1864', *Civil War History*, 39, pp. 305, 311-313 (1993).

29. Wilson, *Rawlins*, pp. 200, 255-256, 261, 263, 265, 270.

30. Ibid., pp. 203, 211, 227-228, 249-250.

31. Ibid., pp. 194-195, Steere, *Wilderness Campaign*, pp. 413, 415; Holden Reid, 'Grant's Crossing of the James', pp. 309-315.

32. Williams, *Lincoln and his Generals*, pp. 295-296; Rhea, *Wilderness*, p. 44; Grant, *Personal Memoirs*, II, pp. 122-123. Rowena Reed, *Combined Operations in the Civil War*, pp. 323-332, University of Nebraska Press, Lincoln (1978, 1993), is critical of Grant's shift of emphasis, but her portrait of him as a muddle-headed lightweight, devoid of ideas of his own, and putty in the hands of a calculating and prejudiced Halleck, is shallow and unconvincing.

33. Rhea, *Wilderness*, pp. 431-436; Wilson, *Rawlins*, pp. 198-199, 209, 227, 249-250; Stephen E. Ambrose, *Upton and the Army*, pp. 30-33, Louisiana State UP, Baton Rouge (1964, 1992). Upton blamed the Corps

Commanders (p. 37). The best discussion of the attritional dilemmas of 1864 is still Fuller, *Generalship of U.S. Grant*, pp. 223-228. More recent conceptual confusion of US historians is discussed in Holden Reid, 'Grant's Crossing of the James', pp. 292-296, 314-315.

34. Wilson, *Rawlins*, pp. 216-217; Catton, *Grant Takes Command*, p. 205.

35. Wilson, *Rawlins*, pp. 312-315, 318-323, although Wilson was right in thinking that Grant, *Personal Memoirs*, II, p. 436, misrepresents Rawlins's views.

36. James M. McPherson, 'Ulysses S. Grant's Final Victory' in Robert Cowley (ed.), *Experience of War,* p. 231, Norton, New York (1992); For a stout defence of Grant, see Williams, *Lincoln Finds a General*, IV, pp. 439-447.

COMMAND IN THE LATE VICTORIAN ARMY

by Ian F.W. Beckett

hen U.S. Grant was appointed General-in-Chief of the Union Armies in March 1864 he was assuming overall responsibility for the direction of some 533,000 men. Exactly seven years later Helmuth von Moltke was directing the efforts of approximately 850,000 men in the closing stages of the Franco-Prussian War.[1] By comparison, between October 1899 and January 1900 Britain despatched only 112,000 regulars to the Cape and, even adding together all those forces eventually deployed in South Africa would still yield a total of only 450,000 men. Yet, of course, this effort was herculean when set beside the usual pattern of Victorian campaigning and, in fact, the largest number of men put into the field between the Crimean and South African wars was the 35,000 or so in what might be termed the Egyptian theatre in 1882. Even then, the actual field force directed by the commanding general, Garnet Wolseley, against Arabi's forces was only some 16,000 strong.[2]

There were those within the Victorian Army who have been described as 'continentalists' to whom, to quote Lonsdale Hale, such colonial expeditions were 'the play of children'. Equally, those characterised as of the 'imperial' school of military theory had a point when, as T.M. Maguire expressed it in 1896,

> while looking at the stars we may tumble in a ditch, and while lost in wonder
> at how to move effectively from Strasburg, Mayence and Metz towards Paris
> with many divisions of cavalry and armies consisting each of from three to
> eight corps, we may forget how to handle a few battalions in the passes of
> the Suleiman Range or in the deserts of Upper Egypt.[3]

Certainly, when discussing methods of command and attitudes towards staff work in the Victorian Army, while it is always necessary to bear in mind the limited scale of the forces involved, sight should not be lost of the considerable professional demands actually being made upon commanders and their staffs.

As noted by the principal theorist of British colonial warfare, Charles

Callwell, Victorian campaigns were waged as much against nature as against indigenous opponents. Wolseley, for example, wrote during the Ashanti campaign of 1873-74 that, 'I always seem to be condemned to command in expeditions which must be accomplished before a certain season of the year begins', reflecting the need to complete operations between December and mid-February before the climate took its toll of his European troops. Earlier, of course, during the 1870 Red River expedition in the Canadian north-west, it had been a case of traversing the 600 miles of wilderness from Thunder Bay to Fort Garry and back before the lakes froze. The route required Wolseley's force to bypass 47 separate unnavigable sections of water or portages while the advance from the Prah to the Ashanti capital at Kumasi needed the construction of 237 bridges.[4]

Similar difficulties were to be encountered in campaigns mounted by the Indian Army. The advance of Sir Robert Napier's expeditionary force, which had 13,000 fighting troops, some 400 miles from the Red Sea coast to the Abyssinian capital of Magdala in 1867-68 required the support of over 14,500 followers and 36,000 draught animals, while two far smaller expeditions on the largely uninhabited and heavily forested north-eastern frontier of India itself – the Lushai expedition of 1871-72 and the Duffla expedition of 1874-75 – required 5,500 and 1,200 coolies respectively. Similarly, climate and terrain were of the utmost significance throughout the Second Afghan War of 1878-81. What could be achieved at the outset, for example, was limited by the necessity of beginning the campaign in November while the lack of transport was a constant nightmare. In February 1879, therefore, it became necessary to reduce the size of Sir Donald Stewart's force at Kandahar, by which time there were also fears that other garrisons would soon need reduction rather than risk troops' health once the weather began to get hot.[5]

One attempted solution to the supply problems was to extend the Indian railway system from the Indus to the Bolan Pass, 133 miles of track being laid in just 101 days. Similarly, railways were constructed elsewhere as at Suakin in 1885 and, later, to support the reconquest of the Sudan in 1896-98. The latter certainly illustrated the benefit of a military railway but far more might have been made of that at Suakin. Moreover, the single track line north into the Orange Free State upon which British forces were dependent once they had advanced to Bloemfontein in March 1900 actually inhibited mobility through its congestion and its vulnerability to guerrilla attack. The transport problems were highly reminiscent of those in the Zulu War of 1879 when it was not only painfully difficult for Lord Chelmsford to assemble the 977 wagons and 10,023 oxen he needed but also impossible to make more than 10 miles a day. Indeed, Wolseley was to complain that, on the move, Chelmsford's baggage train appeared to be at least three or four miles longer than it could actually travel in a day's march.[6]

Such difficulties help to explain Callwell's contention that, while tactics usually favoured British troops armed with modern weapons, strategic advantage most often rested with the indigenous opponent. The enormous variety of opponents, ranging from European-trained armies like the Egyptians of Arabi Pasha in 1882 and highly disciplined native armies like that of the Zulus to fundamentalist fanatics like the Dervishes and primitive tribesmen like the Aka of Assam, against whom an expedition was mounted in 1883, was another complication beyond the experience of a Moltke or even a Grant, who had fought Mexicans and Indians. Moreover, British officers were no less free than their German or Union counterparts from the pressures emanating from politicians and the press.

Moltke famously remarked that he disliked operating with a telegraph wire in his back but such was increasingly the fate of British commanders as a network of submarine cables and land lines stretched across the globe. By 1873 the transmission time from London to Bombay had been cut to just over three hours compared to a month for mail. The telegraph still reached only as far as the Cape Verde Islands when Wolseley was operating in Ashanti but annexation of the Transvaal in 1877 and the Zulu War speeded completion of the link to the Cape by 1887. Nevertheless, with or without telegraphic communications, political considerations could still impede the Army's operations. In South Africa in 1881 both Sir George Colley and his successor, Sir Evelyn Wood, suffered from what has been characterised as the 'tortuous transformation' of the policy of Gladstone's Cabinet towards the Boer republics. The same indecision was equally apparent in the delay in despatching Wolseley's expedition to Egypt three years later, Sir Arthur Hardinge noting of Wolseley's failure to save Charles Gordon that 'it is ungenerous to forget that nowadays military methods are too often the slaves of political expediency'. The relationship between the Viceroy, Lord Lytton, and his Commander-in-Chief in India, Sir Frederick Haines, from 1876 to 1880 similarly offers a case study of contrasting political and military considerations in the formulation of military policy.[7]

The Second Afghan War, which formed the context for many of the disagreements between Lytton and Haines, also demonstrated the need for field commanders to be capable of exercising both military and political judgement. Thus, in November 1878 Lytton preferred command of the Khyber Line Force to be entrusted to Sir Sam Browne rather than alternative candidates such as Frederick Maude and John Ross, not only on military grounds but also in view of Browne's knowledge of the Khyber tribes; Ross, indeed, had 'no political capacity'. Having already rung political alarm bells in the first part of the war by issuing a proclamation in December 1878 seeming to annex the Kuram valley, Frederick Roberts then mishandled the executions in Kabul in January 1880 of those suspected of complicity in the massacre of a political officer, Louis Cavagnari and his escort. As a result, Lepel Griffin was sent to correct 'the stupidity he [Roberts] has shown in all non-military matters'. Clearly irked, Roberts was to insist on full political powers when marching to the relief of Kandahar in August 1880. Nor was he the only soldier to covet political powers, Sir Donald Stewart having complained bitterly in February 1879 that his subordinate, Michael Biddulph, had 'an insane desire to enter into political relations with somebody, and thinks I don't treat him properly, because I do not invest him with specific political powers'.[8]

Wolseley of course, though contemptuous of politicians, was particularly well attuned to the needs of his political masters, writing to his wife in August 1879 that George Greaves, who had succeeded him on Cyprus,

> has yet to learn that it does not do to insert the whole truth in official correspondence. Despatches should always be strictly true, but unpleasant truths that can be made use of by the opponents of the Government you are serving should be reserved for one's private correspondence with ministers.

Not surprisingly, he enjoyed full military and political powers in a number of his campaigns as in South Africa in 1879 when, it can be noted, Chelmsford's fate had been finally sealed through his inability to co-operate with the Lieutenant Governor of Natal, Sir Henry Bulwer. As it happened, Chelmsford's predecessor, Sir Arthur Cunynghame, had also been removed for failure to work harmoniously with the colonial authorities.

Some of Wolseley's appointments, such as his mission to Natal in 1875 and command on Cyprus in 1879, were almost purely political in nature. The readiness of both Liberal and Conservative politicians to send Wolseley on expeditions and missions in itself reflected the increasing significance of public opinion and of the press that informed that public for all commanders. The Secretary of State for War, Frederick Stanley, for example, had specifically ruled out Sir Leicester Selby Smyth for the South African command in 1879 on the grounds that 'his name is hardly well enough known'.[9]

The Ashanti campaign, of course, had attracted an array of war correspondents including H.M. Stanley, while Napier was to remark of the Duffle expedition that, judging by the number of correspondents who accompanied it, it would become better known than Waterloo. Having described such correspondents in his *Soldier's Pocket Book* in 1869 as 'those newly invented curses to armies', Wolseley was predictably hostile to those who accompanied his expeditions although this was manifested more in his private correspondence than in public. Indeed, Wolseley was aware of the need 'to keep my name before the public' and that, as he wrote from Ashanti in November 1873, the press could easily 'turn round and abuse me as roundly as it had previously lavished unmerited praise upon me'. Certainly, it was frequently alleged that he manipulated the press, not least through having his staff write for newspapers. The Army's Commander-in-Chief, the Duke of Cambridge, was equally aware, as he informed Chelmsford in March 1879, that

> in these days the freedom of the press has taken very large dimensions, and anybody that has a relative or friend receives letters and send them to the press giving his version of events as they believe them to have occurred.[10]

It became customary to make all due arrangements for the accommodation of the 'specials' although, at the same time, issuing regulations for the press as in Afghanistan in 1878 and in Egypt in 1882. However, this did not prevent the press from inconvenient disclosure as in September 1879 when Lytton's ADC, George Villiers, was tricked by a correspondent of the *Pioneer* into confirming details of Roberts' Kabul Field Force. Similarly, Roberts, who was himself a conscious manipulator of the press, had earlier had Macpherson of *The Standard* removed from the Kuram Field Force for eluding press controls.[11]

In addition to what might be termed external pressures upon commanders, there was also the internal politics of the Army with which to contend. This was manifested most obviously in the rivalry of the 'rings', such as that associated with Wolseley and variously known as the Wolseley 'gang', the Ashanti 'ring' or the 'Mutual Admiration Society'. The struggle between Wolseley and his various rivals ranged widely. That waged with the traditionalists grouped around the Duke of Cambridge encompassed such reform issues as short service while that fought out with the 'Indians' – increasingly represented by Roberts – principally concerned the Empire's strategic orientation. Perhaps not unexpectedly, neither particular issues nor the positions assumed by individuals with respect to them were necessarily constant but the rivalry between different factions invariably centred upon manoeuvring adherents into particular commands. This in itself is too large a subject to be discussed in any detail here but some aspects of the selection of staff are relevant to consideration of command styles in the Army, as will be illustrated with particular reference to Wolseley.

The selection of staff for the Red River campaign was dictated by those officers available in Canada at the time, the only real exception being the employment of Hugh McCalmont, who made his own way there when his troop was about to be reduced and managed to persuade Wolseley to take him along. Thus, the association of Wolseley with Redvers Buller, William Butler,

Sir John McNeill and G.L. Huyshe was essentially unplanned although he was acquainted with Butler and McNeill from their Canadian service. However, Wolseley claimed in his memoirs that he 'had long been in the habit of keeping a list of the best and ablest soldiers I knew, and was always on the look-out for those who could safely be entrusted with any special military piece of work' and all five together with Assistant Controller M.B. Irvine were to be chosen for the Ashanti expedition. In the same vein, at a time when Butler was proving especially quarrelsome, Wolseley wrote in December 1884 that he would 'drop him from my list'.[12]

Ashanti, therefore, marked the effective beginning of the ring, the initial 36 staff and special service officers sailing with Wolseley in September 1873, including also Evelyn Wood, Baker Russell, Thomas Baker, Henry Brackenbury, Robert Home, Lord Gifford and Frederick Maurice. When McNeill was wounded, he was replaced by Greaves, who arrived in December, as did George Colley. The Red River contingent had proved their worth to Wolseley's satisfaction and others were also known to him personally, Greaves having shared the same room in the War Office and Wood having fortuitously met Wolseley while he was planning the expedition and joked of how his naval knowledge would be of utility on the rivers of West Africa. Most were young and many were clearly courageous. McNeill, Wood and the surgeon, Dr Anthony Home, who also accompanied Wolseley to Cyprus, had all won the Victoria Cross and Buller and Gifford were to win it subsequently.

Others were chosen on intellectual reputation, Brackenbury, Maurice and Colley being on the teaching staffs of Woolwich, Sandhurst and the Staff College respectively. Colley, of course, had passed out first from Camberley with a record number of marks in only nine months of self-tuition while Maurice had won the 1872 Wellington essay prize competition in which Wolseley was placed fifth. Wolseley had commented at the time that men like Maurice must in future be brought to the front and he was to explain in his memoirs that 'I felt that ordinary men could not be good enough for the work I had undertaken'. Accordingly, Wolseley had not simply chosen those at the top of the War Office register for special service and, indeed, stood accused by the Commandant of the Staff College, Sir Edward Hamley, of 'cutting blocks with a razor' by selecting officers with psc (passed Staff College) in particular for campaigning in West Africa.[13]

Hamley's charge in itself gives the lie to the claim by one historian that the failure of the Staff College to attract sufficient candidates at this period could be partly attributed to the greater importance of being a member of the right faction within the Army than a graduate of Camberley. Moreover, it can be noted that ten of Wolseley's original selections had the psc qualification – four of them serving in the headquarters staff – and it was Buller's participation in the campaign that prevented him from completing his course at Camberley. A total of thirty-four, including fourteen in the headquarters staff and five out of seven officers in the intelligence section were to serve in Egypt in 1882, and the Gordon relief expedition initially employed twenty Camberley graduates, six – if one includes Buller – serving in Wolseley's headquarters and seven on the lines of communication staff.[14] Wolseley was also to encourage promising officers to attend the Staff College and to work for the appointment of able directing staff.

Wolseley himself was to suggest on occasions that it was only ability that counted in the selection of staff, pointing out in the autumn of 1884, for example, that his headquarters staff in the Sudan would be different men from those employed in Egypt in 1882:

> This time, as was also the case in 1882, I have, and then had, a host of new men. My idea is to give every Staff College officer and everyone strongly recommended by a good commanding officer a chance in a subordinate position of showing what he can do and what he is worth.

On another occasion he wrote to Cambridge:

> Some think I favour my friends but these are simply officers whom I pick out on active service as very good men. As soon as I find I have made a mistake, I drop than remorselessly.

Similarly, he had also written to his wife in August 1882 'When [Cambridge] can assert that I have appointed a bad man to an office, then it will be high time for him to find fault with my selections.'[15]

In fact, it was widely recognised that Wolseley had the knack of picking able men, Sir Henry Ponsonby for one writing in November 1882, 'He knows a good man and selects him and throws over all other considerations. Therefore his Staff are excellent soldiers.' Thus, new men did indeed appear within Wolseley's circle after Ashanti, Herbert Stewart being a case in point. Wolseley first encountered Stewart as an able but disillusioned young captain close to deciding on premature retirement while employed on line of communication in Zululand. In February 1880 Wolseley was writing to his wife that he hoped 'to have him with me in my next campaign' and, within five years, Stewart was a Major General although that last promotion came only after he had already been mortally wounded with the Desert Column in the Sudan.[16]

It was also sometimes the case that Wolseley did not have altogether a free choice of staff. It had been Greaves rather than McNeill whom Wolseley had first chosen for Ashanti in 1873 but the appointment had been vetoed by the Duke of Cambridge, while Wolseley did not want Sir Archibald Alison as field commander with the white troops eventually sent out. Moreover, Wolseley had actually wanted these troops specially selected themselves but had to settle for the three regular battalions next on the roster for foreign service. On going to South Africa to supercede Chelmsford in 1879, he complained that 'many of the tools I shall have to work with, are not of my own selection, but are men chosen by HRH & the Horse Guards party'. It has to be said, however, that once Wolseley got to the Cape, he swiftly disposed of most of Chelmsford's staff with the exception of a number, including Butler, serving under the Hon. Hugh Clifford, who had been sent out to take over the lines of communication for the second invasion of Zululand. Others Wolseley wished to retain, such as Wood, Buller and Francis Grenfell, chose to go home, while Colley, whose services he secured despite opposition from Cambridge, was recalled to his appointment as Military Secretary to Lytton in September 1879 when renewed conflict broke out in Afghanistan.

In the case of the Egyptian campaign, the principal field commands were taken by those already designated to command the autumn manoeuvres and, while happy with the subsequent performance of Sir John Adye as Chief of Staff, and Drury Lowe with the Cavalry Division, Wolseley was to find fault with both George Willis commanding 1st Division and Hamley commanding the 2nd Division. He also felt compelled to accept Cambridge's son, Major George FitzGeorge, as private secretary and found it politic to take both the Duke of Connaught as a brigade commander and the Duke of Teck as a special service officer eventually confined to supervising foreign attachés. The son of Hugh Childers, Secretary of State for War, was also taken on as an ADC. Three years later, Wolseley had to disappoint a number of associates, such as Baker Russell, while being obliged to accept both Colonel Stanley Clarke as commander of the Light Camel Corps and Lord Charles Beresford as naval ADC at the request of the Prince of Wales, Clarke's appointment being a disappointment for McCalmont who had expected the command.[18]

Attention has been drawn to the staffing of the 1885 expedition with 'comforting relatives, influential courtiers and titled flaneurs', the relatives being Wolseley's brother, George, who took over as Buller's principal assistant when Brackenbury was attached to the River Column, and Wolseley's nephew, Arthur Creagh, who acted as an ADC. In fact, accusing Wolseley of nepotism and snobbery and much else including 'cheap bourgeois habits and sinister Caesarism' merely echoes the claims of his contemporary rivals. The critique of the ring, for example, in the memoir of Sir Ian Hamilton, who was permitted to join the Sudan campaign despite having served most recently as Roberts's Assistant Military Secretary in Madras, is often cited with its condemnation of the composition of the Desert Column. For Hamilton, Wolseley's Camel Corps drawn from the Guards, cavalry and rifle regiments was no more than the result of 'an urge to do something for his pals'.[18]

Wolseley's defence of so frequently choosing the same men was that he could rely instinctively on those familiar with his working methods and in whom he had full confidence. Thus, when urging the selection of Colley, Brackenbury, Butler and Gifford for his Natal staff in 1875 Wolseley stressed the need for 'a few clever men about me whom I could trust implicitly'. Similarly, when Cambridge objected to the likes of Greaves, Brackenbury, Maurice, Baker Russell, Gifford and McCalmont accompanying Wolseley to Cyprus in 1878 he 'pointed out how very desirable it was that in carrying out a difficult job, I should be assisted by men in whom I placed the fullest confidence, etc., etc.'.

As may be imagined, this was not how his opponents saw it. There was the resentment of non-ringers in feeling excluded from campaigns and the glory attached to them and there was also the undoubted vindictiveness shown to non-ringers such as Captain Glover in the Ashanti campaign or to Sir Charles Wilson, who, thrust into command of the Desert Column after the wounding of Herbert Stewart and the earlier death of Stewart's deputy, Burnaby, at Abu Klea, rightly or wrongly provided a ready scapegoat for the failure to reach Khartoum in time. However, the Roberts ring was equally intent on self-promotion, Cambridge remarking on one occasion that Roberts was a 'nimble jobber' and, indeed, when he became Commander-in-Chief in 1900 the War Office was said to have become a case of 'Bobs, Jobs, Snobs & Co'. An added complication in India was the perceived need to balance opportunities between those of the British and Indian service and between the three presidency armies of Bengal, Madras and Bombay. Seen in this regard, for example, the choice of field commanders in 1878 was a matter of some controversy as it was alleged that Haines and his Adjutant General, Sir Peter Lumsden, had unduly favoured those of the Indian service.[19]

A more significant charge against his ring was that articulated to Wolseley by Cambridge in the autumn of 1884:

> of course, if the same officers are invariably employed, you have no area for selecting others, and give no others a chance of coming to the front…if you never go beyond this particular batch of men, you work these and bring nothing on.

There is little doubt that Cambridge had a valid point although there is a certain irony in the source for what most frequently irked him was Wolseley ignoring the claims of seniority. From the point of view of Wolseley, as he expressed it while on Cyprus, the Duke was keeping back younger men and 'delighting to honour those of the old cut-and-dry model from whom nothing new is ever to be expected'. Indeed, when called upon to suggest a field commander in the event of a war against Russia in 1878 and to the dismay of the Secretary of State of War, Gathorne Hardy, the Duke proposed the man who had penned the order that sent the Light Brigade to destruction at Balaclava, the 75-year-old Sir Richard Airey.[20]

Nonetheless, it has been argued convincingly that Wolseley did become something of a prisoner of the initial success of the ring, feeling it necessary constantly to employ the same men lest his rejection of them might reflect adversely on his earlier choice.[21] Certainly, his critisism of some of his followers increased markedly over the years. By 1884 Wood, who was never forgiven for signing the peace treaty with the Boers after Colley's death at Majuba in 1881, was vain and untrustworthy, a man 'who could never run straight...or be true to any Chief'. Butler was exercising considerable powers of prediction but with the unfortunate trait of never giving 'anyone the benefit of his predictions until after the events have occurred'. No longer in Wolseley's confidence, Butler would 'fit in with no one'. Brackenbury, who succeeded to command of the River Column after Earle's death at Kirbekan in February 1885, became 'a little consequential' with his new responsibilities while Buller was building up imaginary difficulties for himself and would not again be employed as Chief of Staff in any future campaign Wolseley might wage.[22]

Wolseley concluded in July 1885 that, 'Nowadays, every man seems to think of himself only, starting with the notion that he is a Napoleon, and apparently entirely indifferent to the interests of the state'. On another occasion during the campaign he also wrote to his wife that:

> as soon as they feel they have an assured footing and can do really good staff
> service they torture themselves with jealousy one of the other and sometimes
> even in their dealings with me are inclined to kick over the traces.

Certainly, as the more prominent members of the ring grew in stature and seniority, their willingness to work together for common goals was subordinated to their own ambitions. Ultimately, one of Wolseley's objections to the establishment of a general staff for the Army was certainly that Brackenbury was the obvious choice to head it. Buller, too, would be portrayed as disloyal by being prepared to accept the office of Commander-in-Chief in 1895 ahead of Wolseley and it was only a fortuitous change of government that saw Wolseley finally grasp the prize. In itself, however, such rivalries were hardly unique. The divisions within Chelmsford's command, largely caused by his abrasive Military Secretary, John North Crealock, are well known. Wolseley himself said of the staff, including McNeill and Greaves, serving under Sir Gerald

Graham at Suakin in May 1885 that

> never was there a force in the field that was less of a happy family: every
> one seemed to desire to play his own hand & to think solely of himself
> whilst he hated and ridiculed his neighbour.

Similarly, the diaries of Roberts's Chief of Staff from September 1879 to August
1880, Charles MacGregor, reveal not only constant manoeuvring by individuals
for preferment but also what Lytton referred to as the 'KCB mania' generally
affecting Victorian officers.[23]

What made such dissension within Wolseley's ring so destructive by 1884
was that his whole command style was built upon the basis of individuals
willingly fulfilling specific roles in a kind of orchestrated military collective.
To the war correspondent, Archibald Forbes, Wolseley appeared to instinctively
assess the right role for a particular individual, be it administration or leading
scout. Thus, the 'gang as an aggregate' was 'a weapon of extraordinary and
diverse force' but, if broken up, its constituent parts would be 'but the withes
of a faggot, with here and there a stick of exceptional stoutness'.[24]

The better known members of the ring invariably filled the same kind of
appointment in each campaign: Colley or Greaves as Chief of Staff, Buller in
intelligence, Brackenbury as Military Secretary, Gifford and Butler in the field,
McCalmont as ADC and so on. Moreover if a particular individual was not
available or became unavailable later in a campaign, Wolseley often detected a
subsequent shortcoming in the standard of work being performed. The recall
of Colley to Afghanistan from South Africa was one such occasion, Wolseley
noting that 'I shall miss him beyond measure. His sound judgement was
invaluable.' Brackenbury did not prove as efficient as Chief of Staff yet, the
year before on Cyprus, it had been Brackenbury's talents as Military Secretary
that had been most missed, Wolseley lamenting that

> When I think of the beautiful regularity with which my books were kept by
> him, I am sad to think of the scrawling hideousness which will be left to me
> as my records of Cyprus.

Again, in South Africa, when Wolseley's private secretary, St Leger Herbert,
was ill, Maurice proved incapable of deciphering telegrams and when Leopold
Swaine's health similarly broke down in the Sudan, Coleridge Grove, in turn,
was not an adequate substitute as Military Secretary since he, too, could not
decipher telegrams with his predecessor's ease.[25]

While Wolseley's command style was highly personalised, he still
depended upon the skills of his staff because of the very nature of colonial

warfare. On the one hand, his campaigns were generally carefully prepared in advance. In the case of the Red River expedition, Wolseley himself supervised detail down to the loading of each individual boat. For Ashanti every potential source of information on the country was combed before Wolseley left England and Brackenbury and Huyshe lectured to the staff on the basic background on the voyage out to the Cape Coast Castle, Maurice and C.E. Webber conducting a similar exercise on the voyage to South Africa in 1879. In fact, Wolseley already had considerable knowledge of the latter country for in 1875 he had taken back to England 'detailed notebooks of technical information concerning topographical and strategic conditions and resources of Zululand'. In much the same way, a considerable amount of preparatory work was carried out in London before Wolseley set sail for Egypt in 1882 and Stewart later told Henry 'Croppy' Ewart that Wolseley had dictated orders for every day of the campaign while still on the voyage out.[26]

On the other hand, considerable attention continued to be paid to detail of campaign itself, in contrast it might be said with Roberts, who was a poor organiser as witnessed by the chaos of transport and medical arrangements in South Africa in early 1900. It is also instructive in this regard to compare Chelmsford's conduct in Zululand with that of Wolseley. For his first invasion attempt, the former had a small headquarters staff of just 14 individuals for a total force of 17,929 officers and men, although each of the five columns into which Chelmsford divided his army also had approximately seven staff. Moreover, although he had issued a pamphlet on the Zulu Army, Chelmsford saw no need to create an intelligence staff and, even during the second invasion attempt, appointed only one civilian in an intelligence capacity. His lines of communication were equally improvised although Clifford them assumed control for the second invasion attempt. When Wolseley arrived, Clifford was given nine assistants while Maurice assumed responsibility for intelligence. In Ashanti, Colley had been brought out especially 'to take upon him the arduous, responsible and comparatively uninteresting duties of organisation and command of transport' and had quite simply brought 'order to chaos'. Huyshe had been responsible for military survey work and Buller for intelligence. Although Wolseley's staff appointments invariably combined the duties of both Adjutant General's department – orders, discipline, etc. – and Quartermaster General's department – movement, reconnaissance, quartering, etc. – in Egypt and the Sudan, there was again a separate lines of communication staff headed by Earle and Wood respectively. Similarly, Buller had six assistants for intelligence work in Egypt and Wilson five assistants in the Sudan, the most prominent of whom was Captain Herbert Kitchener.

Equally important to Wolseley were his ADCs, secretaries and chiefs of staff. While McCalmont regarded his duties as ADC on Cyprus largely superfluous when there were two secretaries and his work in South Africa after the conclusion of hostilities confined to preventing the locals from 'bothering' Wolseley, the role was much enhanced on campaign. In Ashanti, for example, all the ADCs had been effectively plunged into command positions when it was realised that more officers were required to supervise widely dispersed troops in heavily forested terrain. During the hunt for Cetewayo, Wolseley's ADCs had similarly each headed searching groups while all of Wolseley's staff joined in the final assault on Sekukuni's stronghold. The function of the military and private secretaries was to deal with military and political paperwork respectively and thus to draft and transmit both orders and correspondence and they, with the field commanders and the chiefs of staff, have been characterised as the 'central pivots of authority, decision and power' within the ring,[27] although all were clearly subordinate, of course, to Wolseley.

The position of Wolseley's chiefs of staff was a particularly interesting one. Wolseley commented of Ashanti that few could imagine how much work was placed on them

> as the staff duties with a regular army afford no data upon which an opinion can be formed of the labour that devolves upon the Chief Staff Officer of a force such as that under my command.

McNeill in Ashanti and Adye in Egypt were both also designated as Wolseley's second in command in much the same way that Wolseley himself was designated Chief of Staff to Napier in the event of a war with Russia in 1878. Similarly, whatever Wolseley's doubts about Buller's capacity for staff work in the Sudan, once Stewart was wounded it was still Buller followed by Greaves and then Wood whom Wolseley considered in February 1885 as the best sequence of succession in the event of becoming a casualty himself.

However, if the Chief of Staff was technically Wolseley's deputy, the work required of them fell short of participating in real decision making, for all that Wolseley was to claim with respect to Buller in November 1884 that, 'in dealing with a Chief of the Staff in whom one has every confidence I feel too much inclined, I know, to give him a free hand.' Indeed, in October, Wolseley had specifically told Buller that, 'it is a very stupid thing in any position in life to keep a dog and bark yourself' and that 'I had no intention of attempting to be my own Chief of the Staff.' Wolseley explained this on the grounds that too many general officers felt they were not performing their duties adequately if they did not constantly look into matters 'that others have been detailed to do' and that his own experience on the staff earlier in his career had taught him 'what a bore it is to have the man who is your immediate superior doing your work and leaving you idle'.

Nevertheless, it can be noted that Wolseley also charged Buller 'that he must keep me constantly, hourly if necessary, informed of all he was doing' and Buller himself interpreted his responsibilities in a distinctly limited way, seeing his task as one of 'delivery of the advanced base of the striking force'. Indeed, the section in the official history on the work of Buller's department suggests that its only function was to move the field force forward to Dongola and bring up sufficient supplies to enable it to operate beyond. It is not perhaps surprising, therefore, to find Buller located at Wadi Halfa in December 1884 while Wolseley was forward at Korti some 360 miles apart and Buller complaining that, while he had been able to communicate by telegraph, he had seen Wolseley for only eight hours in two months. In the closing stages of the campaign, when Buller had again assumed the duties of Chief of Staff after being sent forward to take over the Desert Column, he again complained that Wolseley had gone back to Cairo while he stayed at Dongola without any clear idea of Wolseley's plans.[28]

Wolseley's attitude to his field commanders was very similar. Again, it is the personalised aspect to Wolseley's command style that is most apparent, Wolseley closely supervising operations while seeming to grant his subordinates considerable latitude. What primarily contributed to the breakdown in the relationship between Wolseley and the notoriously prickly Hamley in Egypt was the latter's temerity in 'suggesting' a plan of campaign to Wolseley, Hamley having decided that 'If I call myself a strategist, I ought to behave as such.' Similarly, although ostensibly leaving the tactical details to his subordinates, Wolseley held a dawn conference of his general officers overlooking what was to be the battlefield of Tel el Kebir and 'there personally explained to them the nature of the intended movement'. In fact, some of the troops did not follow Wolseley's suggested march formations during the night advance but Wolseley was well up with the troops and, at one point, directly controlling the Highland Brigade. He had been under fire in earlier reconnaissances and in Ashanti had been involved in the fighting during an early foray to Essaman nominally under Wood's command and had also been knocked down by one bullet hitting his helmet in the action at Ordahsu before Kumasi.[29]

There were occasions when Wolseley did leave matters to his subordinates and they failed him, Earle fortuitously retrieving some of the errors of supply made by Adye in Egypt. Nevertheless, it was principally only the Sudan campaign in which the system failed comprehensively. For one thing, it was the first campaign in which Wolseley's actual conduct of operations was in any way limited by government, the Secretary of State refusing to allow him to go any further forward than Korti. Wolseley complained that he had not previously been 'chained to the rear in a campaign' and was clearly hard put to contain himself so far from the action. For another, the sheer distances involved – it was 1,600 miles from Cairo to Khartoum – proved too great for the personal control to be exercised over every feature of the campaign. He simply could not be everywhere and it might well be argued that, by maintaining such close control for so long, he had hardly encouraged the development of initiative in his subordinates. Certainly, they did not always thrive when left to their own devices, the elementary blunders of Colley, the most brilliant intellect in the Army, in South Africa in 1881 being a particular example.[30]

Wolseley considered that 'the sun of my luck set when Stewart was wounded' but, in fact, from its very conception the Sudan campaign exposed mercilessly the flaws in the ring as a command system. Wolseley was respected rather than liked and he had associates rather than friends but, despite the detached, aloof manner, the 'Chief' as he was known to his staff, exuded a confidence which seemingly communicated to all around him. To the public Wolseley had a charm and tact conspicuously lacking in his private correspondence and diaries and he was generally able to co-ordinate the diverse talents of his chosen subordinates in a way well suited to the special characteristics of colonial campaigning. But, in the last analysis, improvisation was no substitute for a proper general staff structure and Wolseley's capacity to manage affairs decreased in proportion to the growth in the scale of operations.

Returning in full circle to the point at which this paper began, Wolseley like many of his generation was something of a student of the American Civil War. However, it was not Grant who caught Wolseley's imagination but Lee – the 'ablest soldier of my day'; the 'highly cultivated military genius'; the 'greatest man I ever conversed with' and one who towered even over Charles Gordon, who was the only other man in whose presence Wolseley ever felt awed.[31] That in itself is perhaps adequate comment on the understanding of command by arguably the greatest soldier produced by the Victorian Army.

Notes

1. G.C. Ward, R. Burns and K. Burns *The Civil War*, p. 276, Bodley Head, London (1991); M. Howard, *The Franco-Prussian War*, p. 62, Methuen edn., London (1981).

2. H. Bailes, 'Technology and Imperialism: A Case Study of the Victorian Army in Africa', *Victorian Studies*, 24, pp. 82-104 (1980-81); E.M. Spiers, *The Army and Society*, 1815-1914, pp. 209-10, Longman, London (1980).

3. T.M. Maguire, 'Our Art of War as Made in Germany', *United Service Magazine*, 13, p. 126, (1896); H. Bailes, 'Patterns of Thought in the Late

Victorian Army', *Journal of Strategic Studies*, 4, pp. 29-45, (1981).

4. C.E. Callwell, *Small Wars: Their Principles and Practice*, p. 57, 3rd edn, HMSO, London (1906); Hove Central Library, Wolseley Collections, W/ P 3/17, Wolseley to wife, 16 December 1873; Ibid, 163/iv, Wolseley to brother, 15 August 1873; P[ublic] R[ecord] O[ffice], WO 147/3, Wolseley Ashanti Journal, Entry for 4 January 1874; G.L. Huyshe, 'The Red River Expedition', *J[ournal] of the R[oyal] U[nited] S[ervice] I[nstitution]* XV, 52, pp. 70-85, (1872); Evelyn Wood, 'The Ashanti Expedition of 1873-74', JRUSI XVIII, 78, pp. 331-357, (1874-75).

5. G. Salis Schwabe, 'Carrier Corps and Coolies on Active Service in China, India and Africa 1860-1879', JRUSI XXIV, 107, pp. 815-846, (1880); R[oyal] A[rchives], Cambridge Mss, Add. E1/8407, Haines to Cambridge, 10 October 1878; Ibid., Add. E1/8482, Haines to Cambridge, 26 December 1878; Ibid., Add. E1/8528, Haines to Cambridge, 7 February 1879; Ibid., Add. E1/8550, Lytton to Cambridge, 20 February 1879.

6. Brian Robson, *Fuzzy Wuzzy: The Campaigns in the Eastern Sudan, 1884-85*, pp. 153, 184-185, Spellmount, Tunbridge Wells (1993); Thomas Pakenham, *The Boer War*, pp. 380-381, Weidenfeld & Nicolson, London (1979); John Laband, *Kingdom in Crisis: The Zulu Response to the British Invasion of 1879*, p. 50, Manchester University Press, Manchester (1992); John Laband (ed.), *Lord Chelmsford's Zululand Campaign, 1878-79*, p. xxxii, Alan Sutton for Army Records Society, Stroud (1994); Hove, 'Wolseley Collections', S.A.2, Wolseley to Stanley, 26 June 1879.

7. D.R. Headrick, *The Tentacles of Progress*, pp. 100-107, Oxford University Press, New York (1988); Brian Bond, 'The South African War of 1880-81' in Brian Bond (ed.), *Victorian Military Campaigns*, pp. 199-240, Hutchinson, London (1967); RA, India Letters, N41/78, Hardinge to Queen Victoria, 12 February 1885; R.S. Rait, *The Life of Field Marshal Sir Frederick Paul Haines*, pp. 211-325, Constable, London (1911).

8. R.A. Cambridge Mss, Add. E1/8433, Lytton to Cambridge, 7 November 1878; I[ndia] O[ffice] L[ibrary], Lyall Mss, MSS Eur F 132/24, Lyall to Roberts, 3 January 1879; Ibid., Strachey Mss, MSS Eur F 127/1, John Strachey, 28 January 1880; Brian Robson (ed.), *Roberts in India: The Military Papers of Field Marshal Lord Roberts, 1876-1893*, p. 115, Alan Sutton for Army Records Society, Stroud (1993); IOL, Lyall Mss Eur F 132/26, Stewart to Lyall, 15 February 1879.

9. Hove, Wolseley Collections, W/P 8/19, Wolseley to wife, 8-13 August 1879; RA, South Africa Series, 034/111, Beaconsfield to Queen Victoria, 30 May 1879; Ibid., B61/10, Same to same, 27 May 1879; Sir Arthur Cunynghame, *My Command in South Africa, 1874-78*, pp. 374-375, Macmillan, London (1879); RA, Cambridge Mss, Add. E1/8596, Stanley to Cambridge, 20 March 1879.

10. RA, Cambridge Mss, Add. E1/7516, Napier to Cambridge, 15 January 1875; Alan Lloyd, *The Drums of Kumasi*, pp. 71-74, Longmans, London (1964); Hove, Wolseley Collections, 163/iv, Wolseley to brother, 3 November 1873 and 18 February 1878; Ibid., S.A.1, Wolseley to Frere, 9 December 1879; RA, Army Letters, E27/156, Ellis to Ponsonby, 22 November 1881; Ibid. Cambridge Mss, Add. E1/8593, Cambridge to Chelmsford, 20 March 1879.

11. RA, Cambridge Mss, Add. E1/8476, Baker to Cambridge, 22 December 1878; Ibid., Army Letters, E29/149, 'Rules for the Guidance of Editors of Newspapers, and of Correspondents with an Army in the Field', 28 July 1882; Robson, *Roberts in India*, pp. 17-19, 62-64; N[ational] A[rmy] M[useum], Haines Mss, 8108-9-11, Lytton to Haines, 28 September 1879.

12. C.E. Callwell (ed.), *The Memoirs of Major-General Sir Hugh McCalmont*, pp. 47-48, Hutchinson, London (1924); Field Marshal Viscount Wolseley, *The Story of a Soldier's Life*, II, p. 201, Constable, London (1903); E. McCourt, *Remember Butler*, pp. 173-174, Routledge & Kegan Paul, London (1967).

13. Sir G. Greaves, *The Memoirs of General Sir George Greaves*, pp. 130-131, Murray, London (1924); Field Marshal Sir Evelyn Wood, *From Midshipman to Field Marshal*, II, pp. 254-255, Methuen, London (1906); Wolseley, *Soldier's Life*, II, p. 278; A. Preston (ed.), *Sir Garnet Wolseley's South African Diaries (Natal), 1875,* p. 62, Balkema, Cape Town (1971); B. Bond, *The Victorian Army and the Staff College*, pp. 128-129, Eyre, Methuen, London (1972).

14. G. Harries-Jenkins, *The Army in Victorian Society*, pp. 163-165, Routledge & Kegan Paul, London (1977); Bond, *Victorian Army*, pp. 129-130.

15. A.R. Godwin-Austen, *The Staff and the Staff College*, pp. 207-208, Constable, London (1927); Sir F. Maurice and Sir G. Arthur, *The Life of*

Lord Wolseley, p. 183, Heinemann, London (1924); Hove, Wolseley Collections, W/P 11/13, Wolseley to wife, 31 August 1882.

16. RA, Ponsonby Letters, Add. A36 Box 21, Ponsonby to wife, 4 November 1882; A. Preston, (ed.), *Sir Garnet Wolseley's South African Journal, 1879-80*, p. 224, Balkema, Cape Town (1973).

17. Greaves, *Memoirs*, p. 123; Preston, *Journal*, p. 38; Joseph Lehmann, *All Sir Garnet*, pp. 303-304, Cape, London (1964); M.J. Williams, 'The Egyptian Campaign, 1882' pp. 243-278, in Bond (ed.), *Victorian Military Campaigns*; J. Symons, *England's Pride*, p. 95, Hamish Hamilton, London (1965); Callwell, *McCalmont*, p. 233.

18. Adrian Preston, 'Wolseley, the Khartoum Relief Expedition and the Defence of India', pp. 89-122, in A. Preston and P. Dennis (eds.), *Swords and Covenants*, Croom Helm, London (1976); General Sir Ian Hamilton, *Listening for the Drums*, p. 177, Faber & Faber, London (1944).

19. Lehmann, *All Sir Garnett*, p. 208; A. Preston, 'Sir Garnet Wolseley and the Cyprus Expedition, 1878', *Journal of the Society for Army Historical Research* XLV, 181, pp. 4-16 (1967); RA, W12/10, Cambridge to Ponsonby, 17 February 1890; Lehmann, *All Sir Garnet*, p. 388; RA, Cambridge Mss, Add. E1/8428, Cambridge to Haines, 1 November 1878; Add. E1/8522, Haines to Cambridge, 31 January 1879; Add. E1/8566, Cambridge to Haines, 28 February 1879; and Add. E1/8660, Haines to Cambridge, 8 May 1879.

20. Godwin-Austen, *Staff and Staff College*, p. 207; Preston, 'Wolseley and Cyprus', pp. 4-16; Ibid., 'Frustrated Great Gamesmanship: Sir Garnet Wolseley's Plan for War against Russia, 1873-78', *International History Review*, 2, pp. 239-265 (1980).

21. Preston, *Diaries*, p. 88.

22. Ibid. (ed.), *In Relief of Gordon: Lord Wolseley's Campaign Journal of the Khartoum Relief Expedition, 1884-1885*, pp. 4, 75-76, 112-113, 158, 162, 171, Hutchinson, London (1967).

23. Ibid., *Relief*, pp. 232-33; Hove, Wolseley Collections, W/P 13/38, Wolseley to wife, 23-29 December 1884; Ibid., 13/39. Same to same, 31 December 1884 – 5 January 1885; Sonia Clark (ed.), *Zululand at War, 1879*.

Brenthurst Press, Houghton (1984); Hove, Wolseley Collections, W/P 14/13 Wolseley to wife, 20-27 May 1885; William Trousdale (ed.), *War in Afghanistan, 1879-80: The Personal Diary of Major-General Sir Charles MacGregor*, Wayne State University Press, Detroit (1985); NAM, Haines Mss, 8108-9-5, Lytton to Haines, 3 September 1877.

24. J. Luvaas, *The Education of an Army*, p. 215, Cassell, London (1965).

25. Preston, *Journal*, pp. 109, 149, 224; Sir G. Arthur (ed.), *The Letters of Lord and Lady Wolseley*, 1870-1911, pp. 31, 204, Heinemann, London (1922); Preston, *Relief*, pp. 141-143.

26. The Hon. Sir J. Fortescue, *Following the Drum*, p. 32 Blackwood, Edinburgh & London (1931); PRO, WO 147/3, Entry for 1 October 1873; Preston, *Journal*, p. 41; C. Ballard, 'Sir Garnet Wolseley and John Dunn', p. 130, in A. Duminy and C. Ballard (eds.), *The Anglo-Zulu War: New Perspectives*, University of Natal Press, Pietermaritzburg (1981); J.F. Maurice, *The Military History of the Campaign of 1882 in Egypt*, pp. 4-9, HMSO, London (1887); RA, Ponsonby Mss, Add. A35, Box 21, Ponsonby to wife, 28 October 1882.

27. *A Narrative of the Field Operations Connected with the Zulu War of 1879*, pp. 141-154, HMSO, London (1881); J. Laband, *Companion to the Narrative of the Field Operations Connected with the Zulu War of 1879*, p. 9, N & S Press, Constantia (1989); Bailes, 'Technology and Imperialism', pp. 82-104; H. Brackenbury, *The Ashanti War: A Narrative*, I, p. 368, Blackwood, Edinburgh and London (1874); Wolseley, *Soldier's Life*, II, p. 317; Callwell, McCalmont, pp. 168-169; Preston, *Diaries*, p. 88.

28. Brackenbury, *Ashanti War*, pp. 304-306; Preston, *Relief*, pp. 45-56, 67, 144; C.H. Melville, *The Life of General Sir Redvers Butler*, I, pp. 204, 209, 251, Arnold, London (1923); *History of the Sudan Campaign*, I, pp. 67-69, HMSO, London (1889).

29. Maurice, *Campaigns of 1882*, pp. 20, 73, 84; Luvaas, *Education*, p. 155.

30. Williams, 'Egyptian Campaign', pp. 243-278; Arthur, *Letters*, p. 173; Preston, *Relief*, pp. 67-68; Lehmann, *All Sir Garnet*, p. 367; Symons, *England's Pride*, pp. 128-129, 174-176, 286.

31. J. Luvaas, *The Military Legacy of the Civil War*, p. 50, University Press of Kansas edn. (1988); Lehmann, *All Sir Garnet*, pp. 121, 379; Wolseley, *Soldier's Life*, II, pp. 139-140, Joseph Lehmann, *The First Boer War*, p.87, Cape, London (1972), makes the point that Lee was also Colley's hero.

Quotations from the Royal Archives appear by gracious permission of Her Majesty the Queen. Other use of Crown copyright material in the Public Record Office and the India Office Records is by permission of Her Majesty's Stationery Office while grateful acknowledgment is also given to Hove Central Library for enabling consultation of and quotation from the Wolseley Collections, and to the National Army Museum.

HIGH COMMAND IN THE UNITED STATES: THE EMERGENCE OF A MODERN SYSTEM, 1898-1920

by Ronald J. Barr

T he direction, co-ordination and leadership of the Army was of paramount concern to key American political decision makers during the period 1898-1920. Important political figures such as Theodore Roosevelt believed international conflict was certain as nation states fought over increasingly scarce natural resources. In such a world military preparedness and efficiency of command were essential. The events of the Spanish-American War (1898), Philippine Insurrection (1899-1902), First World War (1914-1918), and the colonial responsibilities which victory in these wars placed upon land forces only reinforced this view among army reformers and imperialist Republicans.

America entered the Spanish-American War with a small, poorly managed Army, ill-equipped to deal with the demands of invading Cuba and the Philippines. The effective Army created during the Civil War was rapidly disbanded at its end. By March 1898, the Army of a country of over 73 million people numbered fewer than 25,000 men. This rapid decline in the Army created an aging officer corps with promotion based solely on seniority. Promotion among army officers between 1865 and 1898 virtually stopped and it was common to find generals of the Civil War serving as captains and majors. According to General Nelson A. Miles in 1889, 110 officers had not received a promotion for two decades, while even in 1895, 279 officers were still Civil War veterans.[1] Slow promotions and the dispersed state of the Army, which had created over 70 operational posts during the various Indian campaigns, discouraged interest in military innovations and provided little opportunity to practice handling larger numbers of troops at divisional, brigade, or even regimental levels.

Confronted with slow promotion and tedious assignments to small Western outposts, many line officers sought staff bureau assignments. Such appointments were permanent, involved promotion by one grade, and allowed an officer to work regular office hours in one of the larger American cities. These assignments were greatly coveted and it was not uncommon for up to 300 of the 600 first lieutenants of the line to apply for a staff vacancy.[2] In these cases the patronage of a particular Senator or Representative who would demand a political favour of the President was important. Such a system of political patronage, combined with poor prospects for promotion in the line and the dispersed state of the Army left most army officers unaware of military reforms instituted in Germany, or the management techniques developed by US business.

The overall command system also discouraged interest in reform and promoted bitterness between staff and line officers and resentment between the top ranking soldier in the Army, the Commanding General, and the Secretary of War and staff officers. Army management departed from planned organisation through the Revolutionary and Jacksonian periods and had been finalised by Secretary of War John C. Calhoun, and the US Senate in March 1821. The structure upheld the President's role as Commander-in-Chief but did not specify the limits of command assigned to the Commanding General of the Army. The Commanding General was allotted control over military discipline and military operations with all orders relating to these issues transmitted through his office. The Secretary of War retained financial control over the Army, under the President, and was directly in charge of the staff bureaus. Such a system gave the Commanding General no control over the powerful staff bureaus who could ignore his orders or issue orders without reference to his office. Once appointed to a staff bureau officers rarely returned to the line, remaining in a particular staff bureau for the remainder of their career. These officers paid scant attention to requests from officers in the field or orders issued by the Commanding General. Such a confused system, with no clear delineation of control, led to constant friction between the Commanding General and Secretary of War.

In 1895 Major General Nelson A. Miles was appointed Commanding General. A Civil War volunteer, he rose in rank to major general of volunteers by 1865 and received the Congressional Medal of Honour for bravery in action at Chancellorsville. After the war he became a colonel in the Regular Army and gained a reputation as an Indian fighter. An exceptionally fine regimental commander, Miles had no interest in the military ideas of Europe which he regarded as irrelevant to the unique American experience. Intensely proud of his promotion to Commanding General, he had no intention of supporting any military reform which reduced the power of this office.[3] Under Miles relations between the Commanding General and the Secretary of War and staff bureaus were to be acrimonious and divisive.

Miles, unlike most of his professional colleagues, also had faith in the state militia system. The National Guard was popular in Congress and was frequently portrayed as a democratic West Point, able to counter professional regulars who might usurp the Government. At state level the National Guard was jealously defended by state political officials who exercised the power of patronage over many senior and middle-ranking National Guard appointments. In 1900, military reformer Colonel J.P. Sanger gloomily summed up the state of the militia when he wrote to the Adjutant General's Office: 'In none of the states are there schools for officers and non-commissioned officers ... and in 42 states, the company officers are elected by the men.' He further criticised the lack of drill, target practice and standardised equipment, concluding the volunteer system was a 'broken reed'.[4] Despite these failings, the National Guard and the concept of a Volunteer Army in times of national emergency retained powerful ideological backing in the Democratic Party and among state politicians.

On 25 April 1898, despite these organisational failings in the Army, the United States declared war on Spain. This war was to highlight the limitations of the Regular Army and National Guard and create the impetus for reform of both institutions. The Army of 24,000 regulars was required to mount invasions in the Caribbean and Pacific. In response to these new demands on the Army, Congress accepted a bill to increase the size of the Army to 120,000 men. However, half were to be National Guard troops mobilised for one year only and Congress refused to adopt any legislation which would address the management and structural problems of the Army. The mobilisation of the National Guard was a calamity. Almost half the guardsmen refused to leave home for an extended length of time and were replaced by hastily assembled volunteers. Most state troops were ill-equipped and less than half of National Guard officers had attended an instructional course, and even fewer had passed a formal command examination.[5] The campaign to invade Cuba highlighted the greatest failings in management and planning. Future President Theodore Roosevelt, who was a volunteer lieutenant colonel in Cuba, described the failures in correspondence to Senator Henry Cabot Lodge. In one letter written while US forces were besieging Santiago in July of 1898 he bitterly summed up the organisational failures:

> The mismanagement has been beyond belief ... We are half starved; and our men are sickening daily. The lack of transportation, food and artillery has brought us to the very edge of disaster; but above all [is] the lack of executive leadership, of any system or executive capacity.[6]

Three weeks into the campaign, men still had no shelter tents and were soaked by the daily rains. In Washington DC the Secretary of War Russell A. Alger and the Commanding General Nelson A. Miles bickered over command jurisdiction and war management, thus diverting attention from the chronic problems in Cuba.

The Army had 12 staff bureaus, all accountable to the Secretary of War, who invariably had no knowledge of army organisation. Army supply was controlled by three bureaus with no overall co-ordination. The largest staff bureau was the Quartermaster's Department, responsible for clothing, tentage, wagons, horses and transportation of troops. The Commissary Department provided food for the troops, while the Subsistence Department delivered accessories such as candles, oil and salt. The Signal Bureau managed army communications, and the Medical Bureau oversaw all aspects of health, including the supply of medicines. The Pay Department paid the troops. The Engineer Corps controlled civil and military construction projects. The Judge Advocate's Office was the legal office for the Army and Secretary of War. The Inspector General's Office conducted examinations into all aspects of army operations. Lastly, the Adjutant General's Office, commanded by Henry C. Corbin, issued all army orders and held many army records. Alger and Miles proved incapable of exercising authority over this system and Corbin was left the impossible task of co-ordinating staff functions, performing as a one-man general staff. The result was independent action by staff bureaus, which created considerable chaos. Despite all these problems General Miles organised an effective invasion force to invade Puerto Rico while General Wesley Merritt conducted a successful Pacific campaign. By mid-August 1898 all Spanish forces in Cuba, Puerto Rico, Guam and Manila had surrendered.

The scandals in army organisation, planning and management led President McKinley to establish the Dodge Commission to look into the conduct of the war. Chaired by Grenville M. Dodge, it convened on 24 September 1898 and conducted five months of hearings on army organisation which, for a while, were followed closely by the press. In February 1899 the Commission published its findings. The report criticised bureaus for ignoring orders from the Secretary of War and for failing to stockpile enough food, medical supplies and money for soldiers' pay. The divided command of the army structure was noted by the committee and the comments of General John M. Schofield, a former Commanding General, who argued for a general staff system, were published in the report.[7] The eight-volume report produced little impact when published. The new Secretary of War, Elihu Root, however, later read the report in his first year in office.

Root was perhaps the finest corporate lawyer in America. He was appointed in 1899 by McKinley after Alger was forced to resign. The President did not appoint Root to reform the Army but to deal with the legal problems envisaged in creating colonial governments in the Philippines, Cuba and Puerto Rico.

The choice was to be the most judicious of all McKinley's cabinet appointments. Root quickly applied his formidable intellect not just to colonial administration but also to the pressing need for army organisational reform. In his first report as Secretary of War he recommended systematic military planning for any eventuality, promotion by merit, posting of line officers to staff bureaus for five-year periods, greater inter-service co-operation and the creation of a war college to co-ordinate all army education and educate the brightest service school graduates. Root realised any plans to federalise the National Guard would be unpopular, and he astutely left this to a separate committee chaired by 'General' Daniel Butterfield of the New York National Guard. Predictably, Democratic congressmen, national guardsmen, state politicians and middle-ranking officers opposed these new ideas.[8]

Root, as a civilian with no military experience, relied heavily on the advice of Major, later Major General, William H. Carter, the Assistant Adjutant General. Carter provided Root with the education he required in matters of military organisation and command and drafted much of the subsequent military reform legislation. The new Secretary of War also read Emory Upton's book, *The Armies of Asia and Europe,* which provided him with a survey of foreign military organisations and exposed him to the ideas of Upton, one of the most influential thinkers in the late nineteenth-century US Army. To gather even more information on military reform Root authorised the creation of a board to study army reform chaired by Brigadier General William Ludlow. Ludlow was a former US military attaché in London and in this capacity he had first come into contact with the British military thinker Spenser Wilkinson, the first Chichele Professor of War at Oxford University. In his book *The Brain of the Army* Wilkinson had provided new insight into how to create an efficient German-style army, while retaining the civilian control of the military so important in a democracy. The text would become highly influential among British and American military reformers and Ludlow was to introduce Wilkinson and his ideas to Root.

In October 1900, the Ludlow Board reported to Root. The board proposed the creation of an army war college headed by a general officer, with the necessary assistants, all with four-year, fixed-term appointments. The war college would co-ordinate a unified army education system and provide advanced learning for selected officers. Five service schools would provide specialist training for certain officers: artillery training at Fort Monroe; engineering at Washington Barracks; submarine defence at Fort Totten; army medicine at Washington Barracks; and staff work at Fort Leavenworth. The last would give officers practical experience with larger military forces in order to prevent a repetition of the command failures of 1898. Root recommended these ideas to Congress and also proposed fixed four-year appointments to staff bureaus and a reorganisation of the artillery which would abolish the regimental system and create a new corps system.

These proposed organisational changes caused great division of opinion in the Army. Nelson Miles, army traditionalists, and most bureau chiefs opposed the introduction of fixed-term assignments for army officers and the disbanding of artillery regiments. Root was forced to compromise. The recommendation on interchange between the staff and the line was applied to only six of the twelve staff bureaus excluding such specialist bureaus as the Engineers or Medical Corps. The reform was further limited when Root agreed to apply the new measure to only new staff positions created by the expansion in the Army. The current members of the army staff were both excluded from re-detail and guaranteed promotion by seniority.[9] These concessions underlined the significant opposition to this reform by Congress and staff officers. The measure endorsed by Congress limited staff service to only 10 per cent of all army officers in their first 20 years of service. The majority of senior officers would continue to have no staff experience. The Senate altered the final reading of the bill by promoting Commanding General Miles and Adjutant General Corbin. Miles was promoted to lieutenant general and Corbin to major general, restoring the traditional rank distinction between the Commanding General, Adjutant General, and the bureau chiefs. On 2 February 1901 the new army bill was finally passed by Congress. Root had achieved only a partial victory. The expansion of the Army from 24,000 to 60,000 regulars was approved, as were the educational reforms and limited staff-line interchange.

In September 1901 President McKinley was assassinated in Buffalo, New York State. The new President, Roosevelt, however, quickly indicated his determination to press for further army reform. On 7 December 1901 Roosevelt delivered a presidential message arguing that America needed a more efficient, better educated army; the United States did not need a larger army but ought to have professional armed forces selected by merit to achieve military efficiency. A general staff, with a Chief of Staff at its head, ought to plan and co-ordinate army actions. He argued that the militia law was obsolete, and recommended a major extension of executive authority. The training, equipment, and organisation of the National Guard was to be placed under federal control. The implementation of general staff and militia reform would complete the successful transformation of the Army into a professional body responsive to central government. Miles claimed that the suggested reforms were more appropriate to a 'military aristocracy' or 'monarchical Germany' than to the American Republic.[10] Angry at Miles's disobedience, Root announced the new chairman of the War College Board would be Major General S.B.M. Young. The Board, approved by Roosevelt, was the first step towards a general staff.

In early January 1902 Carter and William C. Sanger, the Assistant Secretary of War, drafted the new militia legislation. In the Senate, the bill was introduced by Senator Hawley, chairman of the Senate Military Affairs Committee, and in the House by Charles Dick, who had access both to the recommendations of the unofficial Butterfield Committee and to the views of Carter and Sanger. The bill, entitled 'To Increase the Efficiency of the Militia and for Other Purposes', was the first attempt to modernise the militia since 1792. The bill redefined the duties of the National Guard: equipment and training would be standardised to match that of the Regular Army and in times of national emergency the militia would operate under federal control as a national reserve.[11]

Root hoped to introduce general staff legislation in tandem with militia reform and on 14 February 1902 the army reorganisation measures were placed before Congress. Progress on the general staff bill, however, was disrupted by the testimony of Miles who denounced the legislation in Congress. At the conclusion of Miles's testimony, Carter, who had been present throughout, was informed by Senator Hawley that no favourable action on the bill was likely. Miles, confident he had defeated the general staff bill, sailed from San Francisco on a world tour of foreign armies that would take several months. Root and Carter, however, planned a counter-attack against their opponents. Schofield and Merritt were encouraged to testify before the Senate. The generals praised the benefits of army education, the suggested amalgamation of bureaus, and emphasised the benefits of stronger federal control over the Army.[12] The testimony of these two senior army officers and respected Civil War veterans rallied Republican support for military reform. Root had succeeded in reopening the debate on army reorganisation.

On 4 December Root introduced the compromise militia reform bill. In his speech announcing the legislation, he attacked the obsolete basis on which the National Guard operated. Organised without standardised education, equipment, and training, the Guard failed in the Spanish-American War to provide an effective reserve. The new militia bill recognised the National Guard as the first volunteer force, while the remainder of the male population between the ages of 18 and 45 were termed the unorganised reserve. The bill extended federal power. The Guard accepted federal funding; joint Army-National Guard exercises were introduced; militia officers were to attend war college courses; and all equipment was standardised Regular Army issue. This compromise legislation made rapid progress through Congress and was passed as the Dick Act on 21 January 1903. The new act preserved the state organisation of the National Guard but established greater federal control over the reserve. The issue of deploying the Guard abroad remained politically contentious. The Attorney-General, encouraged by Roosevelt and Root, announced that the legislation clearly permitted the President to deploy the Guard abroad.[13] Opposition to the deployment of the militia in foreign wars, however, refused to disappear. Over ten years later, in 1917, Congress challenged the right of President Woodrow Wilson to send the National Guard to Europe during the First World War.

One week after the militia bill was introduced to Congress, the equally contentious army reform bill was tabled before the relevant committees. The bill proposed a general staff and Chief of Staff to replace the divided army command structure. The Inspector General's Department was abolished and the Pay Department, Quartermaster Corps, and Commissary Department were amalgamated into one division of supply. The general staff would consist of officers detailed for four years duty at the discretion of the President. All officers upon completion of their tour of duty would return for at least two years to a field command. Root and other army reformers hoped fixed-term appointments would end animosity and jealousy between staff and line officers. All operational planning would be controlled by the general staff. Unlike the old system, there would be no division of responsibility between the top general of the army and Secretary of War. The proposed legislation was soon in trouble as supply bureau chiefs opposed the amalgamation of their departments and Congress attacked the presidential appointment of general staff officers as an extension of executive authority. Promotion by merit was criticised both by middle-ranking officers as a threat to their rightful promotion and by Congress as a dangerous expansion of presidential authority.[14] In response to this opposition, Carter and Root introduced a modified general staff bill. The proposed merger of the supply bureaus was dropped, and the Inspector General's Office was retained. Vacancies created by general staff detail would not be filled until the general staff proved its use. This compromise removed opposition to reform from powerful bureau chiefs.

On 7 January 1903 the general staff bill achieved unexpected success in the House of Representatives. Root's compromise, which kept the supply bureaus and Inspector General's Office, was passed by 154 votes to 52. General Miles, who was on the Trans-Siberian Railroad, heard the news weeks later when he reached Paris.[15] In early February the bill was approved by the Senate. Brigadier General Fred C. Ainsworth, head of the Army Records and Pensions Department, succeeded in getting one last amendment accepted. In a subtle but significant change to the wording of the bill, the Chief of Staff would 'supervise' but not command the staff bureaus. Carter hoped bureau chiefs would accept the Chief of Staff's authority, and would ignore any ambiguity in the legislation. Unfortunately, bureau chiefs were to utilise this clause in later years to challenge general staff authority.[16] Roosevelt and Root agreed to introduce the staff system, which abolished the rank of commanding general, one week after General Miles retired on 8 August 1903. These final concessions ensured the passage of the general staff bill. The General Staff Act was a triumph for Root and his adviser Carter. The Dick Act and General Staff Act strengthened executive control over the Army and promoted greater professionalism. Individualism and localism no longer dominated army command or training.

The debate on American military reform emphasised a new Anglo-American relationship with information on military reform freely passed between prominent American and British officials. Root was in frequent contact with his British counterpart, H.O. Arnold Forster, as well as Wilkinson, and First Lord of the Admiralty, Arthur Lee.[17] Root underlined the links between American and British military reformers when he wrote some years later to Spenser Wilkinson:

> I do not forget, although I dare say many people do, what a great part your little book, The Brain of the Army, played in bringing to pass that both countries had some sort of an institution of that kind [general staff] in existence when the sudden emergency came.[18]

In the War Department, Root continued the preparations for implementation of the General Staff Act. A review board was established to select candidates for the 42 staff positions available, chaired by Major General Young. Any officer who was a service school graduate, who displayed administrative ability, or who held the Medal of Honour was considered for General Staff duty. The quality of officers selected among the lower grades was remarkably high: Lieutenant Colonel Thomas H. Barry, Major George Goethals, Captain John J. Pershing, Captain Peyton C. March, and Captain Joseph T. Dickman – all appointed to the staff – later became successful general officers. Major General Young was selected as the first Chief of Staff with Corbin as his deputy. The choice of Young was a political compromise. Roosevelt and Root were aware that many opposed the general staff and promotion by merit. By appointing a career officer, Roosevelt and Root hoped to diffuse these criticisms of reform. General Young had been promoted through the ranks and in the Civil War he fought in most of the big battles in the East. He served as Roosevelt's brigade commander during the Spanish-American War and was well liked by the President who took an active interest in his career. A good soldier, he was to prove an inadequate Chief of Staff. This attempt to make Root's army reforms more palatable to many career soldiers weakened the effectiveness of the general staff and war college.

Confident the army reorganisation would prove successful, Root pressed Roosevelt to let him return to his law practice in New York. The President was reluctant to let the most successful member of his cabinet leave and tried to persuade Root to remain in office until the following year's presidential election. The Secretary of War insisted he be allowed to leave as soon as possible. Roosevelt wrote to William H. Taft, Governor of the Philippines, asking him to return home and replace Root.[19] Taft was reluctant to accept. Roosevelt, however, continued to press Taft who did finally agree to take the post. On 15 August 1903 the official transition from Commanding General to Chief of Staff took place. Young became the first American Chief of Staff. A few days later Root publicly announced his intention to resign from the War Department on 31 January 1904.

Section two of the General Staff Act defined the four main goals of the general staff as: planning for national defence, issuing reports on military readiness for operations, providing expert advice to the Secretary of War and field commanders while co-ordinating all action in the field, and performing any other military duties assigned to it by the President. This broad definition of general staff activities and ignorance of staff officers produced an ineffective general staff. Captain Peyton C. March, a member of the first general staff, later claimed no one knew what to do. Numerous committees studied all aspects of the Army without any guiding principle. March only discovered how a general staff actually worked when, as military attaché in Japan, he was able to observe it in the Russo-Japanese War.[20]

The inability of the general staff to perform as expected attracted Root's attention, as pressure to provide an accurate assessment of American defence needs in the Pacific increased. In late November 1903, Root authorised the creation of a new three-man board to consider army administration which included Brigadier General Ainsworth. Ainsworth, who controlled the Record and Pension Office, recommended centralisation of all army records under his control. The Record and Pension Chief cleverly manipulated Roosevelt and Root's admiration of business methods by suggesting that his ideas matched those occurring in business organisation. Root supported this proposal and hoped this amalgamation would provide the general staff with a secretary who would act like the secretary to a company board of directors. In early January 1904, Congress confirmed the abolition of the office of Adjutant General and the appointment of Ainsworth as Military Secretary. Carter, on his way to a command in the Philippines, wrote to the Secretary of War in alarm at this extension of staff bureau power. Root dismissed this warning, confident this measure would relieve the general staff of administrative detail and allow it to function as he envisaged.[21]

On 9 January 1904 Young retired as Chief of Staff and was replaced by Major General Adna Chaffee. Chaffee, like Young, was a strong character, who was untrained in staff work and could not provide the general staff with the necessary guidance as to its role within the Army. In mid-February Taft replaced Root as Secretary of War. Taft was a civilian ignorant of both army matters and the procedures of the War Department. His nomination took place in a presidential election year, and, unlike Root, he found little time to familiarise himself with the problems and responsibilities of his new post. Confronted with the demands of the presidential nomination and electoral process, he was happy to rely on the able administrative abilities of Ainsworth, who made himself readily available to the beleaguered Secretary of War. Ainsworth further strengthened his position when Taft and Roosevelt accepted Ainsworth's contention that the Military Secretary should be one rank above other bureau chiefs.

In November 1904, Roosevelt was easily re-elected President and soon signalled his determination to continue American imperial expansion in the Caribbean, Central America and the Philippines. The general staff meanwhile struggled to assert command over staff bureaus. Taft, swamped with work, was unable to provide the necessary political support the general staff required. In 1905 the Secretary of War, who had also been appointed acting Secretary of State for one month, was placed in overall command of the Panama Canal project and was pro-tem President of the Senate whenever Roosevelt was away. Overworked, Taft rarely mentioned the War Department in his correspondence. The Secretary of War further undermined Root's general staff reforms by putting Ainsworth in charge of the War Department during his frequent absences. This decision made the Chief of Staff responsible to a bureau chief – the exact opposite of what Root had intended in the General Staff Act.[22]

On 16 January 1906 Chaffee retired a few weeks early to allow his friend, Major General John C. Bates, the chance to serve briefly as Chief of Staff before he too retired. Roosevelt initially announced that Corbin would replace Bates and serve the first full four-year term as Chief of Staff. Unfortunately, Corbin was unable to accept the appointment due to a deteriorating heart condition.[23] Roosevelt therefore appointed J. Franklin Bell as the first four-year appointee as Chief of Staff. Bell had impressed the President with his service in the Philippines and had successfully introduced Root's educational reforms at Fort Leavenworth. Born in 1856, he was the first soldier without Civil War experience and the first graduate of West Point to serve as Chief of Staff. Supporters of army reform were delighted that a younger, professionally-trained soldier was to be Chief of Staff. The decision, however, brought about the promotion of an officer who had been openly critical of Taft's policies while Governor in the Philippines, which strengthened Ainsworth's position within the War Department.

The prospect of war with Japan in 1907 forced Roosevelt to reconsider the failure of the General Staff to perform as expected. Root and other army reformers gained the attention of the President for the first time in many months. Ainsworth was criticised for wielding too much power in the War Department and undermining the role of the General Staff. The President agreed to abolish the post of Military Secretary and to re-appoint Ainsworth Adjutant General. In an attempt to increase the authority of the Chief of Staff, Bell was promoted to Major General, the same rank as held by Ainsworth. The sudden flurry of military reform, however, soon ended as Roosevelt's attention again focussed on domestic regulation of big business.[24]

In 1907 Taft began his campaign to secure the Republican presidential nomination. Taft was viewed with suspicion by imperialist Republicans and army reformers. As Governor of the Philippines, and head of the War Department, he had often questioned ideas of American racial superiority, the need for military expansion, and the long-term benefits of colonialism. In an effort to secure Republican support in the primaries, Taft made several speeches giving the strongest endorsements of his career to colonialism and military expansion.[25] In the War Department, the forthcoming presidential election deprived the General Staff of strong political leadership and encouraged independent action among staff bureau chiefs. In July, Taft resigned as Secretary of War to concentrate on his election campaign and was replaced by Luke E. Wright, a lawyer from Tennessee. Wright discovered a War Department unofficially run by Ainsworth, while the Chief of Staff was ignored and bureau chiefs did as they pleased. Bell had failed utterly to assert his authority as Chief of Staff and, to compound his misery, it was discovered he had diabetes.

In the presidential election of 3 November 1908 Taft easily defeated William Jennings Bryan. American politics between 1909 and 1912, however, were dominated by increasing division within the Republican Party. These differences temporarily disrupted the Republican electoral pre-eminence over the Democratic Party. In the Army the concept of a broad-based citizen force re-emerged. The small, professional army of 100,000 regulars was regarded as inadequate. Several European and Asian powers had millions of trained troops and America needed to respond to armies of this size. Army reformers suggested short-term enlistments to create a trained federal reserve, increased money for the armed forces, greater standardisation of National Guard and Regular Army equipment, and more joint training exercises. The policy proposed a trained professional elite which would command a large citizen army with basic military knowledge. Major General Leonard Wood described the new policy as 'military preparedness', which encouraged mass mobilisation around a professional core. In the War Department, staunch imperialist and supporter of military reform Luke Wright was replaced by Jacob McGavock Dickinson. The new Secretary was a corporate lawyer with little experience of government office. Unlike Wright, he had no commitment to American imperialism or army reform. His appointment emphasised Taft's reluctance to accept a view of international relations which stated conflict was certain and that military preparedness was essential.

General Wood was concerned at Taft's willingness to compromise with Japan and spent the summer of 1909 in New York establishing himself as the leading spokesman for army reform. Throughout the summer and autumn of 1909, relations between Wood and Ainsworth, the main critic of reform, remained cordial. Ainsworth often visited Wood's command headquarters in New York while Wood regularly stayed at Ainsworth's home in Washington DC. On 14 December, Taft announced Wood was to be appointed Chief of Staff. The appointment was a major victory for supporters of military reform and imperialism. Ainsworth was one of the first people to congratulate Wood, and he took the opportunity at their first meeting in the War Department to present his ideas on army reorganisation. Wood successfully rejected Ainsworth's ideas but was unable to convince Taft to accept Bliss as his deputy. Carter was promoted to major general and Assistant Chief of Staff.

Throughout the summer of 1910 Wood and Carter worked on a new general staff structure which was approved by Taft in September. The reform eliminated general staff sections. Four new organisational divisions were created: a Mobile Army Division in charge of rapid mobilisation, a Coastal Artillery Division, a Division of Militia Affairs responsible for joint reserve-regular army actions, and the War College Division responsible for strategic planning. Wood and his colleagues also sought to improve the militia system. The Swiss militia system attracted the most attention, since Switzerland was a republic with a locally organised militia and small professional army capable of mobilising 240,000 trained volunteers in less than 24 hours. Wood ordered several reports to be commissioned on the Swiss system and its relevance to America.[26] By late autumn of 1910, these measures had become the foundations of Wood's new proposed military system.

On 8 November 1910 the Democrats gained control of Congress for the first time since 1894. James Hay became Chairman of the House Military Affairs Committee. A staunch supporter of the National Guard and local volunteer forces, Hay distrusted strong centralised government, opposed Root's army reforms, and was a close friend of General Ainsworth. Wood was dismayed by the election results and by Taft's decision to create a War Department Board on Business Methods designed to achieve defence cuts. The Adjutant General was appointed chairman. Wood, like his predecessors, found his authority undercut by Taft's faith in Ainsworth while his difficulties increased with revolution in Mexico.

In 1911 Wood introduced his plan for military preparedness to Congress. The Chief of Staff advocated a new two-year enlistment period in the Army to replace the current five-year term. Under the new scheme, after two years service men would be liable for call-up for the next eight years. Wood hoped this would provide a large trained reserve. The bill re-asserted the right of the President to use the National Guard abroad. A separate measure, introduced days later, suggested commissioning 500 new Regular Army officers to allow the professional Army to expand rapidly in time of war. In the War Department Wood discovered Ainsworth had passed confidential information on to opponents of the new measures, and a serious row erupted over the powers of the Adjutant General. Thereafter the two men were bitter enemies.[27]

The Mexican crisis in 1911 distracted Wood from his attempt to pass new army legislation. A border incursion from Mexico forced Taft to order an army mobilisation in Texas, with Major General Carter in command. The plan was to quickly deploy 20,000 troops on the border, however, the troops were delayed and there were numerous supply problems. The struggle to assemble 20,000 troops in America gave credence to Wood's view that further army reform was essential. In the Senate, Root and Lodge announced their support for Wood's ideas despite Taft's continued opposition to further army reform. Aware of increasing party division, his declining stature in the Army, and increasing opposition in Congress, however, the President decided to replace Secretary of War Dickinson. He offered Henry Lewis Stimson the post. Stimson was regarded as a Progressive Republican, friendly to Roosevelt, and Taft hoped his appointment might reunite an increasingly divided Republican Party. On 12 May 1911 Stimson formally took charge. The new Secretary, like most of his predecessors, was ignorant of army matters and War Department personalities. In a series of meetings, dinners, and a week-long fishing trip, Wood, Root, and Roosevelt sought to educate Stimson.[28]

In Washington the Army remained under pressure from Taft to produce defence cuts. Stimson and Wood initially recommended a post closure plan which was rejected by Congress. In the early spring, however, the General Staff recommended abolishing the muster rolls held by the Adjutant General's Office. The muster rolls, which listed individual members of a unit, could be replaced by a descriptive list which would save money. Wood wrote to Ainsworth for his opinion. After three weeks Wood had still received no reply from the Adjutant General. The Chief of Staff sent a further query to Ainsworth, asking for his comments on the suggestion by the General Staff. Four days later the Adjutant General sent a reply. He accused Wood of arrogance, questioned the objectivity of the proposal and criticised the Secretary of War for bias against his office. A further inquiry from Wood demanding an opinion elicited a sarcastic reply to Stimson. Five days later Stimson relieved the Adjutant General of his command. The following day, faced with a possible court martial and public disgrace, Ainsworth announced his retirement.[29] James Hay and other prominent Democrats were indignant that their friend had been forced to retire and were determined to remove Wood and rescind the General Staff Act of 1903.

In Congress the Democrats, advised by Ainsworth, introduced an amended Army Bill. The Bill proposed a 40 per cent cut in the number of General Staff officers, limited the role of the Secretary of War on post closures, and narrowed the choice of Chief of Staff open to the President in an attempt to exclude Wood.[30] These measures, supported by progressive Republicans and Democrats, easily gained a majority in the House of Representatives. In the Senate, Root and Lodge worried that Taft might not veto the bill. The President, however, required support at the forthcoming Republican National Convention. At the convention Roosevelt needed only 80 more votes to defeat Taft. To win the nomination, the President required the support of Lodge, Stimson, Root, and other Republican supporters of army reform. On 18 June Taft vetoed the Army Bill. The presidential veto included the annual army budget and, in a rare display of support for the Army, Taft defied Congress to leave the Army unfunded.[31] That same day the Republican National Convention began in Chicago. Root was appointed chairman of the convention and his support gave Taft the nomination over Roosevelt. Roosevelt was furious and never forgave Taft, Root and Lodge for denying him the Republican nomination. Roosevelt ignored pleas not to further split the Republican Party and in August at an alternative convention, the Bull Moose Party nominated Roosevelt as its candidate. The split in Republican ranks was complete. Confident of victory in November, the Democrats nominated Woodrow Wilson, the Governor of New Jersey, as their presidential candidate.

In Washington Stimson attended a conference with leading Democrats to design a new army bill. Democrats agreed to remove the provisions from the bill which disqualified Wood from office and prevented the Secretary of War from recommending post closures. A new suggestion to amalgamate the three supply bureaus into one department was accepted. Wood and Stimson reluctantly accepted a cut of one third in General Staff officers and abandoned Wood's planned shorter enlistment periods. Ainsworth advised Democratic congressmen to denounce Wood's plans for national preparedness during the compromise debate, and many did.[32] At the end of August, the compromise bill was presented to Taft, who quickly signed it into law. Wood continued to persevere with his policy of national preparedness. Increasingly, however, the forthcoming presidential election distracted attention from Wood's proposals. Stimson advised the Chief of Staff to concentrate his attentions on preserving the General Staff and army educational reforms already in place. The Secretary of War warned Wood that Taft's administration would not tolerate another Ainsworth controversy before the election.

On 5 November 1912 the election result gave Wilson victory, for Roosevelt and Taft split the Republican popular vote. Republican supporters of army reform responded quickly to the defeat. They were determined both to protect Root's General Staff Act and to ensure that Wood's ideas on national preparedness received consideration from the new administration. In the War

Department Stimson attempted to rush through several administrative reforms before Wilson took office in March 1913. Stimson also sought to convince the incoming President of the value of army reforms already in place. He used his friend, New Jersey lawyer William Osborn, to present his views to Wilson. Osborn was a friend of Wilson's, and the President-elect listened to his advice on matters of defence policy.[33] Wilson appointed Lindley Miller Garrison as Secretary of War. Garrison, a native of New Jersey, was a lawyer and former vice-chancellor of New Jersey and would serve as Secretary of War from 7 March 1913 until 10 February 1916. In the weeks before he took office, Wood and Stimson sought to influence Garrison. The new Secretary became increasingly sympathetic to the idea of army reform and ultimately left office convinced that Wilson's opposition to military preparedness was wrong. In February 1913, violence in Mexico required the mobilisation of American troops and in the process vindicated the Stimson-Wood reforms which consolidated army command. In one short telegram, Stimson mobilised 20,000 fully-equipped soldiers, who were quickly deployed along the Texas-Mexico border. Garrison observed the success of this operation and realised that the mobilisation had succeeded because of forward planning by the War College and the organisational skills of the General Staff. The new Secretary was suitably impressed. Garrison agreed to continue Wood-Stimson policies of closing small western outposts, defending army reform, and consolidating scattered army units through creating brigade and divisional commands.[34] Stimson was delighted with Garrison's promised support for the Army. Wilson provided further good news to supporters of military reform when he announced that Wood would serve out his term as Chief of Staff which allowed Wood to remain until 20 April 1914. The continued influence of those committed to reform of defence policy was assured.

The struggle to preserve the general staff and presidential control over the National Guard continued for many years. The passage of National Defence Acts in 1916 and 1920 rekindled debate on the army best suited to the American republic. The 1916 Act fashioned by Hay, with advice from Ainsworth, virtually destroyed the general staff concept by expressly forbidding command or control over staff bureaus. The general staff was effectively reduced to a war plans division of the Army. Secretary Garrison who had opposed these changes to the General Staff Act of 1903 resigned in March 1916 and was replaced by the pacifist Mayor of Cleveland, Newton D. Baker. The experiences of the First World War, however, convinced all but a small minority in Congress to accept the army reforms suggested in the late nineteenth and early twentieth centuries. The 1920 Defence Act reaffirmed the belief in a small professional army and extended the number of staff bureaus to include a new Finance Department, Chemical Warfare Service, Air Service and Chief of Chaplains. The act, however, accepted the General Staff as a permanent institution and directed it to prepare war plans and report on the efficiency of the Army.[35]

The ideas of Root, Stimson, Wood, Garrison and others which radically altered American defence and foreign policy were finally accepted. These men, confronted by the depression of the 1890s, large European colonial empires, and expanding industrial capacity were convinced American freedom and security depended upon economic expansion abroad. To encourage American exports, the acquisition of colonies and a strong military were essential. War with Spain provided the opportunity to extend American influence in the Caribbean and Pacific. The US experience in the First World War further underlined the importance of effective military planning and command, regarded as so important by military reformers. Throughout the interwar period the struggle between the bureaus and the general staff continued but the legacy of Root's army reforms remained as the basis for the modern professional American Army.

Notes

1. J.L. Abrahamson, *American Arms for a New Century*, p. 48, Free, London (1981).

2. US Cong[ress], House Committee on Military Affairs, 'To Reorganise the Army HR 12224: Hearing Before the Committee on Military Affairs, 56th Cong., 1st sess., statement by Senator Proctor, 14 May 1900.

3. W.H. Carter, 'Creation of the American General Staff System', p. 31, S.Doc., 119, 68th Cong., 1st sess.

4. Memo from Colonel Sanger to Brigadier General Ludlow, 12 September 1900, AGO(Adjutant General's Office), RG (Record Group) 94, NA (National Archives), Washington DC.

5. R.F. Weigley, *History of the United States Army*, p. 229, Indiana UP, Bloomington (1984).

6. Lieutenant Colonel Roosevelt to Senator Lodge, July 17 1898, *The Letters of Theodore Roosevelt,* E.E. Morison (ed.), 8 (2), p. 839, Harvard UP, Cambridge (1951).

7. Report of the Dodge Commission, 8 (2), pp.115-47, S.Doc. 221, 56th Cong., 1st sess.

8. US War Department, 'Annual Reports of the War Department for Fiscal Year Ended 7 June 1899', Report of the Secretary of War, pp. 46-51.

9. US Cong., Senate Committee on Military Affairs, 'For the Reorganization of the Army of the United States, S.4982: Hearing Before the Committee on Military Affairs', 56th Cong., 2nd sess., statement of Secretary of War Root, 14 December 1900.

10. Lieutenant General Miles to Secretary of War Root, 22 November 1901, Nelson Miles Papers, USAMHI (United States Army Military History Institute), Carlisle PA.

11. Secretary of War Root to Mr Wellman, *Chicago Record-Herald*, 27 January 1902, ERP (Elihu Root Papers), LC (Library of Congress), Washington DC.

12. US Cong., Senate Committee on Military Affairs. 'To Increase the Efficiency of the Army, S.3917: Hearing Before the Senate Military Affairs Committee', 57th Cong., 1st sess., statement of Lieutenant General Schofield, 9 April 1902.

13. 'Colonel Sanger's Appointment', *Army and Navy Journal,* 23 March 1901.

14. Secretary of War Root to Senator Proctor, 30 December 1902, ERP, LC, Washington DC.

15. 'Report on Lieutenant General Miles', *Army and Navy Journal*, 31 January 1903.

16. Carter, 'Creation of the American General Staff System', p. 45.

17. Secretary of State for War Arnold Forster to Secretary of War Root, 23 October 1903, ERP; First Lord of the Admiralty Lee to Brigadier General Wood, 21 February 1904, LWP (Leonard Wood Papers), both LC, Washington DC.

18. Root to Wilkinson, cited by J.R. Belshine, *Military Management for National Defence,* p. 206. Prentice Hall, New York (1950).

19 President Roosevelt to Governor Taft, 27 March 1903, William Howard Taft Papers, LC, Washington DC.

20. Interview with General March, conducted by H.D. Cater, 3 October 1947, 'Interviews on the Creation of the General Staff,' USMHI, Carlisle PA.

21. ' War Department Methods', *Army and Navy Journal,* 9 January 1904; Secretary of War Root to President Roosevelt, 2 January 1904, ERP, LC, Washington DC.

22. J.E. Hewes Jr., *From Root to McNamara: Army Organization and Administration 1900-1965,* p. 13, Center for Military History, Washington DC (1975).

23. Major General Corbin, 1710 ACP 1876, OCS (Office of the Chief of Staff), RG 165, NA, Washington DC.

24. Major General Ainsworth, 5042 ACP 1874, OCS, RG 165; Memo to all Bureau Chiefs from Chief of Staff Bell, 13 December 1907, War College Division General Correspondence, AGO, RG 94, both NA, Washington DC.

25. D.F. Anderson, *A Conservative's Conception of the Presidency*, pp. 237-238, Cornell UP, New York (1973).

26. 'Report on the Swiss Military Organization', 25 September 1905; 'Report on the Swiss Army', 5 April 1913, by Colonel F. Edwards, both Military Attaché Records, RG 94, NA, Washington DC.

27. Diary Entry 30 January, 1911, Major General Wood's views on H.R. 28436, 'Efficiency for the Organized Militia' Leonard Wood Diaries, LWP, LC, Washington, DC.

28. Senator Root to Secretary of War Stimson, 19 May 1911, HLSP (Henry Lewis Stimson Papers), Manuscripts and Archives, YUL (Yale University Library), New Haven CT.

29. Diary Entry, 15 February 1912, Leonard Wood Diaries, LWP, LC, Washington DC.

30. Memo by Secretary of War Stimson, 23 August 1912, HLSP, Manuscripts and Archives, YUL, New Haven CT (1973).

31. Diary Entry, 18 June 1912, Leonard Wood Diaries, LWP, LC, Washington DC; Memo, 'On the Provisions by the Conferences', June 1912, HLSP, Manuscripts and Archives, YUL, New Haven CT. 1973.

32. Diary Entry, 20 August 1912, Leonard Wood Diaries, LWP, LC, Washington DC.

33. Secretary of War Stimson to Williams, 31 December 1912, HLSP, Manuscripts and Archives, YUL, New Haven CT (1973).

34. Statement by Secretary of War Stimson at the War Department, 3 February 1913, HLSP, Manuscripts and Archives, YUL, New Haven CT (1973).

35. Hewes, *op. cit.* pp. 50 -51.

HAIG, GOUGH
AND
PASSCHENDAELE

by Andrew A. Wiest

The public perception of the Third Battle of Ypres or 'Passchendaele' in 1917 is of a campaign consisting of little more than mindless, undirected slaughter. Historians, poets, and politicians have often questioned the nature of command at Passchendaele. Field Marshal Sir Douglas Haig, the Commander-in-Chief of the British Expeditionary Force (BEF) has been accused of murder, pig-headedness and incompetence in his direction of the battle. Critics claim that he chose the wrong place to attack, chose the wrong commander in General Sir Hubert Gough, the commander of Fifth Army, chose the wrong tactics and refused to admit his mistakes. Other historians, however, credit Haig with a hard-fought victory. In recent landmark works Tim Travers and the team of Shelford Bidwell and Dominick Graham have dealt fairly extensively with the question of command at Passchendaele. While the present study recognises their conclusions, it will amplify and in some respects revise their versions of events. Though the image of British Great War generals as 'Butchers and Bunglers' is incorrect, this study will argue that the Third Battle of Ypres was indeed fatally flawed at the highest levels of command.

In the controversy that surrounds the battle, the first phase of operations stands alone as the leading example of confused command. The British Army had been in the area of Ypres since 1914, and Haig had been planning and advocating a campaign in Flanders since he had assumed command of the BEF in late 1915. With such extensive planning and local knowledge Third Ypres should have been a model of efficiency. However, Haig seemingly made several blunders that caused the entire campaign to go awry and assume the characteristics of futile, senseless slaughter. Haig chose Gough as operational commander instead of General Sir Herbert Plumer of Second Army, even though Plumer had a wealth of experience of the Ypres Salient and Gough was unfamiliar with the terrain. Moreover, after years of planning Haig remained vague regarding the goals of the offensive: was Gough to attempt a breakthrough to the Belgian coast or was he to engage in an attritional battle? Finally, Haig did not place enough emphasis on capture of the vital high ground on the right flank of the offensive.

A review of the documents dealing with the first phase of the Third Battle of Ypres reveals the true nature of the serious command breakdown between Haig and Gough. Haig, as Tim Travers has demonstrated, practiced a 'hands-off' style of command.[1] At Passchendaele Haig violated one of the basic principles of warfare by not providing Gough with clear orders, limiting himself to advice and somewhat vague hints. Haig realised the need for a step-by-step advance. He also knew well the worth of the ridges that dominated the right flank of the assault. Finally Haig warned Gough that the Germans were using new defensive techniques. Gough and his Chief of Staff, Major General Neil Malcolm were not perceptive enough to incorporate Haig's suggestions into their planning. Haig should have ordered such changes, but did not. The command structure was flawed; the generals made serious mistakes in judgement, and the results were tragic.

Planning began for a Flanders offensive in February 1916. Haig directed General Sir Henry Rawlinson, commander of Fourth Army, to draw up a detailed scheme for an offensive launched from Ypres aimed at capturing the Belgian coast. Rawlinson's resulting plan called for preliminary assaults in the centre on the Pilckem Ridge and on the right on Messines and Observatory Ridges. Rawlinson argued that it was necessary to take Pilckem Ridge to deny the Germans observation of British lines. He advocated preliminary assaults on the Messines and Observatory Ridges to protect the right of the main attack and to deny the Germans opportunity for enfilade fire. Only after successful completion of the preliminary assaults would it be safe to launch the main attack toward Langemarck and Roulers.[2] Thus Rawlinson had advocated an assault in distinct phases, rather than a breakthrough attack. Rawlinson had also stressed the need to protect the right flank of the offensive before launching the main attack. Haig would not forget this advice.

Other obligations, namely Verdun and the Somme, distracted the Allies for the remainder of 1916, and their attention only returned to Flanders during December. The French general Robert Nivelle now dominated Allied planning. He was confident that a massive French assault in Champagne in the spring of 1917, aided by a British offensive at Arras, would break the German lines and restore a war of movement. After these crushing blows the British would launch a follow-up attack at Ypres. Haig directed Plumer to take charge of planning for this new offensive at Ypres. Since events in the south would have weakened and demoralised the German defenders, Haig ordered Plumer to eschew Rawlinson's step-by-step plan to assault the ridges surrounding Ypres. Haig wanted a breakthrough attack.

Plumer's draft scheme represents a second stage in planning for Third Ypres. His plan called for two forces, designated 'northern' and 'southern' armies, to undertake the offensive, suggesting that the Menin Road should mark the boundary between the two armies. Though directed to undertake a breakthrough attack, like Rawlinson Plumer advocated preliminary assaults to capture the Messines, Pilckem, and Observatory Ridges. The southern army would undertake the assault on the Messines Ridge; the northern army would capture Pilckem Ridge; and the two armies would work together to take Observatory Ridge. Once the ridges had been taken, both armies could concentrate on a breakout into the open land beyond. [3]

Some controversy surrounds Haig's reaction to the planning of Rawlinson and Plumer. Even though both men had emphasised the importance of gaining the high ground through limited offensives, such operations were not part of the eventual plan for Third Ypres. In addition, in the final plan, capture of the entire Observatory Ridge fell to the northern army. Did Haig overrule Plumer's suggestions, or was he simply unwise enough to reject the need for systematic preliminary operations? As it happens, neither was the case; rather, a series of General Staff reports and tactical debates altered the nature of Third Ypres.

In January 1917, Brigadier General Launcelot Kiggell, Haig's Chief of Staff and Brigadier General J.H. Davidson, Haig's head of Operations Branch, GHQ (General Headquarters) considered the various plans for operations around Ypres and made recommendations to Haig. Their report concluded that 'There must be no possibility of divided control and responsibility' that could lead to 'misunderstandings and a lack of co-ordination' in the prosecution of the offensive. For this reason they recommended that Haig place the Ypres offensive, as far as possible, under one command. The report concurred with Rawlinson and Plumer in the desirability of launching preliminary attacks to take the high ground. However, Kiggell concluded that the preliminary operations would be too costly and would:

> thus become in themselves important operations including the employment of considerably more troops than could be made available, and it is assumed, therefore, that it will be necessary to forego them as a preliminary to the main attack, desirable though they may be.[4]

The report's conclusions threatened to change the nature of the coming offensive. As might be expected, Haig sought the opinion of both Rawlinson and Plumer regarding the proposed changes in their plans. Rawlinson was the first to respond to Haig's enquiries and indicated that he agreed with the changes proposed by Haig's staff. In his memorandum Rawlinson reiterated the importance of taking the high ground on the right flank, but was concerned that the Germans could concentrate forces against an isolated, preliminary attack against the Observatory Ridge. For this reason Rawlinson informed the General Staff that:

there is little doubt but that the success of the Northern advance is absolutely dependant on the successful execution of the centre attack [on the Observatory Ridge]. I consider therefore that they should be under the same commander, and if possible carried out simultaneously.[5]

Haig read the memorandum and signified his agreement in his marginal comments.

Haig next received advice regarding the Ypres offensive from Lieutenant Colonel C.N. Macmullen of the Operations Branch of GHQ. He informed Haig that there had been suggestions that the capture of Observatory Ridge should be assigned to the southern army, leaving the northern army free to pursue the main attack. Macmullen advised Haig against accepting such a plan. He claimed that any preliminary attack by the southern force would only alert the Germans to British intentions. Macmullen then advised Haig to place the ridge assault and the main attack under the command of the northern force and to undertake both operations simultaneously to disperse the concentration of German defensive artillery fire.[6]

Perhaps the opinion of Plumer was most important in solving the question of preliminary attacks and command of the offensive against the Observatory Ridge. At Haig's direction Macmullen queried Plumer regarding these important issues. In his response Plumer favoured launching the assault on the ridges and the main attack simultaneously. He also preferred placing the all-important assault on the Observatory Ridge under the command of the northern army. He stated:

> if I were commander of the Northern Army I should consider it almost essential that it [the Observatory Ridge assault] be under that command and if the decision rests with me I should place it under the command of the Northern Army.[7]

Haig has received much criticism for bungling the planning for a Flanders campaign. Among the many charges levelled at the Commander-in-Chief is the claim that he assigned Gough an impossible task, that the attacks on the right flank and central ridges should have been undertaken separately. However, only the Messines operation of 7 June 1917 remained as a preliminary to the main offensive, and six precious weeks were allowed to elapse following this operation. On 31 July 1917, without the aid of any other preliminary assaults, Fifth Army attacked along the entire line simultaneously. The effort proved to be too much for Gough's force to accomplish. Haig did not make this blunder on his own. He acted on the advice of Rawlinson, Plumer, and members of his own staff at GHQ.

Though important, planning for an Ypres offensive remained secondary while the Allies prepared for the spring 1917 offensives. When launched in April the British assault at Arras met with some success, but the failure of Nivelle's offensive triggered serious disturbances in the French Army. By late April it had become apparent to Haig that Nivelle could not succeed, and he began to prepare in earnest for his Ypres offensive. Nivelle's failure, though, forced Haig to reconsider parts of his scheme. Since the German defenders around Ypres would not be weakened and demoralised by a great French victory in the south, could the British then still hope for a breakthrough?

In early May Haig placed the main assault from Ypres under the command of Gough. Haig provided Gough with rather vague instructions regarding the offensive. He informed his subordinate to prepare an offensive to wear down the enemy, and that his objectives were to take the Passchendaele Ridge and Roulers.[8] The benefit of hindsight suggests that Haig's appointment of Gough was a serious mistake. Gough had limited familiarity with the terrain around Ypres or with previous planning for the offensive. In addition Gough would prove to be stubborn and unwilling to take advice from Haig and GHQ. Finally, Gough's reputation as a 'thruster' has led many to believe that Haig, even without significant French aid, intended him to carry out a breakthrough attack. Such was not the case.

Gough received copies of relevant Ypres planning documents on 13 May, and thus had access to the opinions of Plumer, Rawlinson and MacMullen as he began to formulate his own ideas. In the early stages of the planning Kiggell provided Gough with important information about the German defensive scheme. Recent experience had demonstrated that the Germans intended to utilise an innovative, new system of defence at Ypres. Kiggell's report informed Gough that the new German system called for a defence in depth. The keys to this system were fortified points that could give each other mutual support. Except for these positions, the General Staff expected the Germans to abandon their front line during an assault. The first two waves of any offensive would penetrate the German lines, but would be cut off by artillery fire and destroyed by German counter-attacks in their second line of defence. Thus Gough should plan for a limited advance, for only a carefully thought out and well-organized attack could overcome such defensive innovations.[9]

That the nature of the German defences still eluded Gough is evident from a memorandum from his Chief of Staff of 7 June. Malcolm informed the corps commanders of Fifth Army of the need to press the coming assault to its fullest potential. He contended that a thoroughly prepared attack could 'break through any defences which the enemy can devise'. The initial attack would confuse and demoralise the enemy leaving a period when British soldiers could advance freely and take much ground 'at slight cost'. At some point the enemy would regroup and again offer stiff resistance, then the attackers should halt and prepare another set-piece offensive.[10] The expectation that the German defenders would be demoralised, and that the attackers should press on as far as possible, portended disaster in the face of the new German defensive scheme.

Having advised Gough of the nature of the enemy defences, Haig forwarded orders for the assault that reflected the Rawlinson and Plumer plans. Haig had learned the value of the Observatory Ridge and was again considering preliminary assaults in that area. Far from ignoring the importance of the high ground, Haig ordered Gough to take it first in order to ensure the success of the main offensive. The order stated:

> As a preliminary to the main Northern operation, the Fifth Army will prepare and submit, as soon as possible, a plan for a minor offensive designed to secure its right flank on the ridge east of YPRES and with the objective of gaining observation about STIRLING CASTLE and depriving the enemy of observation over the low ground east and north of YPRES.

To aid in the assault Haig placed the entire Observatory Ridge in Gough's sector and reinforced Fifth Army with II Corps.[11]

On 7 June, Plumer launched the first portion of Haig's Flanders offensive at Messines. The methodical Plumer realised the formidable nature of the German defences and had planned accordingly. The Second Army utilised a punishing artillery barrage and the explosion of mines dug beneath the German trenches to facilitate its advance. Most importantly, though, Plumer's plans did not exceed the ability of his troops. He did not aim for distant objectives, but seized and held obtainable goals. The success of Plumer's limited 'bite and hold' advance should have attracted Gough's attention, but it did not.

Gough developed his plan for the Ypres offensive during the first two weeks of June. His ideas centered around taking the Passchendaele Ridge and moving on to Roulers as quickly as possible, rather than opting for a series of short, fixed advances. He also decided against launching a preliminary assault on the high ground of the Observatory Ridge. During a conference on 14 June Gough informed Haig that an operation to take the ridge would involve too many men and would only create a salient on the right flank. Gough preferred to attack along his entire front simultaneously.[12]

Haig accepted Gough's plan, although it differed in many ways from those suggested earlier by Rawlinson and Plumer. Gough had declined to launch a preliminary assault on the ridge. Both Rawlinson and Plumer believed in the need for preliminary assaults but had agreed to GHQ staff's suggestion to launch the ridge assault along with the main attack. After the failure of Nivelle's offensive Haig had returned to the idea of the preliminary assault but was now willing to acquiesce to the wishes of the commander on the scene. However, the change in plans caused Haig to worry that Gough would not place enough emphasis on the important right flank of the offensive.

Gough's plan also differed from previous ones in its choice of distant objectives. Even when Rawlinson and Plumer had expected the Germans to be demoralised by a great French victory to the south, their plans had called for a step by step advance. In June and July Rawlinson warned Haig on many occasions to hold in check Gough's tendencies to rush through to distant objectives. Haig did not do so for two reasons. First, Haig himself was not certain about the nature of the attack. He hoped for a breakthrough to the coast supported by cavalry; he did understand the need for a systematic advance, but thoughts of breakthrough were never far from his mind. Second, Haig believed that army commanders should be left to run their own battles.[13]

The result of Haig's confusion was a breakdown in command. During the month before the offensive Haig would make certain that Gough was warned of the nature of the German defences and the danger of attempting to rush through to distant objectives. But since Haig was not convinced that a breakthrough was impossible, his signals to Gough were decidedly mixed. The Commander-in-Chief simply did not give clear, decisive orders to his subordinate commander. Instead Haig relied on a series of hints and suggestions to Gough. It was command at its most confusing and at its worst.

Haig spent the two weeks following the meeting of 14 June in London attempting to win the approval of the Government for his offensive. In his communications to the Chief of the Imperial General Staff, General Sir William Robertson, and during his meetings with politicians, Haig demonstrated his indecision regarding his goals for the coming campaign. In some cases he argued that the Germans were weakening and that British forces would break through to the coast. At other times he emphasised the worth of a partial success at Ypres as part of a long process of wearing down the German Army.[14] Haig would be no more clear on the nature of the coming campaign upon his return to France.

Just before Haig's return from London Davidson produced a response to Gough's plan for what might be termed a 'rush-through' attack. Haig read and approved the report upon his return. In the aftermath of the success of a limited advance at Messines, the report advised Gough that he should not attempt to push his infantry to their maximum distance on the first day of the attack. Such action would leave British forces disorganised and make them very vulnerable to expected German counter-attacks. Gough should instead strive for limited advances. Troops then could consolidate and prepare for the next advance quickly. The report stated that,

> An advance which is essentially deliberate and sustained may not achieve
> such important results during the first day of operations, but will in the long
> run be much more likely to obtain a decision.

German reserves would be brought into the line to prevent any major
breakthrough on the first day of the offensive. Davidson suggested that the
campaign then should be conducted as a series of limited offensives to draw in
and destroy enemy reserves. Once these reserves had been dealt with, then
Gough could begin to plan for attacks that could yield great territorial results.
The risk of aiming for such results on the first day of the offensive were simply
too great. In closing, Davidson reminded Gough that the ridge on his right
flank was the 'most important tactical point on the Army front at the present
moment'.[15]

Davidson was suggesting a 'bite and hold' approach similar to the one
that was to be used with great success by Plumer in his offensives of Menin
Road Ridge (20 September), Polygon Wood (26 September) and Broodseinde
(4 October), yet to Gough such reasoning was produced by a 'somewhat
pedantic, if you like methodical, mind'. Gough agreed that his forces could
only seize the Passchendaele Ridge and Roulers after a series of organised
attacks and did not plan to press through to the Belgian coast in one great push.
He did, however, contend that his troops should advance beyond the German
second line of defences to a depth of 5,000 yards, while Davidson had suggested
advances of closer to 2,000 yards.[16] Thus Gough supported the idea of utilising
a series of organised assaults to push the Germans off the ridge and out of
Roulers. However, he planned to press through as far as possible. His plan also
had the drawback of forcing British artillery fire to disperse over a wide area.
Gough had been warned about the new German defensive scheme and had
been advised to adjust his offensive accordingly. He did not, and it was up to
Haig to force his hand.

A controversial event took place after Haig's return from London. Haig's
diary indicates that Gough came to GHQ on 28 June for a lunch meeting. At
the meeting Haig emphasised the importance of the right flank to Gough:

> It is in my opinion vitally important to occupy and hold the ridge west of
> Gheluvelt in order to cover our right flank, and then push along it to
> Broodseinde. The main battle will be fought on and for this ridge so we must
> make our plans accordingly.

Gough contended that this meeting never took place, and that Haig never pressed
the importance of the right flank or suggested any modifications to his plan of
attack. In Gough's estimation Haig must have written this part of his diary well

after the event, presumably to blame Gough for the failure of the attack of 31 July.[17] Gough's case is questionable. Only during the writing of the British Official History in 1944-45 did he object that the meeting with Haig never took place, and he also denied that he had been given the advice discussed above. The evidence is clear, however, that Haig and his staff had often warned Gough about the importance of the right flank, but Gough rejected Haig's suggestion of a preliminary assault there. In addition, Gough had been warned of the dangers of distant objectives in the face of the improved German system of defence. Gough failed to heed all this advice, but an even greater failure was that of Haig. The latter still hoped for a breakthrough and thus was content merely to advise Gough of the dangers when, as Commander-in-Chief, he should have ordered his Army Commander to alter his plans.

That Gough did not change his plans despite prodding from both Davidson and Haig is evident in a memorandum issued by Malcolm on 1 July that described the plan of the forthcoming offensive. Malcolm asserted that the offensive would take the form of 'a series of organised attacks on a grand scale and on broad frontages'. The first day of the offensive would unfold in one of two ways. The enemy could become demoralised, in which case the British troops would quickly push to their final objectives. After moving the artillery forward a second assault would ensue. 'This would mean that after some 36 hours of fighting we had reached a state of open warfare with our main forces moving forward under cover of advanced guards'.

The second possibility was that the Germans would not break, but would instead offer a determined resistance. The Germans would fall back to and defend a line around Broodseinde and Gravenstafel. Fifth Army would then halt and prepare to attack this line in four days' time.[18] It is plain to see that Gough had not taken Davidson's advice. Fifth Army was to undertake the offensive in stages, but stages which even in the worst case would advance far beyond what Davidson had recommended. Furthermore Gough only assigned one extra brigade to aid II Corps in its assault on the important right flank ridge system.

On 5 July, Haig had a chance to respond to some of Gough's planning. On this day Haig sent instructions to his armies regarding the forthcoming battle. The document is a strange mixture of optimistic belief in a great victory, and warnings to Gough of the dangers inherent in his operation. Haig reiterated that the capture of the Passchendaele Ridge was to be the first overall goal of the campaign. He stated that such a goal was, 'likely to entail very hard fighting lasting perhaps for weeks; but as a result of this we may hope that our subsequent progress will be more rapid.' Haig also went on to remind Gough once again that the high ground on the right flank would be of the utmost importance.

The end of the memorandum is of great interest, for it admirably summarises the mixed signals Haig gave to Gough. With great optimism Haig contended that:

> The general situation is such, however, that the degree of success gained and the results of it may exceed general expectations, and we must be prepared for the possibility of great developments and ready to take full advantage of them.

Haig followed this with a note of caution. He warned that:

> In the attack, more especially in the earlier attacks, each step must be thoroughly prepared and organised. Every advance must be carried out steadily – but none the less vigorously – with thorough combination and mutual support between the troops employed. The tendency of isolated bodies of troops to dash forward beyond reach of support must be held in check.

Thus Gough should be ready to take advantage of any opportunities that presented themselves, but should not attempt to rush through if the Germans did stand staunch in defence. [19]

While Haig wavered and gave conflicting advice, Gough's preparations for an advance to distant objectives proceeded. In 1944, in response to galley proofs of volume II of the Official History for 1917, Gough offered convincing evidence that while Haig approved the plan, the desire to advance as far as possible on the first day was his own. Gough stated:

> Put briefly, the main matter of difference was whether there should be a limited and defined objective or an undefined one. G.H.Q. favoured the former, I the latter. My principal reason was that I always had in mind the examples of many operations which had achieved much less than they might have done, owing to excessive caution . . . In all these operations victorious troops were halted at a pre-arranged line at the moment when the enemy was completely disorganised . . . This was the argument which I used, I claim with complete justification, with Douglas Haig. [20]

During the remainder of July Haig and his staff toured units assigned to take part in the coming battle. Haig also spent time studying the plans of various corps and divisions for the offensive. Though he dropped hints regarding the right flank, Haig seemed to approve of their planning. He had also been receiving reports from his intelligence section that indicated the Germans had supply and morale problems. Haig and his staff, in their estimation, had done what they could. They had warned the operational commander of possible problems in his plan. Now the battle would be Gough's. Haig's natural optimism, belief in German weakness, and confidence in Gough led him to expect a great victory on 31 July 1917.

Gough's attack did not progress as planned. His right made very little progress in taking the important Observatory Ridge and Gheluvelt Plateau. After a heavy bombardment, his centre advanced fairly quickly to take much of Pilckem Ridge, and gains were also made on the left. However, these successes were due to the new German defensive scheme, which emphasised the initial yielding of ground. German counter-attacks then threw the advancing British back with heavy losses. At the end of 31 July Fifth Army had not advanced past its second objective in the centre, and had made no headway on the right. Such small gains were made at the cost of 30,000 casualties.[21]

Neither Haig nor Gough were happy with the course of the first day of the offensive. Haig recorded in his diary that he had expected heavy resistance, and was fairly pleased with the efforts of his troops. He had, no doubt, expected more positive results, and his pleasure could not have been great. Haig also took Gough aside and again stressed the importance of the right flank, pointing out the vital nature of Passchendaele Ridge, emphasising his belief that until this high ground had been taken, Gough would be unable to advance in the centre.[22] In addition to again warning Gough about the importance of the right flank, Haig also had Kiggell send Gough an appreciation of the tactics employed in the offensive. The report stated that, as expected, the Germans had held their front line lightly. Counter-attack groups waited in the second zone of defence and hit British troops once they had become disorganised, weakened, and lost their momentum. Such defensive tactics forced the General Staff to recommend that Gough change the method of his attack.

Many units on 31 July had pressed on with great gallantry, but were thrown back with heavy loss. They had been exhausted, disorganised and no longer had effective artillery support. The answer to the problem was a limited advance. Such tactics would force the enemy to counter-attack fresh forces that had adequate artillery support. Kiggell stated flatly that,

> We must exhaust the enemy as much as possible and ourselves as little as
> possible in the early stages of the fight. Later, when he is so exhausted and
> disorganised that he cannot hit back effectively, we can push our advance to
> its utmost limits and call on our men to the utmost limits of their endurance.

Thus the next stage of the offensive should be limited in its goals and within range of massive artillery support. After defeating the enemy counter-attack, Gough should repeat the process in about four days' time. Kiggell also told Gough to devise better mopping-up schemes and to use machine-gun barrages in both offence and defence.[23]

Thus, after the failure of the first attack of the Third Battle of Ypres, Haig did instruct Gough to place the utmost importance on the right flank. He also told Gough to aim at limited objectives in the face of the German defences. Such advice was not new. Gough had been warned of the importance of the right flank and had been ordered to take it in a preliminary assault. He had refused. Gough had been warned regarding the German system of defence. He had also been told to aim at objectives no farther than 2,000 yards behind the German front line or face disaster. Again he had refused. Haig should have intervened before the beginning of the offensive. He had failed to do so, instead limiting himself to advice and optimism to see the campaign through to victory. Even after the failure of the first day Haig only advised Gough to alter his tactics. That advice, although firm and forceful, was not an order. Haig was, however, becoming concerned that Gough was not the man to lead the offensive.

Gough next planned to advance in two phases. First, II Corps would attack and take parts of the Observatory Ridge and Gheluvelt Plateau. A few days after this, the main attack would fall on the centre of the line. Essentially, Gough planned to do in his second attempt what Haig had requested of the first. II Corps attacked on 10 August but made little headway. Much of the problem was due to Gough's failure to concentrate sufficient artillery fire on the stubborn German defences. The failure on the right flank should have postponed any attempt to take the centre. Gough, however, did not change his plans. His next assault would proceed as planned but would include a renewed effort to take the ridges on the right.

Before the next major action at Ypres, Plumer forwarded to Haig his response to Kiggell's tactical note of 7 August. The note affirmed the methods and ideas implemented by Plumer at Messines. Plumer agreed that special measures must be taken to deal with the new German defensive system. He argued that any new offensive should be limited in scope. The first phase of an offensive could aim at taking more territory than previously, because the Germans held their front line thinly. A punishing barrage and adequate counter-battery fire should accompany the first assault. After taking limited objectives, Plumer strongly suggested bringing forward reserve divisions to deal with the expected German counter-attacks. In essence Plumer agreed to all of the suggestions of Davidson and Kiggell regarding limited advance and the importance of defeating the inevitable German counter-attacks. [24]

Gough did not respond to Kiggell's memorandum, and proceeded with the next phase of his offensive as planned. On 16 August Fifth Army attacked along the entire front. On the left of the line some units made substantial gains and in some places reached their final objectives. On the important right flank, however, forces again penetrated the German front line, only to be thrown back by counter-attack.

Haig's diary indicates that he was not very pleased with the results of the attack and was again bothered by the failure on the right. Gough, for his part, questioned the bravery of some of his divisions. The commander of Fifth Army contended that these divisions had failed to hold the ground gained and had asked for relief too soon. Gough suggested that he should find those responsible for this failure.[25] But he obviously had not learned much from Kiggell's tactical note and placed the blame for failure on divisional commanders rather than on his own flawed methods. The divisions were battered and facing strong German counter-attacks, just as Davidson, Kiggell and Plumer had warned. The fault was no one's but Gough's.

Haig had now began to tire of Gough. Since May Haig and his staff had been advising Fifth Army commander about limited assaults and the importance of the right flank. Gough, however, had launched two major attacks without heeding Haig's advice. The Commander-in-Chief began to contemplate an action he should have taken long before, placing Plumer in command of the main offensive. Without doubt Plumer's response to Kiggell's tactical note played a large part in Haig's thinking. Gough had not responded to the suggestions and had mounted an attack that, like its predecessor, had failed to hold important ground gained. Plumer, on the other hand, had demonstrated a keen grasp of Kiggell's suggestions and had proved his competence at Messines in June. The situation had reached this point because of Haig's indecision. Gough had demonstrated in June in his response to Davidson's appraisal of his planning that he did not grasp the limitations placed on the British by the new German defences. Haig should have done something then. Instead he did not consider replacing Gough until after two failed attacks.

Gough responded to Kiggell's tactical note on 24 August, more than two weeks after receiving it. Only then did Gough advocate abandoning the wave system of attack used hitherto. He reasoned that Fifth Army should advance in columns. Such an advance would be more flexible, leaving troops better able to deal with German strong points. He also advocated a limited advance and keeping reserves close to the front to deal with German counter-attacks.[26] Gough had finally decided to accept the advice he had been receiving since May. But, for him, it was too late.

There is no firm evidence, but Gough's belated response to Kiggell's advice may have finally exhausted Haig's patience. By 26 August Haig had decided to place the capture of the Observatory Ridge and Gheluvelt Plateau under the command of Plumer. Plumer's attacks on the right would become the focal point of the entire offensive. He would follow a step-by-step approach along the lines of Messines and Kiggell's tactical note. Gough retained a part in the offensive. He commanded the forces on the British left, but his role had become strictly subsidiary. The first phase of the Third Battle of

Ypres had come to an end.

The nature of the command breakdown between Haig and Gough is clear. Haig was indecisive regarding goals of the campaign. He hoped for a breakthrough, but also understood the worth of a step-by-step attack to contribute to the wearing down of the German Army. Haig had chosen Gough to command the offensive in the hope that Gough would take advantage of any opportunities afforded by a great success. Gough, however, was not subtle enough to understand the dual nature of the offensive. In the series of mixed messages received from Haig and his staff, Gough chose to ignore those that advocated caution. He had rejected a preliminary assault on the right flank. He had also never come to terms with the nature of the German defences. After Gough had failed twice, Haig, who did not like to intervene directly, took the drastic measure of replacing Gough with Plumer. Gough had not taken his advice and had bungled Haig's beloved Flanders scheme. It seems apparent that Haig held this against Gough for some time.

Thus the first phase of the Third Battle of Ypres represents the nadir of British command. Haig had indeed chosen the wrong commander. He then violated one of the basic principles of warfare by not providing that commander with clear and easily understood orders. Instead, Haig had chosen to offer Gough advice. It is the fault of Gough that he failed to heed important and wise advice. However, Gough should not have been given the chance to ignore advice – he should have been given orders.

Notes

Extracts from Crown copyright material held in the Public Record Office are reproduced by permission of the Controller of Her Majesty's Stationery Office. I am also grateful to the Trustees of the National Library of Scotland for permission to quote from material in their possession.

1. See Tim Travers, *The Killing Ground,* Unwin-Hyman, London (1987).

2. 'Project for operations in Flanders and Belgium, 5 March 1916', WO 158/19, 77, P[ublic] R[ecord] O[ffice]; 'Fourth Army Records, 18: 122-174, 27 February 1916', Rawlinson Papers, I[mperial]W[ar] M[useum].

3. Plumer's suggestions for an Ypres offensive, 30 January 1917, WO 158/38, PRO. This interpretation of this document is at variance with the conclusions of Dominick Graham and Shelford Bidwell, *Coalitions,*

Politicians and Generals, p.108, Brassey's, London, (1993), that GHQ set the army boundary and attack frontage. Close inspection of the document reveals that Plumer stated 'I consider that the boundary between the operations of the two Armies should be the Menin Road.'

4. 'Notes by the Chief of the General Staff on Northern Operations, 23 January 1917', WO 158/214, PRO.

5. Rawlinson to General Staff, 9 February 1917, WO 158/214, PRO.

6. Macmullen's summary of proposed northern operations, 20 February 1917, WO 158/214, PRO.

7. Macmullen's report on an interview with Plumer, 4 April 1917, WO 158/214, PRO.

8. Gough to J.E. Edmonds, 2 February 1944, CAB 45/140, PRO.

9. Kiggell to Plumer and Gough, 24 and 29 May 1917, WO 158/215, PRO.

10. Malcolm to Fifth Army Corps Commanders, 7 June 1917, WO 158/249, PRO.

11. Kiggell to Army Commanders, 8 June 1917, WO 158/249, PRO.

12. Army Commanders' Conference, 14 June 1917; see also J.E. Edmonds, *Official History of the War, Military Operations, France and Belgium, 1917,* II, pp. 128-129, Macmillan, London (1948). While Graham and Bidwell *op. cit..* p. 301, fn. 8 state that Haig made the decision to launch no preliminary attack, the document cited above clearly states that the decision was Gough's.

13. Tim Travers, *How the War Was Won,* pp. 14-15, New York, Routledge (1992).

14. For a discussion of Haig's actions in London see Andrew A. Wiest, *Passchendaele and the Royal Navy,* Greenwood, Westport CT (1995).

15. Davidson's report on the forthcoming attack, 26 June 1917, WO 158/120, PRO. He suggested that troops could only advance 1,500 to 3,000 yards without undue risk.

16. CAB 45/140, PRO; Memorandum by Gough, 26 June 1917, WO 158/ 249, PRO.

17. Haig Diary, 28 June 1917, quoted in J. Terraine, *Douglas Haig The Educated Soldier,* p. 338, Leo Cooper, London (1990 edn.); G.C. Wynne's interview with Gough, 31 May 1945, CAB 45/140, PRO.

18. Fifth Army summary of orders, 1 July 1917, WO 158/249, PRO.

19. Haig's instructions to armies, 5 July 1917, WO 158/249, PRO.

20. Gough to Edmonds, 2 February 1944, CAB 45/140, PRO.

21. Wiest, *op. cit.,* pp. 148-50.

22. Haig Diary, 31 July, 2 August 1917, PRO.

23. Kiggell to Army Commanders, 7 August 1917, Haig Papers, Acc. 3155 (116), National Library of Scotland.

24. Plumer to GHQ, 12 August 1917, WO 95/275, PRO.

25. Notes on an Army Commanders' Conference, 17 August 1917, WO 158/ 249, PRO.

26. Fifth Army tactical memorandum to GHQ, 24 August 1917, WO 95/520, PRO.

BRITISH GENERALS IN THE FIRST WORLD WAR

by J.M. Bourne

The British look back on the First World War with dismay. A.J.P. Taylor delivered the judgement of posterity: 'brave, helpless soldiers; blundering, obstinate generals; nothing achieved'.[1] At the heart of this perception lie the casualties. Nothing in Britain's military experience before 1914 provided any preparation for their scale. British experience in subsequent wars has happily failed to repeat it. A new culture of remembrance evolved in order to provide meaning for the human costs. These made the war seem increasingly futile, at best a Pyrrhic victory, at worst a spiritual and moral defeat, the beginning of the end of Britain's time in the sun. Something appeared to have gone seriously wrong. The search for explanations began even before the war was over. It has often looked no further than the incompetence of the military.

British generalship emerged from the First World War with an evil reputation. Even the crudest charges still have a wide currency. The first of these is that British generals were all stupid (product of a sociological determinism which asserts that British generals were all stupid because only stupid people joined the Army in the first place). The second is that British generals were all cavalrymen (and therefore presumably amateur, incompetent and incapable of responding effectively to the emergence of new technologies). The third is that British generals all hid in comfortable chateaux, miles from the front line, sending brave men to pointless deaths on battlefields from whose squalid realities they were both physically and psychologically remote and which they seldom, if ever, visited. In a survey of the Anglo-American experience of leadership and command in war, the purpose of studying Britain's First World War generals would seem to be that of warning against 'bad practice'.

A true understanding of British leadership and command during the First World War is vitiated not only by deep levels of prejudice but also by deep

93

levels of ignorance. It is worth considering, for a moment, one of the key words in the charges outlined above: the word 'all'. There were a large number of British generals during the First World War. There were 43 corps commanders, 147 infantry division commanders and more than 700 infantry brigade commanders on the Western Front alone. A large number of other men holding general officer rank served as staff officers, artillery commanders and engineers. Very little is known about these men other than gossip and speculation. Few left personal accounts, published or unpublished. Only one British corps commander has a biography,[2] no divisional commander. This reflects a fundamental weakness in the British historiography of the war, which has traditionally concentrated on the activities of GHQ and its relationship with a small number of army commanders, or on the experiences of the ordinary soldier in the front-line trench. The chain of command which stretched between them, especially the key links of corps and division, has been as little studied as the commanders themselves. Filling this gap remains a major task for historians of the First World War. Until the gap is filled, conclusions about the quality of British leadership and command must remain contingent. The parameters of the discussion, however, are clear enough.

Leadership and command are interrelated concepts. The historical baggage which the British Army brought to them on the eve of war in 1914 was, however, very different. 'Leadership' was a concept which the Army was confident it understood. 'Command' was more problematical. Few, if any, had contemplated a command structure for an army larger than the six infantry divisions and one cavalry division envisaged by the planners of the British Expeditionary Force and no one had any practical experience even of that. Existing notions of command and existing command structures were presented with a fundamental challenge by the massive and rapid expansion of the Army. So, in the event, were existing notions of leadership.

Morale is important in all armies. In the pre-war British Regular Army it was at a premium. The British Army was essentially a colonial police force. It spent much of its time abroad in conditions which were politically hostile and physically uncomfortable. An army with low morale had plenty of opportunity to become demoralised. Much attention was therefore paid to keeping morale high. The Army was also a long-service volunteer force. It had to compete for manpower on the open market. It often did not compete very successfully and had to take what it could get. What it could get was usually the poor, the least educated, the least fit and, sometimes, the least respectable members of British society. Turning such people into effective soldiers was something the Army knew very well how to do. The key was leadership and leadership began at the top.

The summit of ambition for most pre-war Regular officers was to command the battalion in which they began their careers. Battalion commanders were usually appointed for a four-year tour of duty, sometime in their mid- to late-forties. Their role was unashamedly patriarchal and quite often authoritarian. The colonel was the 'father of his regiment'. He set the standards of behaviour for all members of the battalion, officers and men. The Regular Army imposed a regime of 'zero tolerance' in matters of behaviour. Unshaven chins, unpolished buttons and boots, dirty uniform and equipment were heinous offences, zealously policed. More serious 'crime', petty theft, drunkenness, insubordination, was met with swift and sometimes draconian sanctions. This system worked well. Every man knew where he stood and what he could expect if he stepped out of line. The battalion commander was the ultimate arbiter. Any soldier brought before the colonel knew that he could expect justice. This might be severe but it would also be fair and impartial. The highest standards applied to all and no one could expect any favours. Least of all the officers.[3]

'They were a remarkable breed of men, those Regular officers,' the poet and painter David Jones, a wartime volunteer, recalled nearly 50 years later.[4] The Army had a clear understanding of the qualities which it sought in its officers. Many seemed born and bred to the role. A high proportion were the sons, grandsons or nephews of soldiers (occasionally, all three). They grew up with an understanding of what was expected of an officer. This was reinforced by public school, by Sandhurst or Woolwich, and by the thorough process of socialisation which took place in the regiment. Hubert Essame wrote:

> In their eyes Courage was the highest of the virtues. Even if afraid, a leader must not show fear, above all in the presence of his inferiors in rank, age or status. Pain, cold, hunger, danger and discomfort must be endured without complaint: self-pity in any form must be treated with contempt. No comrade must ever be let down whatever the risk. Women and children must be protected. Animals must be treated with kindness. A man's duty to his King and Country in the last resort must come before all else. Finally, their faith in Discipline ... had for them all the validity of religion.[5]

The pre-war Army showed enormous faith in sport as a training for leadership and a means of expressing it. Edwin Alderson, a future commander of the Canadian Corps, even wrote a book extolling the virtues of hunting as 'a school for soldiering'.[6] The officer corps was full of fearless riders to hounds, fanatical polo players, cavalier cricketers, rugby internationals, big-game hunters, champion boxers and swimmers. Men like David Campbell (GOC 21st Division during the war), a brilliant horseman who won the Grand National on a horse called 'Soarer' in 1896, and Walter Long (GOC 56 Brigade), twice middle-weight champion of the British Army, were glamorous figures, whose physical prowess and courage met a ready response from their men.

The hunting field and the sports ground, however, were imperfect environments for assessing the leadership qualities of an officer. All peacetime occupations were imperfect. Colonel W.N. Nicholson wrote:

> It is not possible in peace to gauge with certainty the war time qualities of any officer. Those whom we expect will succeed as commanders are not always a success; while some seemingly indifferent peace time soldiers do magnificently. Even courage, the primary virtue in a soldier, cannot be assessed with certainty. Unimaginative courage that goes baldheaded may balk from ignorance; while the imaginative man may find danger a stimulant or a paralysis.[7]

Fortunately, the pre-war British Army offered its officers more than a diet of sport. It offered them also a diet of war.

The pre-war British *Army List* was full of names marked with asterisks. These indicated men who had seen active service. On the eve of war, for example, the Royal Warwickshire Regiment had 13 officers out of 75 who had seen combat, the Lancashire Fusiliers 34 out of 72, the Northamptonshire Regiment 26 out of 76, the Durham Light Infantry 27 out of 69. The British Army was constantly engaged in some corner of the world, often against the warlike tribes of the North-West Frontier and Afghanistan. It had fought a major war in South Africa little more than a decade earlier. The Army also provided opportunities of extra-regimental employment, with the Egyptian Army or the West African Frontier Force, during which ambitious officers could test their powers of leadership in situations which often required personal courage, physical resilience, independence and initiative.

The performance of the British Expeditionary Force in the late summer and autumn of 1914 proved the Army's leadership qualities. Regimental officers displayed courage, resolution and decision of a high order. Failure to maintain the Army's high standards, notably the notorious 'St Quentin Incident', were few.[8] Officers led from the front and their casualties were severe, not least among battalion commanders. Of the 196 battalion commanders who served with the BEF in 1914, 25 were killed in action, 3 died of wounds, 11 were made prisoners of war and 25 were wounded, a total casualty rate of 32.7 per cent. These figures render powerful testimony to the values of Courage, Duty and Discipline which pre-war officers espoused. It remained to be seen whether this leadership 'model', evolved at junior levels for the command of a long-service professional army on active service in colonial wars, would be appropriate for the command of the very different type of armies gathering at home in response to Lord Kitchener's call-to-arms and destined for a very different kind of war.

The pre-war British Regular Army was 'a small family affair'.[9] There were fewer than 250,000 Regular soldiers serving with the colours at the outbreak of war. The officer corps had only 12,000 men. On 11 November 1918, the Royal Regiment of Artillery had the same number of men as the whole of the pre-war Army and twice as many officers. There were more than 12,000 *staff* officers alone. The expansion was also rapid. More than a million men had volunteered by Christmas 1914. The Army's recruitment system broke under the strain and had to be rescued by a display of civilian enterprise and energy coordinated by the Parliamentary Recruiting Committee. The Army's system for making soldiers broke down, too. Normality was stood on its head. Before the war, no more than 37,000 recruits a year entered the Army. It was often difficult to find these. Now, there were too many men to cope with. Instead, of a minority of civilians entering a world of experienced professionals socialised into the Army's way of doing things, the Army was faced by the prospect of inculcating military values into a 'New Army' four times its own size. Only the battalions of twelve New Army divisions had any Regular officers at all. The supply of these soon dwindled. The example of the 21st Division, part of the Third New Army created in September 1914, is telling. All the division's battalion commanders had been 'dug out' of retirement. Only fourteen others had previous experience in the Regular Army. The rest, more than 4,000 men, had been commissioned since the outbreak of war and had little or no officer training.[10] The consequences of this were very great.

The Regular Army was aware from the outset that it was dealing with very different kinds of men from pre-war recruits. Turning them into soldiers in the pre-war Army image was not going to be easy and, perhaps, impossible. 'They are not soldiers and never will be, according to our standards,' Major W.S. Masterman, of the 5th Battalion Welsh Regiment, wrote to his brother Charles, the Liberal politician, in August 1916.[11] Some regretted this and looked back longingly to the pre-war certainties. Captain J.C. Dunn, Medical Officer of the 2nd Battalion Royal Welsh Fusiliers, recalled an inspection by Lieutenant General R.C.B. Haking, GOC XI Corps, in March 1916. The 2nd Royal Welsh Fusiliers was a Regular battalion.

> The General found that many of the men came out in August 1914. He was at home with these – he had just come from inspecting the 20th R[oyal] F[usiliers]. He chatted and chaffed, pinched their arms and ears, asked how many children they had, and if they could be doing with leave to get another. As he passed from one 1914 man to another he dug his elbow into the C.O.'s ribs and exclaimed, 'You're a lucky fellow'. When it was over he said to the G.O.C., 'That's been a treat. That's the sort we've known for thirty years.'[12]

The interruption into the ordered world of the professional military of large numbers of 'citizen soldiers' from the respectable working class and, disproportionately, from the provincial elites of commerce and the professions did not only confuse General Haking. It also confused the Army as a whole. It is difficult, however, to detect a coherent, institutional response to the changed realities. It took the events of 1917, the French Army mutinies in May, the disturbances at the British base depot at Etaples in September, and the Bolshevik Revolution in October, to convince the Army that something more than a lecture on regimental history, fear of the sergeant major and a chat with the padre was necessary to maintain the morale of civilian armies. In February 1918 Field Marshal Haig himself ordered a comprehensive education scheme to be established in order to provide men with a true understanding of the cause for which they were being asked to die.[13] In the meantime, the Army's response was piecemeal. Individual officers were left to their own judgement. The problems which confronted them were very great, not least for general officers. Their response was mixed.

The British officer corps as a whole underwent considerable evolution during the course of the First World War. Nearly 230,000 new commissions were granted. Very few of these were 'permanent'. Most were temporary appointments of 'temporary gentlemen'. The proportion of officers commissioned from the ranks also rose, from 2 per cent before the war to 41 per cent during the war.[14] By 1918, according to Hubert Essame, the British Army was

> for the moment a career open to the talents with only one standard: courage and the capacity to command in battle... No other Army in Europe at this time was drawing its officers from more varied levels of society than did the British, or from so many careers in which individuality, resource and leadership were qualities which were essential to success.[15]

The evolution of the general officer corps was, perhaps, less dramatic but equally real.

The general officer corps evolved in two important ways. First, it became much larger. The BEF put eight infantry divisions into the field by Christmas 1914; there were sixty deployed on the Western Front on 11 November 1918. This expansion, together with a significant turnover of commanders, provided opportunities of rapid promotion for relatively junior officers. Only one divisional commander at the end of the war, Sir George Gorringe (GOC 47th Division), held general officer rank when the war broke out. The majority had been regimental officers, many of them majors and below. One, C.A. Blacklock, though a former regular officer with three years' service, had resigned his commission with the rank of lieutenant in 1904 and was technically a civilian. Blacklock's case was unusual but not unique. A few other 'exotics' managed to break the Regular Army stranglehold on general officer appointments. These included Arthur Hubback, an architect, who rose from Territorial Force major in 1914 to brigadier general in the Regular 2nd Division by the spring of 1916, and the even more remarkable G.H. Gater, Assistant Director of Education for Nottinghamshire when the war broke out, who rose from civilian to brigadier general in just over three years. Second, the general officer corps became, on average, much younger. The average age of divisional commanders on appointment dropped by ten years during the course of the war. The age, on appointment, of those men commanding divisions on the Western Front at the end of the war was just under 47. The youngest divisional commander, at 35, was Keppel Bethell (GOC 66th Division). (Bethell was two years younger than the youngest British divisional commander of the Second World War, Major General R.A. Hull.) The youngest brigade commander, the celebrated R.B. Bradford VC (GOC 186 Brigade), was only 25. He was a mere lieutenant when the war broke out. His substantive rank at the time of his death in action, in November 1917, was only captain. Bethell, too, ended the war as a regimental captain. He did not become a substantive major general until 1930![16]

The increasing youthfulness of the general officer corps and the rapid promotion which many of its members enjoyed meant that the instincts and experience which they brought to the problem of leadership were essentially those of regimental officers, which in terms of substantive rank many of them still were. The impact of this on their styles of command is clear.

'Treat your new brigade as a big battalion,' Major General Oliver Nugent advised Lieutenant Colonel Frank Crozier when the latter made his farewell to the 36th Division.[17] It was sensible advice. Leadership at brigade level was not fundamentally different from that at battalion. The battalion commander's responsibility to display personal courage, to set an example and to uphold the welfare of his men remained valid.

Courage retained its currency in appointments to brigade command. Clifford Coffin (GOC 25 Brigade) and George Grogan (GOC 23 Brigade) both won the Victoria Cross as brigade commanders, two of the highest ranking officers ever to win the award. The list of brigade commanders on the Western Front at the end of the war shows a preponderance of men with decorations for gallantry. W.D. Croft (GOC 27 Brigade) won four DSOs, a record shared with E.A. Wood (GOC 55 Brigade). Wood was an exceptional man. During the course of the war he was Mentioned in Despatches nine times, wounded five, gassed twice and buried once. In September 1918, 'single-handed and unarmed, he captured over twenty Germans by pelting them with chalk and old boots'![18] 'I would not mind going through Hell itself,' observed Private Robert Cude, so long as Wood was in command of the brigade.[19] Commanding a brigade was no 'cushy billet'. Thirty British infantry brigade commanders were killed during the war on the Western Front, eight died of their wounds, sixty-two were wounded (some more than once) and nine gassed.[20] Many were also wounded earlier in the war while commanding at lower levels. They were no strangers to the realities of war.

In matters other than personal courage, the responsibility of setting an example was, perhaps, more ambiguous. Some undoubtedly interpreted 'setting an example' as 'imposing pre-war Regular Army standards', which might include inflicting humiliating 'field punishments' and did not flinch even from the death penalty. In 1916 Brigadier General B.R. Mitford lectured the officers of 72 Brigade, a New Army unit, on

> the unnecessary use of their services in defence of men under court martial for desertion and cowardice, and urged them to impose the heaviest sentences if they were called on to act as judges.[21]

(Mitford had been 'dug out' of retirement to command a brigade. He was promoted to divisional command (42nd Division) in 1917.) It was the constant badgering and lack of encouragement, however, which many New Army and Territorial officers found trying. The encouragement of subordinates is an often overlooked element in leadership. There is little doubt that most general officers favoured the stern, patriarchal approach. Praise often seemed to have gone out of season. Charles Carrington, a wartime volunteer officer who served with a Territorial battalion of the Royal Warwickshires and an acute observer of the war, described Brigadier General B.C. Dent (GOC 143 Brigade) 'as just like the popular image of a brigadier, inclined to find fault as if that were his aim in life'.[22] Carrington much preferred Dent's successor, Gerald Sladen, a fearless big-game hunter and a man of exceptional sartorial elegance under all conditions, who insisted on the highest standards of military efficiency but was more relaxed in matters of what Carrington regarded as irrelevant, nit-picking trivia. Sladen's leadership style was, perhaps, more suited to the peculiarities of a Territorial unit, at least from a Territorial perspective, but Dent's should not be dismissed as reactionary and outmoded. The 143 Brigade suffered very badly during its 'blooding' on the Somme. Dent was forced to rebuild it with new recruits in a short space of time and lead it into battle again, at Ovillers, this time with greater success. During this period he showed considerable powers of leadership, judgement and moral courage.

Leadership embraced not only the encouragement of subordinates but also their selection and training. High Command has been portrayed – accused might be a better word – of having a policy of promoting 'thrusters', leaders prepared to be as careless with their men's lives as with their own.[23] In fact, very little is known about the processes of selection, especially in the later stages of the war, when the Army became far too big and complicated to operate a promotions system based solely on the personal preferences of a few big wigs. There is little doubt, however, that the war did bring to the fore young, ambitious, ruthless leaders, not least at the battalion and brigade levels. This was equally, if not more, true in the much-admired Canadian and Australian armies where GHQ's writ did not run with regard to appointments. Such men favoured their own kind. One of Frank Crozier's first acts as a brigade commander was to remove one of his battalion commanders, whose battalion had suffered over a hundred casualties from trench feet in four days. In Crozier's case, at least, the impetus to appoint 'thrusters' came from the front line, not from GHQ. Crozier had problems finding the kind of battalion commanders he wanted, 'war dogs' like himself. When he did find them, they included a man who had been a regimental sergeant major in 1914, another who had been a private and a third who had been a Second Lieutenant in the Ceylon Volunteer Corps. Crozier believed that aggression saved men's lives. He had no time for commanders, at any level, who could not hold their line with confidence, who did not dominate no man's land by patrolling and raiding, and who were ambivalent about 'slaughtering the enemy'.

A brigade commander's ability to influence operational and tactical planning was strictly limited, though individual officers, notably H.W. Higginson (GOC 54 Brigade),[24] were capable of registering outspoken objections to what they considered ill-conceived plans. It was in the area of unit administration that a brigade commander could make a difference. Frank Crozier was warmly appreciative of his brigade commander in 107 Brigade, W.M. Withycombe. 'We acquire what is probably the best brigade staff in the army,' he noted. 'General Withycombe of the "Koylis"; his old adjutant, Maurice Day, and Teddy Duffin, a Belfast businessman, look after our wants and guide our ways.'[25] There can be little doubt that in the matter of 'looking after wants' and 'guiding ways' many brigade commanders showed outstanding powers of leadership. The welfare of their men remained a priority. But it also brought them into contact with a fundamental contradiction of leadership during war, the certainty that the men to whose welfare they devoted so much attention would one day have to be sent into battle. Crozier resolved this contradiction with his usual brutal acuity when he declared that he had no qualms about sacrificing a thousand men for some useful purpose but that he objected to losing one man for no purpose at all. Nothing in war was more useless than a 'dead body'.

A brigade commander's relationships with his subordinates were essentially face-to-face and day-to-day. Brigade commanders were not isolated from the front line. They were often in the trenches and sometimes beyond them. The title of one of Crozier's most famous books, *A Brass Hat in No Man's Land*, is apt. Cameron Shute (GOC 59 Brigade) was one of many brigade commanders who liked to go and see for himself. Sergeant A.K. Patterson recalled:

> General Shute was the finest offensive officer I've ever come across. He was a man who wanted to be in the line and to know exactly what was going on... [He] was no milksop, no remote, godlike figure so detached from his men that he saw them as pawns or statistics.[26]

Shute felt no ambiguity about his responsibilities as a brigade commander. His place was in the front line, leading, encouraging, cajoling, deciding. Not everyone was convinced. For some, a brigade commander's place was elsewhere. 'Dancing about in No Man's Land' served no purpose and was an abandonment of real responsibility and leadership.[27] This tension increased higher up the command ladder. It was a product not only of the Army's transformed sociology but also the nature of the war itself, especially the difficulties of communication.

'Leadership, above a battalion command, had never been more difficult [than in the First World War]', declared Sir John Smyth, 'and was never to be so again.'[28] The difficulty became much more acute at divisional level. Shute discovered this when he was promoted to command a division in October 1916. Unfortunately, for both parties, the division concerned was the Royal Naval Division. The Royal Naval Division was a distinctive unit. It had emerged from the fertile imagination of Winston Churchill in the autumn of 1914. It was recruited from Royal Naval Reserves and Royal Marines. It prided itself on its naval traditions. Shute's appointment did not go down well. He was determined to 'army-ise' the division. Sub Lieutenant Jeremy Bentham recalled:

> General Shute had no time for the Royal Naval Division and we had no time for him. The first thing he did was to insist that all NCOs should wear army rank on one sleeve as well as their naval rank on the other. They loathed that![29]

Shute's experience highlights the dangers of operating in a heavy-handed Regular Army manner. The need to appreciate different personal and human qualities was one of the leadership skills identified by Field Marshal Wolseley. In this instance Shute failed the test. He also fell foul of one of the Royal Naval Division's most famous sons, the satirist A.P. Herbert. Herbert wrote a devastating song about Shute, provoked by his furious complaint about the 'disgusting' state of the division's trenches. Herbert's verses went round the Army in no time. From that moment, the divisional commander was 'that shit Shute'. His command of the Royal Naval Division lasted only four months before he was put out of his misery and transferred to command the 32nd Division. Here, and later as GOC V Corps, he did much to forward the career of a kindred spirit, Cyril Blacklock, whose appointment in 1918 to command the Royal Naval Division looks suspiciously like someone's idea of a joke.

Other divisional commanders showed more sensitivity and imagination than Shute in recognising 'different personal and human qualities'. One was Major General J.S.M. Shea (GOC 30th Division). Shea was very much a 'driver', but he mitigated this by identifying himself closely with his division. 'As soon as he arrived he struck us as a very nice and undoubtedly a very keen man,' wrote Brigadier General Hon. F.C. Stanley (GOC 89 Brigade).

> At once he entered heart and soul into the Division and became in every way one of us, taking the greatest interest in our doings and welfare.[30]

Shea's driving was thus without that element of 'I am the expert and I am doing my best to knock you useless civilians into shape' which caused much offence to those same civilians who had all volunteered to serve their country and were doing their best as well, often at great personal cost. Shea's visits to brigade headquarters were welcomed, not feared or resented. 'Yesterday [26 June 1916] we had quite a nasty time,' Stanley confided to his diary. 'General Shea has just been up and has been very nice and comforting. His visits and his cheeriness fill us all with confidence, and I very much appreciate it.'[31] After 89 Brigade suffered heavy losses in the attack on Trones Wood, on 16 July 1916, Shea did not hide, but went round the trenches, talking informally to the men and getting them to share their experiences. This story has a curiously modern ring to it which sits uncomfortably with stereotypes about British First World War generals. It is, perhaps, less surprising to learn that Shea was later 'degummed' by Allenby following a violent disagreement over the sacking of Shea's GSO1, Lieutenant Colonel W.H.F. Weber. (Allenby later asked for Shea's appointment to a divisional command in Palestine, where he won a reputation as Allenby's best infantry commander.)

Hugh Jeudwine (GOC 55th Division) was another who identified himself completely with his unit, a second line Territorial division. This made him a natural choice after the war as Director General of the Territorial Association. He was the driving force behind the 55th Division history, one of the first to be produced. He was also quick to defend in print junior ranks of the division from charges that they had bolted during the German attack at Cambrai, an attack which fell heavily on 55th Division and which Jeudwine himself had predicted after personal observation of the German preparations made from a front line trench.

It was far more difficult for a divisional commander to operate on a face-to-face basis than brigade commanders. Nevertheless, many divisional commanders, like Jeudwine, recognised the importance of visiting the front line, for the moral effect, if for no other. Major General Robert Fanshawe (GOC 48th Division) was one of them. Charles Carrington wrote:

> Every soldier got to know that 'Fanny' spent more days in the front line than any of them. He was easy and pleasant-spoken and he liked to drift into a trench wearing an old raincoat over his rank badges so that the men were not intimidated.[32]

Fanshawe's determination to 'get around the trenches' was commonplace. And yet many soldiers, including some who ought to have known better, complained that they had never seen their divisional commander in the front line.[33] There is no real conflict here. The disparity of perception was inherent in the nature of trench warfare. Captain Cyril Falls recalled:

> One day when I was commanding a platoon, I saw my then divisional commander [Major General Oliver Nugent] on his way to the trenches and had to ask who he was. Yet when a little later I went to divisional headquarters as a staff 'learner' I found that he went out five or six days a week, though often not beyond brigade headquarters, so far as I recall, he visited the trenches at least once a week, but as I have suggested the average platoon commander might not encounter him for months on end.[34]

A divisional commander's tour of the trenches was not achieved without costs and a considerable degree of disorganisation. Sir John Smyth recounted a trench tour he made as ADC to Major General Peter Strickland (GOC 1st Division). Strickland began the war as a battalion commander in the Manchester Regiment. He had demonstrated as a brigade commander his desire to get as far forward as possible. At Loos he went to the lengths of hollowing out a tree near the front line so that he could get a better view. Only when a hail of bullets cut a rung of the rope ladder inside did he admit that the idea might not be a good one. Promotion to divisional command did not curb Strickland's instincts. During the tour he made with Smyth, the trenches were assailed by rifle fire and a barrage of *minenwerfers*. Strickland's presence, far from reassuring others present, served only to alarm and concern them. He had shown himself to the troops (he always wore his red cap band, complaining that without it nobody would know who he was and his visit would have no effect), but very few had actually seen him. The trenches were no place for socialising. They were full of men who were working or sleeping. They were cramped and uncomfortable. 'They provided no opportunity at all for the general to say *à la* Montgomery:

"Now gather round chaps and I'll tell you how the war is going". There was nowhere to gather.' 'Was it worth it?' Smyth asked. 'Yes, I think for him it was,' he concluded, 'but I don't think it made much impression on the troops. That was the sort of war it was.'[35]

The problems encountered by Strickland were not unique. They go to the heart of the problems of leadership and command in the First World War. John Terraine has emphasised that the war was the only one ever fought without 'voice control'. Communications during the war were dependent principally upon telephones. These were not of the mobile variety but fixed instruments situated at the end of an incredibly complicated maze of wire, extremely vulnerable to enemy action. A divisional commander who chose to go and see for himself, and to show himself, in the trenches did so at the risk of cutting himself off entirely from his headquarters, usually for hours at a time. Getting up to the trenches and back was a long and exhausting business, much of it necessarily on foot. During that period, in effect, he commanded nothing. And when he got back a commander would have to deal with all the paperwork and enquiries he had missed during his visit to the front. If he stayed at his headquarters, at the end of the telephone, he risked cutting himself off psychologically. It made sense to adopt the Napoleonic model, which Martin van Creveld described as the 'directing telescope'.[36] If you cannot go yourself, find someone you know and trust to go and get him to report back to you. But act vigorously and personally to deal with any problems which are identified. Many divisional commanders eventually made this pragmatic adjustment. But whatever system a commander used, his communications system did not extend beyond the front line trench. Once his troops attacked, they entered a void. The only men who could really respond to events were the ones at the front and their ability to do this depended on their training, their experience and the willingness of their superiors to trust their judgement. None of these elements was brought about easily or quickly.

It was much easier for a divisional commander's personality to make an impact on those with whom he could communicate easily face-to-face, particularly on his headquarters staff and on the training of his brigadiers. Personality did make a difference here. Colonel W.N. Nicholson described the transformation of 51st Division by the appointment of Major General G.M. Harper. 'The magnificent *esprit de corps* of the 51st Division was largely due to "Uncle's" personality,' he wrote.[37] Sir Ivor Maxse concurred, in recommending Harper for promotion to a corps:

His division is organised from top to bottom in all departments and he handles it in a masterly manner in active operations. I knew the 51st Division before General Harper commanded it and then considered it ill-organised and unsoldierlike. It is now one of the two or three best divisions in France and its fighting record is well known. I attribute its success mainly to its present commander.[38]

Nicholson also noticed a similar, if rather less spectacular, impact on the 17th Division made by the appointment of Major General P.R. Robertson. Robertson's career exemplifies the strengths and weakness of pre-war regulars in command of New Army formations. Nicholson considered Robertson 'in every respect a most excellent divisional commander'. He was not a warrior like 'Tommy' Capper (GOC 7th Division) or Keppel Bethell.

> He had no love of war or fighting; he wished with all his soul that 'The Hun would chuck it', and let him go home to his [beloved] family. So did his division, officers and men.

Robertson was never popular. Popularity was something for which pre-war Regular officers had only contempt. But he was admired and, most important of all perhaps in a 'citizen division', trusted. He was clear-minded, conscientious and thorough. He did not waste lives.

> But he was a Regular, with many of the limitations of the Regular who has served nowhere outside his unit; they were slack and ignorant according to his Regular standards and like the sound battalion commander he was he told them so. He had not sufficient insight to deal with the different conditions of the New Army, and enforce his method in a more congenial manner.[39]

Harper's nickname, 'Uncle', is, perhaps, indicative of a particular leadership style. (Generals' nicknames may repay systematic analysis.) He belonged to the school of what Charles Carrington called 'the kind-old-gentleman-British-commander'. Robert Fanshawe was another member, so was William Fry (GOC 30th Division). Others found the 'demanding tyrant' school more congenial. It is difficult to imagine W.C.G. Heneker, long-serving commander of the 8th Division, attracting the soubriquet 'Uncle'. James Jack, a battalion commander in 23 Brigade, described Heneker as a 'fine but exacting chief'.[40] His standards were very much those of the pre-war Regular Army. 8th Division soon felt the effects. All three brigade commanders were removed within three months of Heneker's appointment. Other commanders and staff officers 'also felt the blast'. His job was to keep his subordinates up to the mark, his command style that of an auditor. Nothing escaped his penetrating and unrelenting attention. Hubert Essame recalled:

> He expected to be saluted by everyone within eye range. His eagle eye could detect an unshaven chin, the need for a hair cut, a grease stain or an unpolished

button at a considerable distance. His comments were unequivocally clear, vividly expressed and long remembered.[41]

Sir George Gorringe (GOC 47th Division) was another divisional commander notorious for his bullying insensitivity. Men like this were respected and feared rather than admired, but they were leaders just the same. Popularity was no use in itself. It had to be turned to effect. Passivity is often fatal in war. It was men who made no impact of any kind, who were neither loved nor feared, who neither inspired nor drove who fell by the wayside. Maxse 'degummed' Major General Hew Fanshawe (GOC 58th Division) very much on these grounds. Maxse reported:

> This officer does not in my opinion command his division with either decision or knowledge. In the planning stage he plays a minor part and appears to have little influence on his subordinate commanders... He is not a good trainer, having little knowledge of the subject. But, if he had, I doubt whether he could either teach or enforce his views. I see no sign of grip or drive and think the division would be a very valuable one if placed in stronger hands.[42]

The difficulties of leadership and command faced by divisional commanders were even more severe at corps, army and GHQ level. Corps and army were the operational level of command, during the First World War, responsible for planning and executing individual battles. The Army's inheritance had little to offer. The army level of command did not exist at all before the outbreak of war and was only created at the end of 1914. There was one corps, the Aldershot Army Corps, which existed largely on paper. Only three serving officers in the British Army had commanded this corps. The first, Sir John French, was already commanding above that level. The second, Sir Douglas Haig, was commanding the Aldershot Corps when the war broke out, after which it became I Corps. The third, Sir Horace Smith-Dorrien, was given command of the newly-created II Corps. The dispatch of a three-corps British Expeditionary Force thus exhausted all the experienced officers available. III Corps was given to Sir William Pulteney. He had not been to Sandhurst and had not passed staff college. The best that can be said of Pulteney is that he was the epitome of 'the practical man'. To help him with the 'theory' some of the best staff officers in the British Army were sent to III Corps, including Stanley Maude, George Milne, John Du Cane and 'Tim' Harington. The fourth corps commander to be appointed, Sir Henry Rawlinson, had never commanded a brigade in action and only very briefly a division. At corps, and also at army, level the British Army was forced to make up the rules as it went along.

Very little is known about corps command. There are no published corps histories (other than for the Indian, Canadian and Australian corps), though about half the divisions have them. Corps sectors remained largely static, often for years at a time on the Western Front; divisions were constantly rotated through them. A corps commander would usually have at least 50,000 men under his command. Corps commanders also played a key role in two other areas central to military leadership – training and the selection of subordinate commanders for promotion. They were undoubtedly important figures, yet they have never been systematically studied as a group and many remain 'semi-anonymous'.[43] A few made an impact as leaders, notably Sir Julian Byng (GOC Canadian Corps), the Earl of Cavan (GOC XIV Corps), Sir Walter Congreve VC (GOC XIII Corps), Sir Claud Jacob (GOC II Corps), Sir Ivor Maxse (GOC XVIII Corps), (perhaps the war's most successful 'trainer'), and, in his ineffable way, Sir Aylmer Hunter-Weston (GOC VIII Corps).

Congreve was renowned as a front-line general. Brigadier General Hon. F.C. Stanley recalled:

> I got a message from General Congreve, our Corps Commander, saying he would like to come up and go round the trenches. So off we went in a beastly snow-storm, but really had a most enjoyable time. He was a very agreeable companion, and of course in thick snow we could go to all sorts of places one could not have thought of going to on a clear day; wandering about on top of the ground instead of ploughing through the trenches. He is a most adventurous man, though, and infinitely preferred walking out in full view and quite close to the enemy than anything else. He simply asked for trouble.[44]

Not surprisingly, Congreve was the only corps commander to be wounded during the war, losing his left hand at Arras in 1917. Maxse was a prime example of the enthusiast. Liddell Hart described him as 'bubbling with fiery energy'. He was utterly intolerant of inefficiency, which he sought to expose through relentless inspection and insistent questioning. He loved an argument and admired men who had the courage to argue back. Hunter-Weston ('Hunter-Bunter') was that very British character, a 'card'. More stories were told about him than any other officer in the Army. His flair for self-publicity and his political connections (he was a member of parliament) may explain his long tenure of command. It certainly cannot be explained by his military success. After the disaster which befell VIII Corps' attack at Beaumont Hamel and Serre on 1 July 1916 Hunter-Weston was not trusted with planning a major attack again. Most corps commanders, however, were as anonymous to their men as to posterity and failed to impose a personal style of leadership on their ever-changing commands.

Army commanders were, arguably, more successful than corps

commanders in this regard. Those who did succeed in imposing their personalities on their commands usually belonged to the 'demanding tyrant' school. Allenby was certainly one of these. His temper was awesome, even in an army with no lack of short-fused commanders. Allenby frightened people. Quite senior officers were known to tremble before his assaults. A cavalry squadron commander once passed out while being reproved by him. Gough was equally feared. One of his divisional commanders, Major General W.H. Rycroft (GOC 32nd Division), was said to be 'terrified' of him. Gough admired 'young thrusters' like himself and did much to forward their careers. Allenby and Gough had the power of personality to drive. In Allenby's case, there is no doubt that this contributed materially to the success enjoyed by the polyglot armies he commanded in Palestine in 1917 and 1918. Leadership, however, is sometimes about listening as well as driving. Neither Allenby and certainly not Gough was very good at this. There was a particularly unattractive streak of arrogance and contemptuousness in Gough, which was a weakness in a commander. All great commanders are formidable, but those who are also unapproachable run a real risk of isolating themselves from unpleasant truths.

If any army commanders fell into the 'kind-old-gentleman' school it was Byng and Plumer. Both represented the best of what the old army had to offer: lack of personal ambition; an austere sense of duty; a thoroughgoing professionalism and attention to detail. Horne, also, shared these virtues, but it would be stretching the meaning of words to describe him as 'kindly'. Horne was another 'driver' who drove no one harder than himself. His nervous sensibilities were subjected to iron control. He led a life of almost monkish dedication, eating little, drinking nothing, restricting himself to only two cigarettes a day, selfless, honourable but ultimately impenetrable even to the fellow professionals who worked most closely with him. Horne is one British general of the First World War in whose face it is possible to read the personal costs of command.

Field Marshal Montgomery complained that he had served on the Western Front for four years under two commanders-in-chief and never seen either of them. Field Marshal Sir John French, the first of Montgomery's C-in-Cs, has been described by David French as an 'over-promoted Victorian cavalry colonel'. He brought the instincts of a regimental officer to his command on the Western Front. He liked to 'get round the troops'. His visits to the line in 1914 may have done much to restore his own morale (which was often low), but seem to have had little impact on his men. His visits were received with the puzzled enquiry 'Oo's the ole bloke, then?' His disappearances also caused consternation among his staff and a vacuum in command. French's successor, Douglas Haig, inherited an expeditionary force much larger than the one French took to war in 1914 and one which continued to grow until it became the second biggest organisation in the British Empire after the London County Council. Even if Haig had the temperament of a showman, which he did not, it is difficult to see how he could have imposed his personality on the mass of ordinary soldiers. In the event, he did not even try. 'No doubt Haig's character did influence those immediately around him,' wrote Lord Moran. 'But we in France knew nothing of this man until he was explained to us after the war. Haig with us was not even a legend.'[45] The importance of the first part of Moran's statement should not be underestimated. Haig, unlike French, never lost the support and confidence of his immediate subordinates or of his military and political superiors, with the important exception of the Prime Minister, David Lloyd George. But Haig's apparent remoteness and detachment from the realities of war brings us, at last, to the crux of the problems posed by leadership and command in the First World War. Is it possible to command without leading?

J.F.C. Fuller was one of those who thought not. He accused the British High Command of surrendering to bureaucratisation, withdrawing from the line of fire, severing the Army's head from its heart and destroying its moral authority.[46] What substance is there to these charges?

The British Army's system of command and control during the First World War has not had a good press. It has been portrayed as rigid, hierarchical and inflexible, vitiated by snobbery and favouritism, backward-looking and reactionary, hostile to technology, preferring a costly 'human solution' to the problems of the battlefield and fatuously determined to overcome the chaos of war by highly detailed and structured planning emanating from above.[47] This unhappy state of affairs has been unfavourably compared with the task-oriented methods of the German Army, initiative-encouraging, risk-taking, tactically innovative and flexible, a 'bottom-up' system capable of speedily absorbing, digesting and responding to battlefield realities.[48] The most that can be said in favour of the British system is that, in 1918, it broke down under the impact of the German offensives and the semi-open warfare which followed, to be replaced by 'useful anarchy'.[49] The 'villain' of this account is not any one individual but the pre-war British Regular Army itself. In this peculiar institution, initiative and independent thought were not encouraged. Intellect was despised, professional curiosity largely absent and frank and open discussion suppressed. The Army's only sustained intellectual activity appeared to be the protection of senior officers' reputations.[50]

The problem with this explanation is that it explains too much. Its severe strictures are difficult to reconcile with what actually happened. The British Army did embrace technology, much more than did the German. By 1918 it had created the world's largest (and, soon, first independent) air force. The Royal Flying Corps had no greater supporter than Douglas Haig. Armoured warfare had also been developed. The recent work of Paul Harris has clearly demonstrated the positive reception which GHQ gave to the development, introduction and use of the tank.[51] British artillery tactics were not only innovative but also, arguably, revolutionary. Creeping and box barrages, sound ranging, flash spotting, silent registration, aerial gun control, the deep battle ushered in the 'modern style of war'.[52] After the disaster of the first day of the Somme, infantry tactics also responded. Infantry continually developed its firepower. Its method of attack became less stereotyped. Initiative was increasingly delegated to increasingly experienced junior officers and NCOs.[53] And all this was achieved in a relatively short space of time by an historically small, ill-equipped army, weak in doctrine and staff work, in constant contact with a powerful enemy. These were not the achievements of a mindless and somnolent bureaucracy incapable of responding to events.

Defence of the British Army's command system in the First World War, however, rests for the moment largely on these a priori arguments. The depth of analysis carried out on thinking at GHQ has not been fully extended to lower levels of command. But it is now clear, at least, that the British Army did evolve considerably during the First World War. New weapons, new men and new tactics emerged. The most impressive account of the process is Robin Prior and Trevor Wilson's *Command on the Western Front*.[54] This study began as an attempted rehabilitation of Sir Henry Rawlinson. It ended as a rehabilitation of the British Expeditionary Force. Rawlinson was part of the BEF's learning process not the cause of it. No one individual was the cause of it. The expeditionary force itself was too big and the endeavour in which it was engaged too complex for that. The learning process was undoubtedly messy and piecemeal. Many mistakes were made. GHQ and army commanders often found it very difficult to know when to interfere with subordinate formations and when not. Commanders at army, corps and divisional level oscillated between over-control and allowing uncoordinated subordinate initiative. Considerable confusion resulted, some of it very costly indeed. Failures of leadership led, even in 1918, to a paralysis of command.[55] Effective systems for ensuring that lessons were learned were not really put in place. Experience was the BEF's greatest teacher, not GHQ. The SHLM Project on British divisional performance during the war suggests that 'useful anarchy' began much before 1918.[56] The BEF was the passive victim neither of the German Army nor of its own High Command. Tactical initiatives emanated from army, corps and divisional level, not least from the 9th Division, under its outstanding commander Major General Hugh Tudor. A new breed of young, experienced, determined commanders, a few of them not even professional soldiers, conspicuous not only for the traditional virtues of personal courage and a high sense of duty but also for ruthlessness and aggression, took advantage of the opportunities for rapid promotion. At battalion, brigade and, to a great extent, at divisional level the

BEF eventually became a meritocracy. Had the war lasted longer, the rising tide of change would surely have engulfed the Army's corps commanders, many of whom seem less impressive than their subordinates and too many of whom were maintained in position for too long. Those men who emerged at battalion, brigade and divisional level understood the relationship between leadership and command. They were experienced front-line commanders who had lived – and continued to live – in what Clausewitz called 'the realm of danger'. They recognised that there was more to command than issuing orders down a telephone line. They were, in short, leaders.

Notes

1.   A.J.P. Taylor, *An Illustrated History of the First World War*, p. 105, Penguin, Harmondsworth (1965).

2.   J. Baynes, *Far From a Donkey: The Life of General Sir Ivor Maxse*. Brassey's, London (1995).

3.   J. Baynes, *Morale: A Study of Men and Courage: the Second Scottish Rifles at the Battle of Neuve Chapelle, 1915*, Cassell, London (1967).

4.   A. Hine (ed.), *David Jones. A Fusilier at the Front*, p. 122, Seren, Bridgend (1995).

5.   H. Essame, *The Battle for Europe 1918*, p. 110, Batsford, London (1972).

6.   E.A.H. Alderson, *Pink and Scarlet, or Hunting as a School for Soldiering*, Heinemann, London (1900).

7.   Colonel W.N. Nicholson, *Behind the Lines. An Account of Administrative Staffwork in the British Army 1914-1918*, p. 146. Cape, London (1939).

8.   P.T. Scott, *Dishonoured*, Tom Donovan, London (1994).

9.   Lord Moran, *The Anatomy of Courage*, p. 60, Constable, London (1945).

10. P. Simkins, The Four Armies 1914-1918, p. 250. *The Oxford Illustrated History of the British Army*, D. Chandler and I. Beckett (eds.), Oxford University Press, Oxford (1994).

11. W.S. Masterman to C.F.G. Masterman, 27 August 1916. Masterman Papers, Birmingham University Library.

12. J.C. Dunn, *The War the Infantry Knew 1914-1919*, p. 185, Jane's, London (1987).

13. S.P. MacKenzie, *Politics and Military Morale. Current Affairs and Citizenship Education in the British Army 1915-1950*. Clarendon Press, Oxford (1992).

14. J. Gooch, The Armed Services, p. 190, in S. Constantine *et al*, *The First World War in British History*, p. 190, Arnold, London (1995).

15. Essame, *Battle for Europe*, p.111.

16. J.M. Bourne, British Divisional Commanders during the Great War: First Thoughts. *Gun Fire. A Journal of First World War History*, 29, 22-31 (n.d.).

17. Brig. Gen. F.P. Crozier, *A Brass Hat in No Man's Land*, p. 131, Cape, London (1930).

18. P. Simkins, The War Experience of a Typical Kitchener Division: The 18th Division, 1914-1918, p. 304, in H. Cecil and P.H. Liddle (eds.), *Facing Armageddon. The First World War Experienced*. Leo Cooper, London (1996).

19. *Ibid*, p. 306.

20. For full details of British senior officer casualties, see F. Davies and G. Maddocks, *Bloody Red Tabs. General Officer Casualties of the Great War, 1914-1918*. Leo Cooper, London (1995).

21. L. James, *Imperial Warrior. The Life and Times of Field Marshal Viscount Allenby 1861-1936*, pp. 324-325. Weidenfeld, London (1993).

22. C.E. Carrington, *Soldier from the Wars Returning*, p. 101. Hutchinson, London (1965).

23. T. Travers, *The Killing Ground: The British Army, the Western Front and the Emergence of Modern Warfare, 1900-1918*, p. 13, Allen & Unwin,

London (1987).

24. R. Prior and T. Wilson, *Passchendaele, the Untold Story*, p. 288, Yale, London (1996).

25. Crozier, *Brass Hat*, p. 62.

26. L. Macdonald, *Somme*, pp. 230-231. Joseph, London (1983).

27. See the comment by Lieutenant Colonel H.M. Davson on Brigadier General F.W. Lumsden VC DSO, in Davies and Maddocks, *Bloody Red Tabs*, p. 87.

28. Sir J. Smyth, *Leadership in Battle*, p. 55, David & Charles, Newton Abbot (1975).

29. Macdonald, *Somme*, p. 321.

30. Brig. Gen. Hon. F.C. Stanley, *The History of the 89th Brigade 1914-1918*, p. 117, *Liverpool Daily Post,* Liverpool (1919).

31. *Ibid*, p. 120.

32. Carrington, *Soldier from the Wars Returning*, p. 103

33. The future Field Marshal Alexander was one, see C. Falls, Contacts with Troops: Commanders and Staffs in the First World War. *Stand To! The Journal of the Western Front Association*, 47, 21 (1996).

34. *Ibid.*

35. Smyth, *Leadership in Battle*, pp. 12-13.

36. M. Van Creveld, *Command in War*. Harvard UP, Cambridge, Mass. (1985).

37. Nicholson, *Behind the Lines*, pp. 140-141.

38. Lieutenant General Sir F.I. Maxse, Report on Major General Harper CB DSO. Maxse Papers, Imperial War Museum, 69/53/12/, Box No 54.

39. Nicholson, *Behind the Lines*, p.122.

40. J. Terraine, (ed.), *General Jack's Diary*, p. 197, Eyre & Spottiswoode (1964).

41. Essame, *Battle for Europe*, p. 109.

42. Maxse, Report on Major General H.D. Fanshawe CB, *ibid*.

43. Terraine, *General Jack's Diary*, p. 155.

44. Stanley, *89th Brigade*, pp. 112-113.

45. Moran, *Anatomy of Courage*, pp. 203-204.

46. J.F.C. Fuller, *Generalship: Its Diseases and their Cure*, Faber, London (1933).

47. See Travers, *Killing Ground, passim*.

48. M. Samuels, *Doctrine and Dogma. British and German Infantry Tactics in the First World War*, Greenwood, Westport, CT. (1992).

49. T. Travers, *How the War Was Won. Command and Technology in the British Army on the Western Front 1917-1918*, London, Routledge (1992).

50. Travers, *Killing Ground*, pp. 3-37.

51. J.P. Harris, *Men and Ideas and Tanks: British Military Thought and Armoured Forces 1903-1939*. Manchester UP, Manchester (1996). See also, Harris, The Rise of Armour, pp. 113-137, in P. Griffith (ed.), *British Fighting Methods in the Great War*. Cass, London (1996).

52. J. Bailey, *The First World War and the Birth of the Modern Style of Warfare*, pp.13-21. Strategic and Combat Studies Institute Occasional paper No 22 (1996). See also, Bailey, British Artillery in the Great War, pp. 23-49, in Griffith (ed.), *British Fighting Methods*.

53. P. Griffith, *Battle Tactics of the Western Front. The British Army's Art of Attack*, Yale, London (1994).

54. R. Prior and T. Wilson, *Command on the Western Front. The Military Career of Sir Henry Rawlinson 1914-1918*, Blackwell, Oxford (1992).

55. Travers, *How the War Was Won*, pp. 50-110.

56. J. Lee, The SHLM Project: Assessing the Battle Performance of British Divisions, 1914-1918, pp. 175-181, in Griffith (ed.), *British Fighting Methods*.

LEADERSHIP IN THE BRITISH ARMY IN THE SECOND WORLD WAR: SOME PERSONAL OBSERVATIONS

by Michael Howard

T he chapters in this book deal with the distinct but overlapping subjects of Command, Control, and Leadership. The first two are normally combined; in German they are known simply as *Kriegsführung*. Leadership, or *Führerschaft,* is rather different. The first two demand a capacity for comprehending often highly complex factors and thus require minds of above average intelligence. The last consists almost entirely of what Clausewitz termed 'moral' qualities, of a kind that can often coexist with a complete absence of any significant intellectual capacity at all.

Leadership is the capacity to inspire and motivate; to persuade people willingly to endure hardships, usually prolonged, and incur dangers, usually acute, that if left to themselves they would do their utmost to avoid. It is essential at the lower levels of command, where danger and hardship are at their greatest, but the need for it does not diminish at higher levels. It is true that young officers endowed with 'leadership qualities' and precious little else will reach their ceiling of command fairly rapidly – if indeed they survive to reach it at all. It is the additional capacity for intellectual grasp of all the complexities of their profession that will determine how far they can – or, rather, how far they should – ascend the ladder of promotion. There is certainly plenty of room in the higher ranks for officers with good minds whose capacity to inspire their followers into risking their lives may not, at the lowest levels, have been very evident. Such men are usually best employed in the general activity of 'control', for command decisions at every level require moral strength as well as intellectual grasp. The capacity not just to take decisions but to follow them through and make them stick requires leadership of the very highest quality. It is one thing to be able to inspire men to risk their lives and endure prolonged hardship if one is sharing those dangers and hardships. To be able to do so by remote control demands qualities of personality possessed by very few.

During my service as an infantry officer in the 3rd Battalion The Coldstream Guards during the Italian campaign in 1943-45, I was lucky enough to experience leadership at both levels. I also learned that of all the qualities of leadership listed by the pundits (Clausewitz for one cites courage – physical and moral – physical stamina, *coup d'oeil*, imagination, determination, energy, self-control, boldness, perseverance, cunning and calm)[1] by far the most valuable is the last: *calm*. My own battalion commander, George Burns (later Major General Sir George Burns, GCVO, CB, DSO, OBE, MC) was a model of his kind. Whenever the situation was, in the parlance of the time, 'sticky'; whenever we were being heavily shelled or subjected to counter-attacks, or felt particularly demoralised from cold, damp, hunger or sheer fatigue, Colonel George would miraculously appear, beaming cheerfully, armed only with a large walking stick, nursing an unlit pipe and demanding a match. His very presence dispelled fear and fatigue, making us feel that all was well and there was nothing to worry about. He was like a mobile service station moving around among his troops and filling them up with courage, energy and good humour. He was far from unique: young officers from different battalions would hotly compete with stories about the leadership qualities of their own battalion commanders. It was one of the many advantages of the regimental system – of which more later – that it could breed such men.

Colonel George and those like him could do this by personal contact. It might be supposed that such direct contact is necessary for the magic to work, but it is not necessarily so. At the crisis of the Salerno campaign, when it seemed quite possible that German counter-attacks would push us back to, if not off, the beaches on which we had landed a few days before and the situation looked very sticky indeed, we learned that General Alexander had landed in the beachhead. General Alex was not even the Army Commander; that was the egregious American General Mark Clark, who was rumoured – later we learned, entirely correctly – to be making arrangements to evacuate the American forces on our right flank. Alexander commanded something even more stratospheric, the Army Group. Very few people apart from staff officers and senior commanders can have actually seen him during his visit, let alone talked to him. But the very knowledge that he was there at once made everything seem all right. He had performed the same miracles at Dunkirk and in Burma, and was later to do it at Anzio, providing a calm, gentle, friendly presence whose influence, like an oil slick, spread outward from the small number of people with whom he made contact to the rest of us who only heard about his visit, dispersing the terrors of the battlefield by a kind of urbane normality.

This 'urbane normality', in my experience, was very much the style of

British military leadership during the Second World War. British officers above the rank of company commander seldom carried arms, apart from pistols issued for personal protection, and even those were normally discarded by general officers. The contrast with the American Army, where the style was set by General Patton with his helmet, breeches and pearl-handled revolvers, or General Ridgway with his hand grenades, was rather striking. The American generals were warriors, and like to show it. British generals were professionals, brisk, competent and totally unromantic. They obtained results not by heating their troops up but by cooling them down – those, that is, who made any impression on their troops at all. Not all of them did.

But how could generals during the first half of the twentieth century make any impression on their troops? The qualities defined by Clausewitz were all very well in the days of Napoleon, when the commander really could impress his personality on every man on the battlefield. Then the mere presence of Napoleon could be the equivalent, as Wellington put it, of a couple of divisions. The presence of Wellington himself (whose calm, understated style of command perhaps set the pattern of British leadership for two hundred years) could make the different between victory and a rout. But how can this magic work when an army consisted, not of 60,000 men spread over a front of six miles, but ten times as many on a front of three hundred? Even Napoleon failed to do it during the campaign of 1812. The elder von Moltke solved the problem half a century later by devolution of command responsibilities under the supervision of a highly-trained General Staff. He exercised command through the advice he gave his Commander-in-Chief, and control through the hierarchy of the General Staff. He himself remained known only to a few intimates. Leadership was still exercised at the level of personal contact by unit or divisional commanders.

A generation later, by the time of von Moltke's successor Alfred von Schlieffen, the problem was even greater. Armies could now be numbered in millions, and battlefields extend over five hundred or more miles. Under such circumstances, as Schlieffen confessed in a famous article of 1909, all the commander could do was sit in a comfortable chair behind a large table and send 'inspiring words' down the telephone. That effectively was all that Haig, Foch and von Falkenhayn were able to do in the First World War. Given the conditions of trench warfare, what else was possible?

The result was to create armies whose troops would hardly have known even the names of their generals if they had not learned about them from the newspapers. Even in the Second World War the horizon of the average soldier was narrow to a degree now very difficult to visualise. During the First World War, given the lower level of education and literacy, it must have been narrower still. While some work has been carried out on the level of 'command recognition' among troops on the Western Front (see editor's introduction and J.M. Bourne's chapter), we need to find out more about this subject. I would assume that the average soldier would have certainly known his battalion commander. He would also have known, if only from the press, that the commander of the British armies was General Sir Douglas Haig. But what about intermediary commands? Did the average Tommy know in whose brigade, division, army corps, or even Army he was serving? Did the rank of the generals who inspected them out of the line register at all, except for the intensity with which they had to clean their kit? It was bad enough in the Second World War, except in such relatively closed communities as the Eighth Army in the Western Desert or the Fourteenth Army in Burma. As a very young platoon commander in Italy I knew my brigade commander, but I cannot speak for the men under my command. I knew the name of the divisional commander, though I never clapped eyes on him. I never knew at any given moment even the name of my corps commander; and I knew about the Army commander largely though the press.

In my experience, leadership in the British Army during the Second World War could be effectively exercised at three levels. First was that of the battalion, and this, thanks (as I have indicated) to the regimental system, was on the whole pretty good. Then there came the division, the largest unit to have any sense of corporate identity and on which a strong-minded commander could impose his personality. Finally there was the Army; but it must be admitted that it was largely the skill with which Montgomery in Europe and Slim in Burma used the press to give themselves salience that the Army stood out as a significant level of the command structure. Even the Army, under Montgomery's predecessors in the Western Desert and successors in Europe, did not mean all that much.

To understand why this should have been the case, it may be useful at this stage to get away from a purely anecdotal approach and establish a simple typology of armies for our guidance.

Broadly speaking there are three types of armies: professional, volunteer, and conscript, each demanding a different type of leadership. In professional armies, leadership is almost a function of built-in 'followership'. Well-disciplined troops are trained to do what they are told and to have confidence in their equally professional leaders. Like well-trained horses, they can carry even indifferent or incompetent riders. Volunteers usually need continual inspiration from charismatic leaders to bridge the gap between their romantic motivations and the usually horrible conditions in which they find themselves. And conscripts?

Conscript armies will differ according to the type of society from which they are drawn. Those taken from rural and illiterate communities, such as those in Eastern Europe during the First World War, may bring with them deferential qualities that make them as biddable as professional soldiers, but will always require stern discipline to ensure that they do not desert. But if they come from complex, urban and rather unmilitary societies such as the United States and the United Kingdom, they will require very careful handling indeed. In 1914 Britain started with a professional army rapidly swollen by volunteers, which after two years was further reinforced by conscripts. By 1918 every unit probably contained men drawn from all three categories. But the upper levels of command were held throughout the war by officers whose minds had been shaped by regimental service overseas with the small pre-war professional army, and who found it very difficult to adjust to the new circumstances. In his excellent novel about that war, *The General*, C.S. Forester draws a sympathetic picture of their predicament. His hero starts the war as second in command of a cavalry regiment in which he had distinguished himself during the Boer War. Courageous, dutiful, energetic and no fool, he performed so brilliantly at the first battle of Ypres that he ended up in command of the brigade. He was then given command of a division of enthusiastic volunteers in the New Army on which he was able, during a prolonged period of training, to set the stamp of his personality. He led that division at Loos and on the Somme with unremitting devotion and energy but found himself increasingly out of his depth in the new form of warfare. His total reliability, combined with a fortunate marriage, brought him to the command of an army corps in 1917, and in 1918 his career was ended by a shell at the beginning of Ludendorff's offensive; a disaster to which he responded by ordering up his horse, drawing his sword, and riding towards the front line. As he rose in command, the superb leadership qualities that he had displayed in the earlier stages of his career became less and less relevant, both to the kind of war he was having to fight and the kind of army that he had to command.[2]

Although both the volunteers and the conscripts of 1914-18 came from a predominantly urban society, they were still responsive to traditional patterns of leadership by the landed classes from which army officers were still very largely drawn, although there were increasing problems of adulteration, both of officers and of other ranks, as the war went on. Leadership was thus facilitated by a deferential 'followership'. Officers above battalion level did not see it as their role to provide charismatic leadership, and those who did, like the egregious Aylmer Hunter-Weston, were generally regarded as buffoons. Given the circumstances of trench warfare, it is difficult to see what kind of leadership they could have provided, except Schlieffenesque 'inspiring words' over an unreliable field telephone. Yet given other circumstances, they could still do extraordinarily well. Consider the case of Edmund Allenby: a fairly ordinary general of his generation who did not do particularly well on the Western Front, but who, given his head in Palestine, proved quite outstanding. He had that most precious of Napoleonic qualities – Luck. Might not some of his contemporaries – Rawlinson, Byng, Gough, Horne – have done just as well if they had had similar luck?

Second World War generals were drawn from very much the same social and professional background as their predecessors in the First World War, but there was one major difference. Most of them had experienced that war as regimental officers on the Western Front, and been lucky to have survived. They thus had a sympathetic understanding of the troops under their command such as First World War generals frequently lacked. They had lived with them in the trenches and experienced the remoteness of the High Command. They therefore knew the importance of personal contact for effective leadership, and made it whenever they could. Open warfare and improved communications made it far easier for them to get to the front if they so desired. More important, they were determined not to get their men unnecessarily killed. This led to a caution in their conduct of operations that was remarked on both by their German adversaries and by their American allies, but for which those who served under their command have every reason to be grateful. We were often placed in conditions of hideous discomfort, but we never felt that our lives were being pointlessly thrown away. Attacks were always carefully prepared, fully supported with firepower, and – perhaps most important – we were always told why they were taking place and what they were expected to achieve. Even at the lowest levels of command we felt that we were being treated as intelligent human beings, and were expected to treat those under our own command accordingly.

Most of our leaders, in short, were very conscious that they were commanding a citizen army, even if some of them found it difficult to learn how to handle it. The man most conscious of all was probably the Adjutant General, General Sir Ronald Adam, whose efforts to accommodate the civilian mentality through encouraging activities such as unit newspapers, forces radio, education in current affairs, and entertainment at all levels earned him the reputation among many of his colleagues as being a 'thorough bolshie'. He was a remarkable man whose influence has never been fully appreciated, and whose biography has still to be written.

Yet probably the most effective mechanism for reconciling civilians to army life was that most characteristic feature of the Regular Army, and one that remained defiantly unchanged: the regimental system. Even in an unadulterated form, with regiments expanded to a dozen or more battalions, the regiment gave conscripts a sense of belonging. Regimental loyalty provided group cohesion, regimental rivalries the most effective form of motivation. Regular officers did not have to change their approach: they were still commanding Bombardiers or Halbardiers, the finest body of men in the world, and it was their responsibility to see that they remained so. More remarkable was the number of National Servicemen who came to believe in it, and still do. In consequence the 'followership' built in to the Regular Army was to a large extent transmitted to the National Servicemen as well, making the task of 'leadership' a great deal easier for amateurs like myself. So long as you wore the right cap badge, you were given the benefit of the doubt.

If we look at the American Army, of which we saw a great deal in Italy, we can see all the advantages of the regimental system. In that army troops were regarded as interchangeable units in a kind of gigantic production line. Manufactured according to a common pattern – GI, Government Issue – they were regarded as freely interchangeable and replaceable. They served with strangers and were commanded by strangers. They barely knew their company officers, while their generals seemed to regard their lives with the callous indifference that had characterised the British High Command in the First World War. Morale in American infantry units was low, desertion rates high, and horror stories abounded.

If we look at the German Army, however, we can see the other side of the coin. The disadvantage of the British regimental system was its inflexibility. The strong bonds within the regiment were built up at the cost of alienation from everyone else. We hated serving with other units. If hospitalised or posted away, we pulled every possible string to get back to our own mob. One of the few mutinies in the Second World War occurred on the Salerno beaches when reinforcements were told that they were being posted to units other than their own. Nothing of the kind happened in the *Wehrmacht*. There the unit of loyalty was, if anything the division; but German troops seemed ready to serve at a moment's notice under any appropriate operational command. During the chaotic aftermath of Allied attacks a few squads of infantry could reform round a couple of tanks and a self-propelled gun, commanded probably by a NCO, and fight as if they had been trained together for years. Given long enough, and under similar pressures, we might have learned to do the same; but we had a very long way to go.

The British Army also developed strong divisional loyalties, which were especially significant for support troops who did not belong to combat units. These perhaps showed themselves at their strongest in the Western Desert, where warfare occurred on a small enough scale for divisional commanders to display traditional 'leadership qualities'. For those who served in 1st Armoured Division under Herbert Lumsden, 7th Armoured under 'Strafer' Gott and later John Harding, 51st Highland under D.M. Wimberley or 4th Indian under Francis Tuker were very conscious of the impact made by those commanders. These were men of attractive and often unusual personalities, with mild eccentricities in behaviour and dress that awoke amusement and imitation among their followers. Their fly-switches, silk scarves and desert boots became the trademark of officers in the Eighth Army. Their leadership preserved a remarkably high degree of morale in their formations in spite of acutely uncomfortable campaigning conditions and a constant succession of setbacks and defeats.

But such leaders had defects to their qualities. For one thing they were highly resistant to control from above, ruling their divisions almost like feudal baronies. For another, few of them – John Harding was a notable exception – showed any capacity for higher levels of command. They displayed in fact all the good and the bad qualities of the Regular Army: excellent in looking after their men, brilliant in small-scale actions requiring flair, dash and leadership, but out of their depth when confronted by the serious professionals of the *Wehrmacht*, and inept at the higher levels of command for which they had done nothing to prepare themselves in peacetime. In March 1942, three months after taking over as CIGS, General Sir Alan Brooke (who was, be it noted, a gunner) looked at the material at his disposal and despaired:

> Half our Corps and Divisional Commanders are totally unfit for their appointments, and yet if I were to sack them, I could find no better! They lack character, imagination, drive and power of leadership. The reason for this state of affairs is to be found in the losses we sustained in the last war, all of our best officers who should now be our senior commanders.[3]

This, alas, was almost certainly true so far as it went, although one would like to see some comparative figures for casualties among German officers during the First World War. But a more fundamental reason was that between the wars the British Army had not trained itself, and had not been required to train itself, for *la grande guerre*. Not until 1932 was a committee set up by the War Office to study the lessons of the First World War. As before 1914, the highest level to which British army officers could aspire was command of a division; anything beyond that was, if not inconceivable, then certainly rarely conceived. The irony was that not until 1988 did the British Army get round to establishing the kind of Higher Command and Staff Course that was common in continental and the United States armies, to train commanders of large formations; at the very moment when it *did* become almost inconceivable that Britain would field a mass army ever again.

There was of course one notable exception to Alan Brooke's strictures – Bernard Law Montgomery, who took command of the Eighth Army in August 1942 and completely transformed it. About Montgomery we must notice two things. First, he had trained himself for higher command in war; trained *himself,* be it noticed, as there was no one to train him. He thought about war and not about 'soldiering' – that agreeable and gentlemanly occupation to which war

124

came as such an unwelcome interruption. Montgomery was, in fact, in the dismissive words with which I came so familiar during my military service, 'a military shit'; someone who took his profession really seriously. Goronwy Rees, an Oxford don who briefly served on his staff, wrote that:

> the difference between him and the other commanders I had come to know was that he actually thought, in the same way that a scientist or a scholar thinks. His subject matter happened to be war but the mental processes, of definition and analysis, of coming to conclusions on demonstrable evidence, were the same…[W]hen he was thinking about war, which he did with wonderful lucidity and concentration, he seemed to me to come as near as any could to exemplifying the dictum of my old tutor H.W.B. Joseph, that the will is reason acting.[4]

Montgomery's concept of major operations was that which he had learned during the First World War as a staff officer, serving in Plumer's Second Army: the meticulous preparation of highly complex operations, depending on the maximum use of firepower to achieve strictly limited objectives, with careful staff work that left as little as possible to chance but provided equally little scope for independent initiative. If it was to fulfil its objectives, the Eighth Army would have to fight as an *Army*, not as a group of quasi-autonomous divisions. Its prima donnas had to learn to sing ensembles under his baton rather than improvising their own arias. If they could not learn he sacked them and imported his own men – Oliver Leese, Brian Horrocks – who were content to operate in his shadow.

The second thing to note about Montgomery was that he thoroughly understood the men that he was commanding. They were basically civilians in arms: intelligent, literate, fundamentally unmilitary and longing to get home. Their music was not the cheerful marching songs of the First World War but the nostalgic, homesick refrains crooned by Vera Lynn. Most of them were not in combat units or elite divisions, but in supporting or base formations, often doing civilian jobs within the huge support corps of Signals, Ordnance, Services, Engineers or REME: but they needed motivating none the less. The way to communicate with such men, Montgomery quickly realised, was not through the 'usual channels' of command but through the press: their own press organ, *The Eighth Army News*, and the national newspapers they all read, particularly the *Daily Mirror*.

The attitude of the military to the press in both world wars was one of great suspicion. They tolerated it as at best a necessary evil whose activities should be so far as possible circumscribed. A few senior figures, Ronald Adam foremost among them, realised the vital part it could play in sustaining morale; but Montgomery went even beyond this, and deliberately used it as an instrument of his own leadership. To the horror of his colleagues, he deliberately set out to make himself a press personality, with his own instantly recognisable trademarks and his own 'sound bites'. He gave his own press briefings and made himself freely available to favoured war correspondents. Further, he learned how to 'chat up' the troops, treating them not as warriors itching to get into action (which they were not) but as a workforce doing an unpleasant but necessary job that had to be completed before they could go home. He behaved in fact in a way that most of his gentlemanly predecessors would have found impossible, and many of his contemporaries considered intolerable. But then, Montgomery was no gentleman – that was his great strength.

He was also inimitable. His successor in command of the Eighth Army, Oliver Leese, tried to use the same techniques but became in consequence a figure of fun. Brian Horrocks might have achieved it in his own way had he been given the opportunity. But Horrocks apart, Montgomery established a reputation in whose shadow nothing else could grow. His subordinates in north-west Europe were grey figures – even those who, like O'Connor and Pip Roberts, had made their reputation in the Western Desert. The commander of the British Second Army, Miles Dempsey, was a thoroughly competent professional, but one whose main qualification for the job was that Montgomery could trust him to do what he was told. Montgomery did not like competition.

The contrast between the command techniques of Montgomery and Alexander is endlessly interesting. Alexander did not compete; a gentleman to his fingertips, he did not see the need. But one cannot visualise Montgomery intervening so effectively as did Alexander at Salerno. He would not have seen the need for that. When he made plans, he ensured – as he always insisted – that they were the best possible, and then withdrew to his caravan and let his subordinates get on with it. It used to be said in Italy that whereas Alex was a man for whom one would happily die, Monty made quite sure you would not have to die if he could possibly help it. They made an excellent team, Alexander providing the charisma, Montgomery the technical competence. Officers on the whole appreciated the former, but other ranks emphatically the latter. They did not see themselves as heroes, but as men doing a necessarily dangerous job. It was efficiency they appreciated – not charm.

About the Far East I know only from hearsay. There Mountbatten exercised triphibious leadership by a use of publicity and a kind of film star glamour so shameless that he put even Montgomery in the shade. He certainly cheered up the troops under his command by making them feel that they were not forgotten, but I doubt whether it made them fight better. Divisional loyalty, especially under such commanders as Messervy, Rees, and Ouvry Roberts, probably mattered a great deal more. But the true hero of the campaign was Bill Slim.

Slim, like Montgomery, was something of a maverick. His father had been a small businessman. Slim served in the ranks of the OTC and was commissioned as a 'Temporary Gentleman" in 1914. Between the wars he had made ends meet by occasional journalism, and knew how to write as well as how to speak. He was a man of high intelligence and great humour, with the gift, as his biographer Ronald Lewin put it, of 'commanding affection while communicating energy'.[5] As with Allenby in Palestine, the limited size and comparative isolation of his theatre of war enabled his personality to get through to every man under his command, and like Montgomery he knew how to make use of the media to make this happen. He combined, to a remarkable extent, Montgomery's professionalism with Alexander's charm. I like to think that he was very much more typical of the kind of officer who was to command in the Army after the war than those who were in charge when it began.

Notes

1. C. von Clausewitz (M. Howard and P. Paret, eds.), *On War*, pp. 100-12, Princeton UP, Princeton NJ (1976).

2. C.S. Forester, *The General*, Michael Joseph, London (1936).

3. D. Fraser, *Alanbrooke*, p. 297, Collins, London (1982).

4. G. Rees, *A Bundle of Sensations*, p. 149, Chatto and Windus, London (1960).

5. R. Lewin, Slim: *The Standardbearer*, p. 1, Leo Cooper, London (1976). This phrase was originally used of Marlborough by Liddell Hart.

'A BRIGADIER IS ONLY A CO-ORDINATOR': BRITISH COMMAND AT BRIGADE LEVEL IN NORTH-WEST EUROPE, 1944: A CASE STUDY.

by Nigel de Lee

This paper is based mainly on a series of interviews with Brigadier Sir Alexander Stanier Bt. DSO MC.[1] Sir Alexander was unfailingly diligent and frank, and encouraged careful exploration of intriguing questions which arose during the interviews. An examination of these interviews, dealing with the latter part of his military career, has provided this account of the art of command at brigade level: the middle management of military operations. The basic question put to him was, how did he spend his time in the performance of his duties?

Sir Alexander was born in 1899. He went to the Royal Military College Sandhurst in 1917, where, amongst other things, he learned ground appreciation. In spring 1918 he was commissioned into the Welsh Guards, and joined the 1st Battalion on the Western Front. In summer 1918 he was awarded the MC for taking a village during the Allied advance. Shortly afterwards he was wounded while leading a reconnaissance patrol on the river Selle. Between the wars he was occupied with the routine of public duties and training. In 1939 he was given command of the 2nd Welsh Guards, forming and training this battalion. In May 1940 he took the battalion to Boulogne as part of 20th Guards Brigade, under the command of Brigadier W.A.F.L. Fox-Pitt. Brigadier Fox-Pitt eventually decided to withdraw his Brigade, in accordance with latitudinarian orders from Lord Gort and the CIGS, General Ironside, but against the wishes of Churchill.[2] Sir Alexander approved of his brigadier's decision, and gave him full and open support. Subsequently Sir Alexander commanded 223 Infantry

Brigade and then 181 Infantry Brigade in England. By January 1944 he believed that his military career would be devoted to training and he was unlikely to command in action.

However in February 1944 he was appointed to command 231 Brigade, part of 50th Division. 50th Division had seen action on the continent in 1940, and subsequently in North Africa and in the Mediterranean. The Division was earmarked to assault GOLD Beach on D-Day. Sir Alexander was selected for the appointment by General Montgomery on the grounds that he had proved himself to be an excellent trainer of soldiers, using competitive schemes and games based on field skills to motivate his troops. He was surprised by the appointment, particularly because he had not attended the Staff College, thinking himself not bright enough to complete the course. He was reassured when he was given a very intelligent Brigade Major, who was destined to join the directing staff at Camberley. It is very likely that Montgomery believed that Sir Alexander had other qualities that would prove invaluable in commanding troops engaged in exceptionally complex and dangerous operations. One was his eye for ground, developed at Sandhurst and demonstrated in the field in France in 1918, and again in 1940. Another was coolness in action, a quality in senior officers which reassured and encouraged all their subordinates. Finally, his open and sociable character fitted him well for liaising with the Royal Navy, RAF and the Americans. Sir Alexander himself was a firm believer in the primary importance of human factors; that command skills were less important than the ability to inspire and sustain enthusiasm in soldiers. He said 'the best plans are unworkable if the troops do not have the will to fight.'

Upon appointment, his first tasks were to prepare his troops for amphibious assault, and plan his own Brigade operation. He started by training himself, and attended the Inverary Battle School as a student. Subsequently he accompanied each of the units of his Brigade through the school, landing amongst the soldiers as the directing staff pelted them with rocks and thunder-flashes.

For the purposes of Operations NEPTUNE and OVERLORD, 231 Brigade was a large Brigade Group. The core was provided by three infantry battalions, 1st Royal Hampshires, 1st Dorsets and 2nd Devons. These battalions were battle hardened and experienced in amphibious assault, but also weary. On first inspection the Brigadier detected a mood of 'oh, have we got to do it all again?' The remedy was to post most of the officers, and about half the men, and new officers and young fresh soldiers were brought in. This measure was intended to achieve a balance of expertise and enthusiasm in the battalions. The process was consolidated by hard and realistic training, and particularly familiarisation with the 'funnies' of the 79th Armoured Division. In addition to the battalions mentioned, the Brigade included 6th Borders, a battalion intended to act as a beach brick for labouring and administrative duties but also capable of all infantry tasks; the Sherwood Rangers, a yeomanry regiment equipped with Sherman tanks; the Essex Yeomanry, a self propelled field artillery regiment; Finally, 147 Field Regiment Royal Artillery; a Royal Engineers Field Company; a Royal Army Medical Corps Field Ambulance; and other detachments. Finally, 47 Royal Marine Commando was attached to the Brigade for purposes of landing and artillery support.

Once all the units had done their amphibious assault training, they proceeded to take part in SMASH I and SMASH II, rehearsal exercises at Studland Bay. They went to Portsmouth for Exercise FABIUS to test their logistic arrangements.

Meanwhile, as the troops trained, plans were sketched, discussed, drawn, adapted and issued. The geographical intelligence was profuse and of perfect quality; the Brigadier was given maps, photographs, panoramas and models of the ground. These showed the terrain and the location of enemy installations. The assessment of enemy forces was less accurate; some fortifications and installations specified as objectives were unoccupied on 6 June. The estimate of the quality and morale of the German troops was also defective; Sir Alexander was advised that they were poor and not expected to fight hard. In the event some of them fought with great resolution.

The planning process was consultative and most thorough. In the first stage, Sir Alexander received outline orders from headquarters (HQ) 50th Division. As he remembered these orders, the essentials were: 'You will land to the east of Le Hamel-Asnelles, you will proceed in as far as the village of Ryes, and you will then turn right and capture the high ground towards Arromanches, and then continue along the coast until you have joined up with the Americans just to the west of Port en Bessin.'

The plan was for 69 Brigade to land to the left of 231 Brigade; in the second wave, 56 Brigade would pass through 231 en route to capture Bayeux, whilst 151 Brigade followed 69 and moved inland. General Graham, commanding 50th Division, put particular emphasis on the importance of the high ground above Asnelles, where a German battery was located overlooking GOLD beach.

Having got his orders, Sir Alexander devised his Brigade outline plan. This took two days. The main elements came to his mind very quickly and clearly, being dictated by the lie of the land. He indicated his intentions in broad terms allotting sectors, axes and objectives to the battalions and their supporting units, with particular attention to the tasks of the 'funnies' from 79th Division. Artillery and armour were allocated to the battalions, in effect providing three 'battalion groups'. One regiment of artillery was retained as Brigade reserve. The plan was intended to be simple and flexible, with two battalions landing simultaneously, followed up by the third to exploit.

The outline plan was considered at a Brigade conference attended by all battalion and company commanders. The implications and details of the plan were discussed and worked out. Next, the battalions and regiments produced their own plans, which gave outline orders to companies, batteries and squadrons. These were submitted to Brigade HQ, which ensured that they were in accordance with the Brigade plan and compatible with each other. The finalised Brigade plan was submitted to Divisional HQ, which approved it without amendment. Formal orders to implement the Brigade plan were written and issued by the Brigade Major.

The Brigade Major also dealt with other details and technical matters. He liaised with 21 Army Group staff to settle mounting and loading plans, in particular the tactical loading of landing craft for the assault. Arrangements for naval gunfire support were handled at divisional level. The Brigade submitted a list of targets to the Commander Royal Artillery (CRA) who selected them and allocated them in order of priority. Divisional HQ also advised on the deployment and use of the HEDGEROWS, the landing craft armed with rockets intended to drench the enemy fortifications with high explosive just before the assault troops landed. In the event, the sea conditions on the morning of 6 June made the HEDGEROWS highly inaccurate and their rockets were wasted.

The Brigadier concerned himself with only one matter of detail: the choice and employment of 'funnies'. He was advised by Divisional HQ of the capabilities and limitations of these specialised vehicles but had to choose what types to have in the Brigade. He eventually decided to have AVREs (Armoured Vehicles Royal Engineers), Flails, Flamethrowers and Bridges.

He was more occupied with higher level tasks. A special briefing gave him an outline of the Corps plan, so that he understood the big picture. Armed with this information, he spent much of his time on liaison work. He was in direct contact with Brigadier Knox, commanding 69 Brigade. He went to Dorset to visit the American 1st Division, who were due to land on OMAHA beach, and meet 231 Brigade near Port en Bessin. Their confidence, which seemed to be based on their wealth of material resources, was boundless. Relations with the Royal Navy were very good. The sailors of Force G, which was to transport the Brigade across the channel, worked with it during the rehearsal exercises. The Navy were sociable; officers met informally at cocktail parties, soldiers and sailors met in football matches. Military questions were settled *ad hoc* by conversations on the telephone or face to face. The Royal Air Force had a different attitude and outlook. Liaison with the airmen was minimal and strictly formal. There was no social contact at all; the RAF declined all invitations. Sir Alexander remarked 'I never met any of the airmen, it was frightfully difficult to know when to call on them, how to call on them.' The machinery for practical co-operation in the field remained cumbersome; once ashore Sir Alexander was accompanied by a RAF signaller who passed signals requesting air support back to an officer at Divisional HQ, who sent them back to England. The process was subject to friction, and aircraft did not appear over the targets for hours, which was no use at all in a fluid battle.

As D-Day approached, the Brigade had to nominate targets for naval and air bombardment. Sir Alexander was most concerned to arrange for the destruction of a blockhouse at Le Hamel. He said 'that was the only thing that was going to beat me because it was defiladed from the front and it could fire straight down the beach.' This meant that guns in the work could enfilade troops landing all along GOLD beach. The Navy could not see or hit the blockhouse, because it was protected by a building to seaward which had been gutted then filled with reinforced concrete. RAF aircraft bombed the village, but the blockhouse was a very small target in amongst the buildings and they missed it.

On 6 June 1944 the Brigade HQ was organised in three articulated components. Sir Alexander was with his tactical HQ, accompanied by a Liaison Officer, Intelligence Officer, local CRA, Forward Officer Bombardment (a naval officer to co-ordinate naval gun support), signaller, orderly, and BBC commentator. This HQ, with a universal carrier and jeep, was embarked in HMS *Nith*. The Reserve Tactical HQ, led by the Brigade Major, was in another ship, ready to take command of the Brigade if necessary. Main HQ was in a third vessel, under command of the Staff Captain. The Reserve Tactical HQ went ashore shortly after the Brigadier; the main HQ landed at 1600 hrs on 6 June.

The first wave of the infantry landed at about 07.30 on D-Day. Sir Alexander and his HQ followed them at about 08.30. Their landing craft was damaged by a beach obstacle in the surf, and the vehicles were lost. The wireless was immersed, but it was preserved by its waterproof bag, and found to be in working order. The landing plan had been disrupted and delayed by the rough sea conditions. The troops from the landing battalions had been driven eastwards in their landing craft by wind and current. When they got ashore, the battalions were intermingled. Tanks, which should have arrived before the infantry using their amphibious capacity to swim ashore, had proved unable to navigate in the heavy swell, and had to be delivered, late, by landing craft. As they landed, some tanks were hit and knocked out by the gun in the blockhouse at Le Hamel. The Brigadier found that the beach was under mortar and machine-gun fire, with many soldiers lying in the sand. He felt that smoke from the burning tanks would screen him, so walked up the beach at Les Roquettes, and on into the dunes to find his forward troops.

He found the Hampshires in a most difficult situation. They were in an area of drained marshland, to the east of Le Hamel, in full view of the village, pinned by machine-gun and mortar fire. The Commanding Officer, Second in Command, Forward Officer Bombardment, commander of the attached field battery, and all but the most junior company commander, were casualties. Perceiving a situation of genuine emergency, in which 'for a moment...co-ordination was rather lost', Sir Alexander took charge and issued verbal orders. In his own words, 'I directed the Hampshires to send a company round to the back of Le Hamel, and also told the Dorsets they must attack Le Hamel from the rear.' A and C companies of the Hampshires were amalgamated into a composite company, and set off inland, accompanied by a company of Dorsets, self propelled guns from the Essex Yeomanry, and an AVRE. The Brigadier also urged the Dorsets and Devons to get inland, onto the downs overlooking the beach. He said:

> I was more keen on getting the Devons and Dorsets onto the higher ground above Asnelles, if I could knock them [enemy troops on higher ground] out they couldn't give supporting fire to the people in Asnelles; if the Dorsets could get up to Ryes that would cut off any reserves coming up for any counter-attack, which I thought might come at any moment, but it didn't luckily.

The attack on the high ground was also directed to take a battery at Puits d'Herode, which had caused some anxiety to Major General Graham. The battery was reached and found to be fully constructed but unoccupied. A battery of field guns at point 54, above Asnelles, was attacked and taken by the Dorsets. The Germans in Le Hamel were isolated from their supports, and their line of communication was cut off. The Hampshires fought their way through the village house by house, with fire support from the Dorsets inland. The resistance was overcome and the village was secured in the late afternoon. Meanwhile the Devons moved inland and captured Ryes, which proved to be a local HQ for horse-drawn transport. Sir Alexander, having studied the ground, had decided that Ryes, which is in dead ground from the beach and downs to its north-west, would be an ideal place for a counter-attack to assemble and form up.

The reorganisation and reinvigoration of the attack was the only command decision he made on D-Day, according to Sir Alexander. But he was not idle, and found plenty to do. He saw 47 Commando approach the beach, lose landing craft to swamping, and struggle ashore. The commandos had expected to land earlier than they did, and find a beach secured and cleared. Instead they were delayed by the rough seas and disembarked into the middle of a firefight. Time was vital to them; their orders were to move inland, then westwards evading all enemy, and assault Port en Bessin at 14.00. This assault would be given strong naval and air support. Sir Alexander went to offer the commandos his assistance . They had lost their wireless sets while landing, and the Brigadier offered to provide replacements. This would have enabled them to call on the Brigade's field regiment of 25 pounders, and to maintain indirect contact with the Royal Navy and RAF. But the commander of the commandos was anxious to keep to his schedule, and moved off inland very quickly. It is conceivable that Sir Alexander should have ordered them to wait until equipped with a wireless set, but he did not think this appropriate. As he remarked: 'They were very independent. They knew what to do and were quite happy to get on with it. They advanced very quickly....' Unfortunately, the commandos were delayed by snipers and small parties of enemy, and were not at Port en Bessin in time to benefit from their naval and air support.

Meanwhile the beach was badly congested. There were patches of glutinous clay on the beach, which obstructed movement. Immediately inland there were minefields. Many of the mines were dummies, but all had to be treated with respect. As soon as the Dorsets had reached the crest of the Manvieu ridge, Sir Alexander moved inland and up onto the high ground:

> the beach was absolutely congested, it was being fired upon, and I went to the... highest point of Manvieu ridge; the Germans had kindly dug some slit trenches there which we jumped into, and two shells practically landed on top of us, I thought "Oh my God they've seen us arrive, that's the end" but actually no more came...

From his Tac HQ on the ridge, Sir Alexander could see the Brigade area. He watched the Devons attack Ryes, working their way up a stream, delayed by snipers hiding in cornfields and clumps of willows.

Having established his pied à terre, he went visiting. Upon entering a battalion or battery command post, he made an instant, instinctive assessment of the atmosphere. If there was a sense of optimism and activity, he would give some words of encouragement and move on quickly; he 'kept out of the way'. This he considered essential, in order to show confidence in his junior commanders, and avoid distracting them from their own work. However, if he sensed doubt or hesitation, he instantly offered help. The assistance he could give was substantial; he could task the Brigade artillery regiment, under his command, or call for naval bombardment from the ships in support. His attempts to organise support from the RAF were futile, because of the delays involved. He estimated that he could lay on a regimental artillery shoot at fifteen minutes notice, and a naval bombardment in half an hour; but tactical aircraft were available only at two hours notice due to complications in the chain of command.

By his visits, Sir Alexander kept a close feel on the development of the fighting. Quite often he discovered that battalion commanders were out seeing their companies, so he was able to get information about the action at company level by consulting battalion HQ maps and signal logs. His own liaison officer travelled with him and marked all information on the maps as it was acquired. His signaller was in the jeep, to keep in touch with other stations. Every half hour he sent a minimal situation report to 50th Division HQ 'to keep them happy', and ensure the units in his Brigade were not bothered by demands for information from the divisional commander. The manoeuvres of the Brigade conformed in a general way to the plan, but not to the schedule, because of the disruption caused by the German defenders and that other more ancient enemy, the weather. By late afternoon Le Hamel and Asnelles were clear and secure. The Hampshires set off westwards, and attacked Arromanches. Here the enemy were less resolute than they had been in Le Hamel, and the port was taken by about 18.00.

Sir Alexander was happy with his day's work on 6 June. He remembered, 'I was quite satisfied that I'd got the high ground, I'd got Ryes, I'd got Arromanches, and I'd got a company on the beach as a backstop in case of a counter-attack between us and 69 Brigade.' The high ground between Asnelles and Arromanches had been cleared of enemy observation posts, and patrols were out searching for snipers and stragglers. Content with his dispositions, he settled down for the night in a garden and slept soundly. Contrary to expectation, the Germans made no attempt to counter-attack 231 Brigade. The enemy withdrew during the night; patrols found very few Germans still in the area.

According to his own account, he made only one important intervention on 7 June 1944, which was to organise support for the attack by 2nd Devons on the Longues Battery. This battery was still firing, although it had been repeatedly bombed and intensively bombarded by warships. Like all the German coastal batteries, it was strongly garrisoned and protected by elaborate defence works. Sir Alexander saw the battalion commander and 'I said, "well now, how do you propose to do this?" He told me what he was roughly going to do, but I left him to carry on with it.' Having been briefed on the battalion plan, for an attack on the rear of the battery by two companies, he arranged for support. The RAF was to lay on an air strike to last five minutes; the RN provided a bombardment with six inch guns for fifteen minutes; the Brigade artillery regiment and a platoon of Vickers guns from the Cheshires fired during the assault. The battery was taken and cleared by 11.00.

The Dorsets were detached from the Brigade, and sent south with a column based on 8th Armoured Brigade. The Hampshires and Devons pushed on westwards, and took over Port en Bessin from the Commandos. The Devons swung inland to assault and capture a German naval HQ in a château. The Brigade remained in the area of Port en Bessin on 8 June. On that day the first Americans arrived from OMAHA beach. They were in a bad way, exhausted by two days and nights of intense fighting, but their arrival connected the Anglo-

Canadian and US beachheads.

On 9 June 231 Brigade advanced south-eastwards heading towards Bayeux. Bayeux had been taken by 56 Brigade, and the plan was for 231 Brigade to exploit beyond, pressing on south from east of the town towards Villers Bocage. But *en route* they were checked by a counter-attack near La Belle Epine and halted. Next day they found that the way forward was blocked by German positions skilfully sited and prepared to take every advantage of the *bocage*. The enemy were intent on holding a quadrilateral with strong points at Tilly sur Seulles, Lingèvres, Hottot and Juvigny. 231 Brigade made repeated attacks on Hottot, but according to Sir Alexander 'whenever we captured it, before we could consolidate it, bang, in came a counter-attack and we were pushed back.'

During the days in the *bocage*, the Brigadier established a regular routine. He spent the nights sleeping, in order to have a clear head for thinking, but always out of doors. He rose at first light, ate his breakfast, then went to his HQ to hear reports from his staff, in case anything of significance had happened during the night. Then, as soon as possible, he went out:

> I was hardly ever in my HQ. I relied on my Brigade Major to stay there, and Staff Captain. I went round with my L[iasion] O[fficer]. My I[ntelligence] O[fficer] remained at HQ or went out on his own ... to get the information, and when I came back I could get it. I spent most of the day touring round. But I am a great believer in not staying too long with commanding officers and people because you're delaying them from getting on with their own job. All you can do is to come in and say 'I hope you're alright, is there anything I can do?'

These visits were made as far forward as possible. The help offered and given varied. Often, he would go forward to do reconnaissance for commanding officers who were short of time. On occasion he acted to resolve logistic difficulties, such as obtaining an extra supply of anti-tank mines when the local commander anticipated an armoured attack. Very occasionally he would give advice to junior officers. In one case he was concerned that a platoon in defence was too dispersed, and advised the subaltern in charge to make sure that all his men were within shouting distance.

He also conducted his own personal reconnaissances, being a great believer in studying the ground. By going right forward he also set an example to his officers and soldiers of personal steadiness. This course of action entailed risks; on 6 June Brigadier Senior, commanding 151 Brigade, went too far forward, and was captured. He eventually managed to escape from this predicament, but lost his command party in the process.[3] In September 1944, his successor, Brigadier Gordon, moved too far forward into the Gheel bridgehead and his whole HQ narrowly avoided a head-on collision with an enemy panzer column.[4] Sir Alexander felt that a senior commander must take risks, and be seen to do so, but not to the extent that he lapsed into the foolishness of bravado. He was always aware that if spotted he and his party might give away his own Brigade locations, or attract mortar and artillery fire. He also knew that the Germans had a policy of using snipers to 'separate' the officers from their men.Once he had paid his visits and made all necessary reconnaissances he returned to his HQ. There he refreshed his knowledge of the situation by studying the IO's map, reading signals and talking to the Brigade Major.

If a major operation was in prospect, Sir Alexander would call a Brigade conference. All such conferences were *ad hoc*, and not routine. Conferences usually followed a pattern. The Brigadier would brief all those present, summoned for operational reasons, on the planned action. He then listened to the opinions of commanding officers, the CRA, CRE and logistics officers. After considering their views, he made his decisions and issued orders. The latter were usually verbal, and delivered using the map to make his intentions absolutely clear. If the operation was to be an integrated part of a large and complex whole, the Brigade Major would prepare and disseminate formal written orders.

Complex large-scale operations were usually preceded by a Divisional or Corps conference, but those tended to be infrequent, as were visits to the Brigade from senior officers. Sir Alexander remarked 'General Graham was extremely good; as long as you didn't bother him, he didn't worry you, but if you wanted his help he was there.'

After the breakout from Normandy, the routine had to be abandoned. The Brigade moved swiftly to occupy the south bank of the Scheldt at Antwerp. Subsequently it acted as a flank guard for the advance on Arnhem from the Neerpelt bridgehead.

In these mobile operations, Sir Alexander travelled light, with his tactical HQ. He kept in touch with his main HQ and units by wireless, and acted as a troubleshooter. Visits were generally fortuitous rather than planned. He said that the situation was so fluid that planning was impossible, as he was often not fully aware of the locations of his units, and they were sometimes intermingled with the enemy. The important thing was to conform to the general intention of the strategic plan in the light of local circumstances. His personal rôle was to convey enthusiasm and reassurance to his subordinates who might otherwise have been confused and disorientated by the inevitable confusion of such operations.

Sir Alexander held the opinion that real, active command was concentrated at battalion level. He saw his own functions as essentially auxiliary: planning in advance, the supervision of administration, the maintenance of morale, organisation of support in action, and occasional direct interventions in cases of dire emergency. His behaviour to all was governed by an instinctive code of gentlemanly conduct. He was courteous to all. To senior officers he accorded obedience, but it was not unquestioning or uncritical. Whilst on the south bank of the Scheldt at Antwerp he saw elements of von Zangen's German Fifteenth Army withdrawing from Zealand along the north bank, and proposed to General Roberts (commanding 11th Armoured Division to which 231 Brigade was attached) that his orders be changed to allow the Brigade to intercept the enemy line of withdrawal. Roberts told him curtly to 'get on with your task'. He did so, and Fifteenth Army escaped to fight another day. He felt that General Bucknall, who had commanded XXX Corps early on in Normandy, was a good staff officer, but lacked the nerve to command effectively in action. As for General Horrocks, who succeeded General Bucknall, he was 'good as far as Paris'. After Paris, enfeebled by his wound, he was exhausted and his judgement deteriorated. Stanier approached every decision in a pragmatic way, with no reference to doctrine or any developed system of principles. Having received orders, he would examine and study the ground, listen carefully to the opinions of all concerned, then make a decision on the basis of his own experience and judgement. The decision made, he believed in relying on his subordinates to carry it out without close supervision, and to adapt it in detail if the circumstances required. His own duty during action was to go forward to give encouragement without interference. The method worked; in action his brigade undertook very complicated and dangerous operations and succeeded despite very adverse conditions and strong opposition.

Notes

1. The interviews are deposited in the archives of the Sound Records Department of the Imperial War Museum, reference 7175/7, and are quoted here by kind permission of that institution.

2. Interview with Major General Sir W.A.F.L. Fox-Pitt CVO, DSO, MC, in Sound Records Department of the Imperial War Museum reference 7038/4. It is quoted by kind permission of the Imperial War Museum.

3. E.W. Clay, *The Path of the 50th, The Story of the 50th (Northumbrian) Division in the Second World War,* p. 246, Gale and Polden, Aldershot (1950); D. Rissik, *The DLI at War, the History of the Durham Light Infantry 1939-45,* p. 242, Depot of the DLI, Brauncepeth Castle (n.d.).

4.   P.J. Lewis and I.R. English, *Into Battle with the Durhams, 8 DLI in World War II,* p. 238, London Stamp Exchange, London (1970).

COMMAND AND LEADERSHIP IN THE CHINDIT CAMPAIGNS

by David Rooney

The Chindit campaigns in Burma during the Second World War provide excellent case studies of the peculiar problems of command and leadership of irregular forces in war. These campaigns can usefully be divided into three: the first campaign, Operation LONGCLOTH (February to May 1943); Operation THURSDAY (5 March 1944 until the death of Wingate 19 days later); and the final Chindit campaigns from then until Special Force was evacuated in August 1944, then shortly afterwards disbanded.

The Chindits were remarkable in being the brainchild of one man, Major General Orde Wingate. He constantly developed, tested and honed his ideas on the theory and practice of irregular warfare from the time of his successful campaign with the Special Night Squads in Palestine in 1938, for which he received the first of his DSOs. As a captain and divisional intelligence officer, he had watched in dismay as two British infantry divisions – 5th and 8th – were frequently outsmarted by the Arab terrorists who blew up the Haifa pipeline or attacked the Jewish settlements and then disappeared into the countryside, while the military and the police, even with motorised units and aircraft, lumbered up the road and failed to catch them. Thanks to the support of Wavell, Wingate was given his head and was able to develop his own theory of Special Night Squads. This was really the start of the concept which came to fruition in the Chindits.

The Special Night Squads were armed groups, based in the Jewish settlements, made up of the young men, whom Wingate trained in basic infantry work. These squads were strengthened by cadres of British officers and NCOs drawn from the Royal Ulster Rifles and the Royal West Kent Regiment. Wingate personally led the squads and swiftly turned the tables on the Arab terrorists. From this experience, Wingate began to develop further his ideas about irregular warfare. In doing so he was highly critical of the orthodox and regular approach, and from then until his death six years later he was to build up a strong body of antagonism and resentment among his more orthodox colleagues. Always thinking of the future, Wingate criticised the tactics of the Army, which appeared to be tied to the roads and rarely took to the country. The military never used air support effectively, and this initiated Wingate's thoughts on the role of air power in modern infantry battles. His ideas also ranged over the role of irregular forces and their relations with the indigenous people. The failure of the military operations in Palestine was partly due to the Arab terrorists getting advanced information from the clerks and cleaners who worked in the barracks.

Wingate also learnt valuable lessons from his own battles with the terrorists. There was one major clash at Dabburiyah in July 1938, when he led an attack on a terrorist position, but during the attack the Special Night Squads fired on each other, and Wingate himself was wounded. Colonel King-Clarke, who took part in the fight, considered it a 'cock-up of the first order', but the lessons of control in battle were not lost on Wingate.

The next opportunity to develop his ideas on the operation of irregular columns, came when he was posted to Cairo in October 1940. As GSO2, he was given a general brief to liaise with General Platt's forces operating from the Sudan, and with the patriots in Ethiopia who were supporting the Emperor Haile Selassie. In the Gojjam province of Ethiopia, a Colonel Sandford had been operating successfully for some months. Unfortunately, because Platt never defined their individual roles, Sandford and Wingate clashed bitterly, and the legend of Wingate as a very odd and difficult man gained strength. As the campaign proceeded Wingate led 'Gideon Force', consisting of two battalions of Sudanese and Ethiopian troops, together with some artillery and 3-inch mortars.

During the brief campaign of Gideon Force, which operated in several different columns, Wingate, with just a handful of men, succeeded in bluffing 12,000 Italian troops to surrender to him. At the same time, his acute observation both of his own forces and the enemy enabled him to build up a body of ideas which came to fruition in the plans for the Chindits. To keep in touch with his columns Wingate established effective wireless communication, and this was the key to all future Chindit operations. On several occasions, having identified a good Italian target, he called for an air strike, but his demands were rejected as fanciful. In spite of this, Wingate's ideas matured and developed, helped by watching and learning from the enemy, who in supporting their own columns used their air superiority effectively.

Wingate and Sandford had serious differences because of divided command and disputes over the allocation of supplies – problems which Wingate tried to eliminate when the Chindits were established. At the end of the campaign in June 1941, to the chagrin of Platt's two divisions advancing from the north, and Cunningham's three divisions coming up from their base in northern Kenya, Wingate stole the limelight and personally escorted the Emperor Haile Selassie into his capital, Addis Abbaba. Wingate had learnt valuable lessons, but he had made very powerful enemies among senior military officers, and this reputation preceded him to India, where Wavell had once again asked for his services.

In early 1942, Wavell – by then Commander-in-Chief India – asked Wingate to organise guerrilla warfare behind the rapidly advancing Japanese troops. Wingate carried out a preliminary reconnaissance, and flew to Chunking to discuss guerrilla warfare with Chiang Kai-shek, but by this time the Japanese advance had reached Imphal, so Wavell's original plan came to nothing. None the less, in May 1942 Wingate gave a lecture at GHQ Delhi on the subject of Long Range Penetration (LRP). He believed that LRP groups of brigade strength could go into the jungle behind the Japanese lines and, supplied by air, could remain there wreaking havoc on roads, railways, bridges and all the enemy lines of communication with marauding columns, and, given control of the air, the possibility of using air power as a substitute for artillery. The majority of Wingate's audience at GHQ thought his ideas were impracticable, dangerous or absurd, and he soon realised that he faced formidable opposition to his plans for an LRP operation.

With Wavell's support, the planning and training for the first LRP operation went ahead under Wingate's direct leadership and control. 77 Brigade were subjected to a training programme of savage severity. The brigade was organised into eight columns, each of which could operate independently, with their own mule transport, and supplied entirely by air. The key to this and to all subsequent Chindit operations was effective wireless contact between columns, between each column and the commander, and between each column and their air support. Wingate's leadership and attention to detail shone through his training directives: the boldest measures are the safest; always take the offensive view; attack with surprise; concentrate to strike and disperse for security; leave scope for commanders to adapt or exploit success.

After several weeks of strenuous training, the Chindits held a major exercise in December 1942 to test the effectiveness of command and control in this totally new form of guerrilla warfare. Three thousand men in eight columns were controlled effectively by signals and cyphers. Mistakes were made and valuable lessons learned. Liaison with the RAF worked well, and wireless communication was effective, though it threw a heavy burden on the overworked signallers in the columns.

The handling of signals and intelligence matters remained a heavy and crucial task for the Chindits because their operations were not keyed in to normal corps or divisional intelligence. The operations room – 25 feet square – had the wall covered by maps and air photographs, and the floor covered by one inch to the mile maps of specific areas. Close by lay the sand table room where officers and NCOs alike were trained in aggressive tactical thinking. In the operations room was concentrated each element of command and control for every Chindit operation.

At the start of 1943 Wavell planned a general offensive in north Burma, with IV Corps advancing down the Chindwin; Stilwell and his Chinese divisions driving south towards Myitkyina; and Chiang Kai–shek's armies advancing from Yunnan. With this overall strategy, the Chindits were to be launched behind the Japanese lines to disrupt their communications while these three major attacks took place. However, in February 1943, Wavell came to see Wingate in Imphal to tell him that none of the planned offensives would take place. Wingate argued strongly and successfully that in spite of this the Chindit operation should go ahead, in order to prove and test the whole concept of Long Range Penetration and the control and command of major units operating behind enemy lines. Wavell agreed to this and gave specific orders to the Chindits: to cut the railway between Mandalay and Myitkyina; to attack the Japanese in the Shwebo area; and to cross the Irrawaddy river and cut the rail link to Lashio.

Operation LONGCLOTH started on 13 February 1943 with eight Chindit Columns. 1 and 2 Columns ostentatiously drove south in order to confuse the Japanese, while the remaining six Columns moved east towards the Chindwin. The deception worked perfectly, but problems soon arose. 2 Column and 4 Column were both ambushed by the Japanese and dispersed, while the decoy Column failed to regain contact. By the beginning of March Wingate faced a crisis: 2 and 4 Columns had ceased to exist as fighting units, 6 Column had been dispersed among the other Columns, and 1 Column was still out of touch. At this critical stage, Major Michael Calvert (3 Column) and Major Bernard Fergusson (5 Column), carried out successful attacks on the railway at Nankan village and on Bonchaung Gorge, thus completely destroying the railway. Major Walter Scott with 8 Column made a successful diversionary attack on Pinlebu.

The successful attacks by Calvert and Fergusson on the Myitkyina railway had carried out the first of Wavell's orders. Wingate, in his HQ located roughly between Calvert's and Fergusson's Columns now had a difficult decision to make. He consulted Calvert, Fergusson and Scott, and they all agreed that the whole force should cross the Irrawaddy and proceed eastwards. This was a dangerous move, since with no general British advance, all the Japanese forces could concentrate on wiping out the Chindits. Throughout this very difficult time, Wingate, himself present in the field, kept complete control of his Columns and the system of supply drops by the RAF. All worked admirably.

Towards the end of March, just when Calvert was about to blow up the Lashio railway, IV Corps Headquarters ordered the whole Chindit force to return to India. After earnest discussions with all the Column Commanders, on 27 March Wingate gave out his orders for the whole force to dump their heavy equipment, to recross the Irrawaddy, and then to break up into small groups and make for home. This gave considerable flexibility to the Column Commanders. The Japanese turned out in force to annihilate the Chindit groups, and most of them suffered severely. Most groups made for the Chindwin where the forward units of IV Corps were on the lookout for them, but some marched north, and one intrepid Column travelled eastwards and reached China, from where they were flown home by an American aircraft returning from its supply trip over the 'Hump'. Clearly, after 27 March, Wingate had no control over the different Columns, but each Column had wireless contact with Force HQ at base, and with the RAF for their supply drops. The close links with the RAF were illustrated when one Column found a long stretch of flat land, and printed out a message 'PLANE LAND HERE NOW'. The intrepid pilot landed and took off all the sick and wounded.

In February 1943 three thousand Chindits had marched into Burma and by the beginning of June just over 2,000 shattered and emaciated men returned; 450 had been killed and over 400 lost or taken prisoner. A heavy price had been paid, and valuable ammunition had been given to Wingate's critics, but the concept of Long Range Penetration had been proved. As Louis Allen wrote: 'The first Chindit expedition had panache, it had glamour, it had cheek, it had everything the successive Arakan failures lacked'.[1]

The media, hungry for any success in the Far East, seized upon Operation LONGCLOTH and made Wingate and the Chindits into heroes. Churchill joined in the euphoria. He sent for Wingate, and took him to the Quebec Conference in August 1943. Here, Wingate gained the support of Roosevelt, Churchill and the Combined Chiefs of Staff for a large-scale Long Range Penetration operation involving six Chindit brigades. The American attitude was 'Here is a Limey who is keen to fight the Japanese, let's back him'. The great American commander 'Hap' Arnold was so impressed that he offered the First Air Commando so that the Chindit brigades could be flown rather than march to their objectives, and would have adequate supply and support aircraft throughout their campaign.

Auchinleck, who had replaced Wavell, had the full backing of India Command in objecting strongly to the Quebec decision, and particularly to the break-up of the British 70th Division to form Chindit brigades. When Wingate, as a newly-appointed Major General, returned from Quebec to GHQ in Delhi he met implacable opposition at every level. This added substantially to the difficulty of setting up Operation THURSDAY, but with fanatical determination he finally succeeded. By September 1943 he had laid the foundation for the organisation and training of six Chindit brigades. In spite of a dangerous attack of typhoid from which he returned to duty only in December, the training and preparation continued under the dedicated leadership of Calvert, Major Derek

Tulloch and Major General G.W. Symes, the former commander of 70th Division.

Wingate's performance in the Chindit operations illustrates in exemplary form all the qualities of effective command and leadership. He conceived the role of Long Range Penetration in the widest strategic context; he planned the whole operation down to the last detail; he set up the staff and administrative backing for a massive operation in terms of supply, logistics, air supply and air support; and his demands for perfection moulded the training of the Chindit forces. Here was leadership and command in its rawest sense. The most significant comment on this aspect of the Chindit operations came from Bernard Fergusson, who took part in both Chindit operations:

> No other officer I have heard of could have dreamed the dream, planned the plan, obtained, trained, inspired and led the force. There are men who shine at planning, or training, or at leading; here was a man who excelled at all three, and whose vision at the council table matched his genius in the field.

Later Fergusson made another telling comment when he wrote:

> Those who are now saying Wingate was not all he was cracked up to be, remind me of the mouse who takes a swig of whisky and says 'Now show me that damned cat'.[2]

Operation THURSDAY centered on Wingate's new concept of the 'Stronghold'. The Stronghold, of roughly brigade strength, would be established in wild country remote from railways and main roads in order to prevent attack by enemy tanks or heavy artillery. Essential to the Stronghold concept was a good supply of water and sufficient flat ground for landing strips for Dakotas and light aircraft to enable supplies to be flown in and the wounded to be flown out. The Stronghold would be heavily defended by mines and wire and detailed fire plans would be drawn up for the 25-pounder batteries, Vickers machine-guns and – the most effective weapon of the Chindit campaign – the 3-inch mortar. From the secure base, aggressive patrols would range far and wide to destroy roads, railways, bridges, convoys and supply dumps, while floater groups hovered outside the base to harass and destroy any enemy units which approached the Stronghold.

The actual launch of Operation THURSDAY at 1700 hours on Sunday 5 March 1944 highlighted every aspect of command, control and leadership, and produced one of the most dramatic moments of the Far Eastern war. 77 Brigade (Calvert) and 111 Brigade (Brigadier Joe Lentaigne) were trained to a high pitch of perfection. The RAF and the Air Commando had their Dakotas and gliders neatly lined up ready to fly to the secret landing grounds – code-named Piccadilly, Broadway and Chowringhee. General Slim, Air Marshal Baldwin and senior American officers stood by. Thirty minutes before the start, an American pilot rushed up to the command group with photographs showing that Piccadilly was blocked with tree trunks. This was the moment for decisive command and leadership. Was the operation compromised? Were the Japanese waiting at the landing sites? Should the whole thing be called off? At that moment Brigadier Calvert made an incredibly brave decision, and said he would change the plan and take his whole brigade into Broadway. Despite the substantial reorganisation that resulted, the operation started just over one hour late. After the war Brigadier Scott, who as a lieutenant colonel commanded the 1st Battalion The King's Regiment, wrote: 'If ever I saw greatness in a human being, I saw it in General Wingate that night.'[3] Wingate had planned the whole scheme, it was his show, and he knew that if it was called off the concept of Long Range Penetration would be lost. Yet, what weighed with him at that moment was the thought that he was asking the Chindits to go into a dangerous situation when he was not going with them. For a very large majority of Chindits the issues of command and leadership were reflected in an intense personal loyalty to Wingate himself.

As the gliders were towed off, Wingate, Slim, Baldwin and Tulloch waited in the control tent for news. Some gliders ditched while at Broadway, other gliders crashed into unseen obstacles, but, after a harrowing night Calvert signalled for the operation to go ahead. From that moment, the control of the whole unique and complex Chindit operation centred on that tent.

While 77 Brigade achieved outstanding success at Broadway – the classic example of a Stronghold – Fergusson led 16 Brigade on the long march from Ledo to Indaw. Simultaneously, 111 Brigade under Brigadier Lentaigne flew in to Chowringhee. As a part of Wingate's plan, a section of Lentaigne's brigade (know as Morris Force) was detached to destroy the major trunk road from Bhamo to Myitkyina, the sole supply route for all the Japanese units fighting Stilwell in the north. All the Chindit units, scattered over north Burma, were linked by wireless to the control centre at Force HQ and depended on it for all supplies, and all air support from the RAF and the Air Commando. Mountbatten considered that the liaison between the Chindits and the Air Commando to be the best example of inter-Service and inter-Allied co-operation of the whole war. This was achieved because the Chindits and the men of the Air Commando gave their strong support to the concept of Long Range Penetration, and their loyalty to Wingate's leadership.

Derek Tulloch, Wingate's old friend and loyal supporter, masterminded the whole complex operation for all the Chindit brigades in the field, while Wingate divided his time between Force HQ and visiting the units behind the

Japanese lines. He visited 77 Brigade at Broadway, as well as the block on the road and rail centre at Mawlu – known as White City because of the parachutes festooning the trees. He flew in to visit Fergusson and 16 Brigade as they struggled southwards towards their target of Indaw. Fergusson said that Wingate may have appeared as an ogre, and was a fearsome man to cross, but he had only one standard – perfection. When he visited units in the field, they were strengthened and uplifted. Later the universal tribute to his leadership, from brigadiers to privates, was that 'He would never ask you to do something he would not do himself.'

On 24 March, 19 days after the launch of Operation THURSDAY, Wingate visited Broadway, White City, and Fergusson's new Stronghold at 'Aberdeen'. Later in the evening his aircraft crashed into the hills near Bishenpur and everyone was killed. The death of Wingate highlights all the problems of command and leadership, particularly in an independent and irregular force, and even more when, as in the Chindits, that force was one man's concept from the beginning. The key to the future of the Chindits at this critical juncture was the appointment of his successor. Clearly, someone was needed who had the experience of operations in the field with the Chindits, and who wholeheartedly accepted Wingate's philosophy. There were suitable candidates: above all Calvert, Tulloch or Symes. To the amazement of nearly all the Chindits, Lentaigne was appointed. This appointment was almost tailor-made to illustrate the theme of this whole book – command, control and leadership.

Wingate had created the Chindits, moulded the force in meticulous detail, and imbued it with a passionate loyalty. In the same way, the North Vietnamese commander General Giap in Vietnam – perhaps the most successful military leader of modern times – built up, from absolute basics, a force which was totally imbued with his own ideas and philosophy. Giap lived to achieve victory over both the French and American forces, but Wingate was killed just when Operation THURSDAY was starting and before his own ideas had been fully proven.

THE FINAL CHINDIT CAMPAIGN

Lentaigne, who had reluctantly transferred with his brigade to the Chindits, had never fully accepted Wingate's ideas. Richard Rhodes-James, who was Brigade Cypher Officer, recorded a deep antipathy between Lentaigne and Wingate.[4] Within the brigade, Lentaigne had two close friends, Major Jack Masters and Lieutenant Colonel 'Jumbo' Morris, and these three had a critical and derisory attitude towards Wingate.

Lentaigne had landed with 111 Brigade at Chowringhee, and in the couple of weeks after that his nerve had gone. His officers considered him to be 'excessively timid', and just before the fateful 24 March, Masters, the Brigade

Major, had considered ways of getting Lentaigne flown out because as a leader he had clearly crumpled. In this delicate situation the signal arrive appointing Lentaigne to command the whole force. From that moment, three men who were strongly antagonistic towards Wingate's whole philosophy held senior positions in the Chindit operation: Lentaigne took over command; Morris was already in charge of Morris Force on the Bhamo road; and Lentaigne appointed Masters, over the heads of more senior colonels, to command the remaining and larger part of 111 Brigade.

The destiny of the Chindits had, from the Quebec Conference onwards, been closely associated with Stilwell and his Chinese/American divisions in north Burma. Their joint aim had always been to drive the Japanese from northern Burma and to re-open the Burma Road up to Kunming – hence the significance of Mogaung and Myitkyina, the capture of which was to cost so many Chindit lives. Within this context, the antipathy of Lentaigne to the rationale of Operation THURSDAY quickly became apparent. He proposed to abandon Broadway and White City and move 77 Brigade and 111 Brigade north to assist Stilwell. Calvert protested strongly against the intention not to engage in further Chindit-type operations – later admitting that he had become dangerously insubordinate. Tulloch, equally imbued with the Chindit ethos, was absolutely horrified at the proposals of Lentaigne and Masters to move 111 Brigade to Hopin (codenamed 'Blackpool'). Tulloch threatened to resign because he considered that Lentaigne's plan ignored every precept that Wingate had laid down, and he thought, correctly, that the establishment of Blackpool would be a disaster. Here we see the true pressures and realities of command.

At his appointment, Lentaigne was pitchforked into high-level squabbles with which he found it difficult to cope. The organisation of Operation THURSDAY had involved Wingate in fearsome clashes with Slim, Gifford, Pownall and to some extent Mountbatten. Mountbatten, like Wingate, had been appointed at the Quebec Conference, and he supported his wayward and difficult subordinate as far as possible. In fighting his corner for men and supplies, Wingate antagonised many. The vicious in-fighting is vividly described by Pownall.[5] Pownall hated Wingate, as did Gifford, GOC 11 Army Group, and many others, although Stilwell, who rarely had a good word for the Limeys, saw Wingate as a real fighter. To hold his own and to get his way in that company is itself a tribute to Wingate, but when his abrasive determination was removed, the cause of the Chindits and Long Range Penetration had no protagonist at that level. Calvert had said 'Who will look after us now?'[6] How right he was to wonder!

Lentaigne, a broken man by the time he was appointed Force Commander, was no match for Slim or Stilwell, and in May 1944 he meekly acquiesced in the decision to place the Chindits under the command of Stilwell. This decision condemned them to death and annihilation. As they suffered and died in their hundreds in the gruesome struggles of Blackpool, Mogaung and Myitkyina, the overall feeling of the Chindits was that they would never have been placed in that position if Wingate had lived.

A few days before he died, Wingate had put forward a plan for another Chindit operation to be based at Pakoku, west of Meiktila, when the Japanese started retreating after their defeat at Imphal.[7] This would have been a classic Chindit operation. In 1945, during the battle for Meiktila, Slim gained great credit for an operation based on this plan without acknowledging the origin of this idea. By then the Chindits had been slaughtered at Mogaung and Myitkyina in fighting for which they were not trained or equipped. All of this took place because at the top level there was no-one to champion the Chindits' cause. Had Slim or Gifford believed in Long Range Penetration, as least some of the Chindit brigades would have been taken out after the success of Broadway, and used again in their designated role to drop behind the Japanese lines during their massive retreat southwards.

As the defence of Broadway came to an end, and the brigades prepared to move north, the Chindits soon noticed a dramatic change in the style of command. Although Lentaigne was making substantial changes to the actions of five brigades, except for a brief initial conference at Aberdeen, he did not once fly in to discuss the plans with his brigadiers. Masters, his old friend, disagreed with the orders he had been given, but felt there was no point in protesting. Later he wrote: 'The hand that pulled us away was not that of Joe (Lentaigne) but of Slim acceding to Stilwell.'

After a long and frustrating march north with 111 Brigade, Masters chose the site for Blackpool. He ignored Wingate's precepts about enemy artillery, and even before the site was established on 8 May, the Japanese guns were pounding the brigade. The Japanese assault continued relentlessly until 25 May and Masters waited desperately for the other brigades to come to his rescue. He reacted bitterly: '40 flaming Columns of Chindit bullshit sat on their arses.' As no help came, Masters increasingly had to think about abandoning Blackpool to save the remnants of his shattered men, and he signalled urgently to Slim and Lentaigne but received no reply.[8]

From early May, the Chindit brigades focused on three main objectives. Masters with 111 Brigade at Blackpool was wilting under sustained Japanese pressure. Calvert and 77 Brigade had two roles: first to try to reach Blackpool, and second to march north and capture Mogaung, a heavily defended Japanese base. Further east, and under Stilwell's direct command, Morris Force was heavily involved in the assault on Myitkyina. In addition, 14 Brigade and 3 West African Brigade, after closing down Broadway and Aberdeen, had also marched north and had reached Nammun, which was just south-east of Lake Indawgyi, and fairly close to Blackpool. Lentaigne moved Force HQ to

Shadazup, Stilwell's own HQ, close to the action at Mogaung and Myitkyina.

In this situation vigorous command and control were urgently needed, but Lentaigne totally failed to provide them. He deserves some sympathy. His nerve broke in the weeks after the landing at Chowringhee, but he merely exchanged the physical tensions of moving behind the enemy lines, for the even greater pressures of high command. When he reached Shadazup, 111 Brigade were still holding Blackpool. The two brigades at Nammun, 14 and 3 West African, were within possible reach of Blackpool, and the brigade commanders were furious and frustrated when they received no orders to move. Yet with his own brigade close to annihilation at Blackpool, at no time did Lentaigne come from his HQ at Shadazup to visit or to see the situation on the ground. Nor did he even send a staff officer to assess the position and report to him. Meanwhile 77 Brigade was trying desperately to reach Blackpool but was prevented by a river made impassable by monsoon floods. There is no doubt that, given positive direction, 14 Brigade and the West Africans could have taken action in support of Blackpool. One more factor must be mentioned – if Blackpool had not been wrongly sited in the first place, the three other brigades could all have come to its assistance.

The war in Burma has many examples of orders given from behind the front line proving irrelevant or even ludicrous because the officer giving the order had not seen the ground. In the aftermath of the battle of Kohima, the whole advance of 2nd Division, the spearhead of XXXIII Corps, was held up at the Naga village despite angry orders going up from brigade, division and corps headquarters. They had not seen the ground. It took a young CO – Lieutenant Colonel Horsford, 4/1 Gurkhas – to view the ground, to reject the order for a frontal assault, and work out a plan to capture the strongpoint and the village. So at Blackpool, having no response to his urgent entreaties, and no visit from Force HQ staff, Masters decided to pull out the broken remains of his brigade – to the fury of Stilwell who saw powerful Japanese forces released for the battles of Mogaung and Myitkyina.

The debacle of Blackpool tragically illustrates the problems which arise when command, control and leadership are lacking, for whatever reason. Chindit veterans have maintained from that day to this, that Wingate would not have allowed Blackpool to be sited at the place Masters chose, and would have been in with the brigades assessing the situation on the ground. They believe, too, that had he lived, the Chindits would never meekly have been handed over to Stilwell to be used as normal infantry attacking strongly fortified towns without artillery or armour support. All of these developments were the result of weakness in command, control and leadership.

The Chindit campaigns illustrate another aspect of leadership in war. While Wingate organised and trained the force to a high pitch of readiness, he did not have the time or opportunity to assess and establish which commanders would have the type of leadership qualities needed in the demanding situation of a Chindit Column behind the enemy lines. Lentaigne, who had proved himself a brave and intrepid leader during the retreat of 1942, was a failure in the different context of a Chindit operation. In the operations of Morris Force on the Bhamo road, there is ample evidence that Morris himself was a failure in terms of command and leadership, while Peter Cane, a lieutenant colonel in 4/9 Gurkhas, was an outstandingly successful and aggressive Column Commander. In the other brigades, Calvert, the doyen of all Chindit leaders, Scott, Vaughan and Upjohn all provided sound leadership, while others who had had experience of action in traditional formations failed the test.

From the withdrawal from Blackpool (25 May) the Chindit brigades were drawn more closely into Stilwell's web. He vented his fury at the abandonment of Blackpool on the unfortunate Lentaigne, who in turn sent a curt and petulant order to Calvert and 77 Brigade to take Mogaung. While Calvert moved his brigade towards Mogaung, Morris Force came directly under the control of Stilwell's HQ and in particular the egregious Boatner who was typical of the sycophants with whom Stilwell surrounded himself. Morris Force then became heavily involved in the attacks of Myitkyina.

Although 14 Brigade and 3 West African Brigade continued vigorous action with the Japanese in the aftermath of the Blackpool surrender, throughout this period they sensed very clearly that 77 Brigade were in a fight to the death at Mogaung and needed support. Instead of moving as rapidly as possible to Mogaung, they were left deeply frustrated near Nammun. Their commanders, Brodie and Vaughan, made frequent comments about the inexcusable waste of time, and their annoyance at the passive inactivity forced on them by the absence of direction from Lentaigne at Force HQ.[9]

In contrast, Calvert's attack on Mogaung with 77 Brigade is a classic example of sound leadership, excellent planning and effective control, but here too there was no direction or support from Lentaigne. As the brigade approached Mogaung, fighting hard most of the way, they received no message from Lentaigne, but were greatly heartened by warm congratulations on their achievement from Mountbatten.

In a series of hard-fought actions at the approach to Mogaung (9 to 13 June) the South Staffordshire Regiment, the Lancashire Fusiliers and 3/6 Gurkhas drove back the Japanese defenders and seized several crucial positions ready for the final attack. Calvert, in the front line and controlling the battle on the ground, had to face several additional imponderables. All signals now had to be processed through Stilwell's chaotic HQ, and consequently air support attacks could rarely be relied on, the wounded were not flown out swiftly enough and were often left to die, and supplies, especially of 3-inch mortar ammunition, became increasingly unreliable. Intelligence had come to Calvert that he was to have the support of strong Chinese forces for the final assault on Mogaung. These reinforcements were vital because the brigade had suffered very heavy casualties. The South Staffordshires had had 40 officers killed or wounded; only two of their subalterns had survived the campaign, and they had been wounded seven times between them.

The difficulties for the fighting units on the ground, caused by the inadequacies in the headquarters, were compounded by the attitudes of Stilwell's staff. They fed him only information they thought he wanted to hear, and rarely left the headquarters to see the ground. Stilwell himself had sterling qualities as a fighting general, but he had a contemptuous attitude towards the British which caused anger and frustration among the Chindits.

At Mogaung a Japanese artillery post was causing heavy casualties among the Chindits, and on 18 June Calvert put in a well-planned attack with a company of the King's (Liverpool) – now reduced to 70 men. This assault supported by a Mustang attack at dawn, together with 4.2 mortar, 3-inch mortar, Vickers and Bren gun fire finally overcame the enemy strongpoint – a good example of clear orders and co-ordination because the commander was on the ground at the front.

A few days before this a Burma Rifles officer had been despatched to attempt to bring in the long-awaited Chinese regiment. Rather to Calvert's surprise, they turned up just after this successful attack. He had some experience of Chinese forces from his buccaneering days in pre-war Shanghai, and he personally welcomed the regiment even though they produced another problem of control. Calvert was wise enough to realise that, although they were technically under his command, the Chinese had been fighting the Japanese since 1931, and they had a very different attitude to war. He therefore adjusted his tactics, realising that the Chinese would be unlikely to meet an exact deadline. He had hoped to capture Mogaung before the Japanese in the town received those reinforcements released by their victory at Blackpool, but unfortunately fresh enemy units arrived there before he was able to put in his attack on 24 June. Then, after three days of bitter fighting, in which the Chinese did take part, although in their own good time, 77 Brigade finally drove the last of the Japanese out of Mogaung. Initially 2,000 strong, the brigade's fighting strength after the battle was a mere 800 men.

A few days after the battle, Lentaigne and Calvert were summoned to Stilwell's HQ, where an incident took place which illustrates that indefinable factor of personality and character which is such a significant ingredient of leadership. Lentaigne, tense, worried and apprehensive, begged Calvert not to antagonise Stilwell. Stilwell started aggressively: 'You send very strong signals, Calvert.' Calvert replied, 'You should see the ones my Brigade Major would not let me send.' After a tense moment, Stilwell roared with laughter, having met a man of his own mettle. This instantly wiped away weeks of duplicity and false information which his staff had fed him. He awarded Calvert an immediate Silver Star.[10]

By the end of June 1944, after the victory at Mogaung, the Chindit brigades were in such bad physical shape that they had to be flown out to India for prolonged medical treatment and recuperation. They had fought bravely and had survived the stress of serving for months behind the enemy lines. In addition to the actions of 77 Brigade at Broadway and Mogaung, Morris Force on the Bhamo road, 111 Brigade at Blackpool, 14 Brigade and 3 West African Brigade at Nammun, 16 Brigade had made its historic march from Ledo to attack Indaw. In addition 23 Brigade, which had trained as Chindits, had been used by Slim to guard his flank north of Kohima, and they had acquitted themselves well.

When all the Chindits had been flown out a command decision had to be made about their future role. In March 1944, in one of their last meetings, Mountbatten had asked Wingate for his views on the wider strategic possibilities for Long Range Penetration. In a remarkable memorandum, Wingate outlined a scheme for LRP brigades to leapfrog eastwards from Burma as the Japanese withdrew.[11] In fact the war developed in a different way, but in considering the decisions of August 1944 about the future of the Chindits, it must be remembered that the original idea of the Stronghold and the Chindit operations based on it applied to a situation where the British were advancing and the enemy retreating. The Chindit brigades had proved their worth, and had amassed vast and valuable experience in the field of irregular warfare. Long before Mogaung they should have been taken out and re-equipped ready for the great advance after the victory of Imphal. In that advance, Fourteenth Army could have been dramatically assisted if Chindit brigades had been dropped behind the Japanese lines as they fell back.

What was the command decision at that critical moment? It is clear that Slim was never fully convinced of the value of Long Range Penetration. Indeed, in spite of his terrific successes he never really approved of the use of airborne troops, which could also have helped the Fourteenth Army advance. Mountbatten did believe both in Wingate and the LRP concept, but he was not strong enough to overcome the opposition of Slim and the phalanx of establishment figures whom Wingate had antagonised. So, at a high level the decision was made to disband the Chindits and to disperse their units throughout the army. In the American forces, Merrill's Marauders, based and trained on the Chindit concept, were virtually destroyed by Stilwell just as the Chindits had been. They too were disbanded. So both the Chindits and Merrill's Marauders suffered from having inadequate support at the top level where long-term command decisions are made.

Wingate had shown his outstanding leadership qualities in creating the Chindit force from scratch, based in every detail on his own carefully planned ideas, and against the almost complete opposition of the Delhi establishment. He created the system, obtained the supplies, trained the men, led the expedition, and then paid with his life just when his whole concept had been proved and justified at Broadway and White City.

The Chindit campaign emphasised other aspects of leadership under the difficult conditions of operations behind the enemy lines. Some brigade or column commanders possessed those essential qualities of stern resolve and determination, but, as Colonel Carfrae observed, fear 'could reduce officers to pitiable ineptitude'.[12] Certainly, there were some who became excessively timid and imagined a Japanese sniper behind every jungle tree. Until the day of his death, Wingate used his leadership qualities to establish complete and effective control of the Chindit operations. With the appointment of Lentaigne, problems of command and leadership emerged. Lentaigne had openly derided Wingate's ideas, but had no coherent philosophy to put in their place. Masters, too, rejected Wingate's lead and consequently he and his brigade suffered severely.

The Chindit campaigns illustrate one thing above all – that for an irregular military force to survive and prosper, it must have determined backing at the highest level. After Operation LONGCLOTH, Wingate had won the support of Churchill, and after a brilliant exposition at Quebec, had also convinced the Combined Chiefs of Staff. With very few exceptions, he carried his own staff and men with him, as well as Cochran and Alison, the leaders of the Air Commando, but his abrasive personality, which he exploited to the full to forward his cause, created too many enemies, especially among the staff at GHQ in Delhi. When he died there was no-one to assume his mantle, and the Chindits were swiftly handed overt to Stilwell and used disastrously in fighting for which they were not prepared. The rejection of Wingate's ideas was noted by the *Observer* as early as 16 April 1944 – less than a month after his death – when their military correspondent regretted that his ideas should be shelved because 'they were not liked by official Delhi'.[13] The correspondent was warned that the Secretary of State considered Wingate was no longer sane at the time of his death. That shows clearly enough where command and control of irregular forces really lies.

Notes

1. Louis Allen, *Burma: The Longest War*, p. 118, Dent, London (1984).

2.   Bernard Fergusson, *Beyond the Chindwin*, p. 242, Collins, London (1945). This passage is reproduced with kind permission of Collins.

3.   *Wingate: An Appreciation*, The Chindit Old Comrades Association, p. 66.

4   Richard Rhodes-James, *Chindit*, p. 63, Murray, London (1980).

5.   Brian Bond (ed.), *Chief of Staff*, p. 112, Leo Cooper, London (1974).

6.   David Rooney, *Wingate and the Chindits – Redressing the Balance*, p. 207, Arms and Armour, London (1994).

7.   Memorandum, Wingate to Slim, 13 March 1944, Wingate Papers, Imperial War Museum.

8.   John Masters, *The Road Past Mandalay*, p. 219, Joseph, London (1961).

9.   Rooney, op. cit., p. 174.

10   Michael Calvert, *Fighting Mad*, p. 212, Bantam, London (1990).

11. Memorandum, Wingate to Mountbatten, March 1944, Wingate Papers, Imperial War Museum.

12. C. Carfrae, *Chindit Column*, p. 101, Kimber, London (1985).

13. Rooney, op. cit., p. 217.

For further details on this campaign, see David Rooney, *Burma Victory*, Arms and Armour, London (1992).

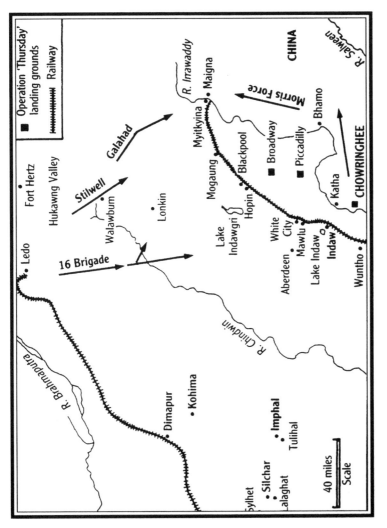

Chindit Operations, March – July 1944.

COMMAND AT ANZIO AND IN THE FALKLANDS: A PERSONAL VIEW

by Julian Thompson

A member of Mrs Thatcher's War Cabinet in 1982 is alleged to have drawn attention to his concern at the apparent slow progress of operations in the Falklands by likening the situation to that at Anzio in 1944. Both were amphibious operations, followed by battles on land, and it is interesting to compare the two, to see where, if at all, they have similarities, particularly in command methods and styles at several levels. Our examination will be restricted to command and leadership in the amphibious and land battle phases, from the perspective of the land force commanders, leaving aside naval and air aspects except where they impinge on the land commanders' decisions and actions. There will be no discussion of the purely maritime or air matters connected with Anzio or the Falklands.

It is necessary when examining command and control to include some narrative to give an idea of the context in which decisions were made, and also to comment on the higher command whose actions can help or hinder the commander in the field.

By the time of the Anzio landings in January 1944, the British and Americans together had conducted three successful major amphibious operations, and a number of minor ones. The techniques were well proved and practised. The commanders, particularly the senior British, had years of warfighting behind them: as junior officers in the First World War, and as divisional, corps, and army commanders, or their naval and air equivalents, for up to four years in the Second. The command chain for the landing was straightforward and conventional, as shown in Annex A (p. 188). Vice Admiral Hewitt, as well as commanding the Allied Naval Force at Anzio, was United States Navy commander in the Mediterranean Theatre in his own right. Admiral Sir John Cunningham was British and Commonwealth C-in-C Mediterranean. The senior land and air commands were inter-allied. General The Honourable Sir Harold Alexander's 15th Army Group (from 9 March 1944, he was C-in-C Allied Armies Italy), comprised Lieutenant General Mark W. Clark's United

States Fifth Army, and Lieutenant General Oliver Leese's British Eighth Army. Lieutenant General Ira C. Eaker USAAF was Allied Air C-in-C Mediterranean Allied Air Forces. In the case of land forces at Anzio, the chain of command ran from Alexander, to Clark, to the American Major General John P. Lucas, commanding VI Corps. Overall responsibility in the whole theatre was vested in Allied C-in C Mediterranean Theatre, General Sir Henry Maitland Wilson (from 9 March 1944, Supreme Allied Commander Mediterranean Theatre). The senior commanders charged with strategic and operational matters in the theatre were situated in the very theatre of operations, and were thus able to go forward to see for themselves and discuss problems face to face with the commanders in the field. Finally the troops who took part in the Anzio landing were almost all battle experienced.

It was very different in 1982. Very few of the British troops and commanders who actually fought in and around the Falklands had any previous experience of high intensity war, although many were well versed in 'brush-fire' wars and counter-insurgency. A handful of the most senior officers based in Britain and charged with the overall direction of the Falklands War had been very junior officers in the Second World War or Korea, but none had commanded a battalion or ship in battle, let alone a formation; some had never heard a shot fired in anger. Perhaps most significant, none of the senior officers in overall charge had personal experience of the command and control imperatives of even an amphibious exercise at formation level, let alone the real thing.

During the Falklands War, the Task Force Commander charged by the Chiefs of Staff with day-to-day direction of operations in the South Atlantic was a naval officer; he was shrewd, resilient, and quick brained; but his last experience of any kind of active service was as a very junior officer at sea 37 years previously. Throughout the Falklands War he was located in Northwood, just outside London. From here, 8,000 miles from the action, he and his staff, the overwhelming majority of whom had never been near a battle in their lives, were in overall command of that most complicated operation of war, an amphibious landing followed by a land campaign. Both were closed books to every single officer on the Northwood staff. No one in Task Force Headquarters, other than a handful of Royal Marines and Army officers posted in specially for the occasion, had any experience of land warfare whatever. Yet, as always, the land campaign would decide the outcome. The admirals, generals and air marshals charged with overseeing operations from their desks and operations rooms in Whitehall, Northwood, and Wilton in 1982 were faced with a very steep learning curve indeed compared with their predecessors in 1944.

The command organisation for the Falklands War (Annex B, p. 189), although superficially straightforward, was flawed. There were three task groups in the theatre of operations: the Carrier Task Group, the Amphibious Shipping

Task Group, and the Land Force Task Group. The commanders of these Task Groups (CTGs), reported direct back to the Task Force Commander (CTF) in England. The flaw, and a major one, was the lack of an overall commander in the theatre of operations. Rear Admiral Woodward, commanding the Carrier Task Group, as the senior of the three, was given the responsibility of co-ordination. Beloved of NATO staffs because it panders to international sensitivities, 'co-ordination' can mean all things to all men and is no substitute for command. Personalities aside, the Carrier Group Commander, however able and experienced, would not have been well placed to bear responsibility for overall command in the theatre of operations in addition to his other duties. Before the landings took place, he was anything up to 4,000 miles away from the other two task group commanders. After the amphibious operation, the tactical situation usually required him to be positioned up to 250 miles away from the beachhead, and in any case command of the Carrier Group was a full-time job, allowing little leeway for detailed considerations of the problems and needs of the other two commanders. Major General Michael Wilkins, the Chief of Staff to the Commandant General Royal Marines, made strong representations in the Ministry of Defence that a three-star, in-theatre overall commander should be appointed. Wilkins's experienced eye had spotted the flaw, but he was ignored. The lack of a theatre commander with experience of amphibious and air operations and an appreciation of the demands of land operations was a potential source of disaster, which fortunately was never realised.

Operation SHINGLE, the Anzio landing, was an amphibious hook intended to outflank the Gustav Line, the main German defensive barrier from Minturno to Ortona, guarding the approaches to Rome. Alexander's 15th Army Group had been stalled on this Line since November 1943. When detailed planning for SHINGLE started in early January 1944, some misconceptions surfaced. One of these, the aim of the operation, remained unclear well after the landing took place. Lucas, the land force commander for the operation, was given:

> a tentative 'planning' mission as follows:(1) Seize and secure a beachhead in the vicinity of Anzio, (2) Advance and secure Colli Laziali [the Alban Hills], and, (3) Be prepared to advance on Rome.[1]

These objectives were in accordance with Alexander's expectations at the time.[2] The purpose was to cut, or at least threaten, the German line of communication to their formations facing Fifth Army on the Rivers Rapido and Garigliano. He hoped that the Germans would react by pulling troops out of the line to face the new threat, thereby enabling Fifth Army to break out. Clark, after his experience at Salerno the year before, had misgivings about VI Corps advancing too far inland.[3] There were only enough landing craft to land Lucas's two infantry divisions on the first day: United States 3rd, commanded by Major General Truscott, and British 1st commanded by Major General Penney. Combat Command A (the equivalent of a brigade group) from Major General Harmon's United States 1st Armored Division would not land for at least three days. In Clark's orders to Lucas for SHINGLE the mission was given as:

a. To seize and secure a beachhead in the vicinity of ANZIO.
b. Advance on the COLLI LAZIALI.

There is a considerable difference between advancing on Colli Laziali and seizing it. Expressing orders to a subordinate in this way leaves them open for him to interpret as he sees fit, including exactly what constitutes 'advancing on Colli Laziali'. Clark's Chief of Staff delivered the orders to Lucas in person, and made it clear that the primary mission was to seize and secure a beachhead. The orders, he said, had been worded so as not to force Lucas to push on at the risk of sacrificing his corps. He was free to move to and seize Colli Laziali should it be possible. Lucas was also concerned:

Colli Laziali is the first terrain feature north of Anzio, but is distant therefrom [sic] some twenty miles. The term 'advance on' indicated in itself that the Army questioned my being able to reach this feature and at the same time, hold a beachhead.[4]

The ambiguous wording of Lucas's second task filtered down through the chain of command. In British 1st Division's operation order it emerged as: 'An advance to Colli Laziali may take place'.[5]

The aim of Operation CORPORATE in 1982 was:

To bring about the withdrawal of the Argentinean forces from the Falkland Islands and the Dependencies and to re-establish the British Administration there as quickly as possible.[6]

The Task Force Commander's Despatch, quoted above, states:

It was always accepted that because of its vital role as the seat of government and the only centre of communication, Port Stanley held the key to victory; he who held Port Stanley, held the Falklands. The aim therefore was to secure the capital as quickly as possible.[7]

It was also clear to both Brigadier Thompson, commanding 3 Commando Brigade, the land force for the initial landings, and Commodore Clapp, commanding the amphibious shipping, that Port Stanley must be the ultimate objective. But, despite the statement in the Task Force Commander's Despatch, written with the benefit of hindsight, the requirement for an advance to the capital immediately after getting ashore was not included in any orders issued by Task Force Headquarters back in Northwood in the days leading up to the landing. Indeed, before landing, Thompson received a directive from Major General Moore, cleared by the Task Force Commander, which read:

> You are to secure a bridgehead on East Falkland, into which reinforcements can be landed, in which an airstrip can be established and from which operations to repossess the Falklands can be achieved.
>
> You are to push forward from the bridgehead area so far as the maintenance of its security allows, to gain information, to establish moral domination over the enemy, and to forward the ultimate object of repossession. You will retain operational control of all forces landed in the Falklands until I establish my Headquarters in the area. It is my intention to do this aboard *Fearless*, as early as practicable after the landings. I expect this to be approximately on D+7. It is then my intention to land 5 Infantry Brigade into the beachhead and to develop operations for the complete repossession of the Falkland Islands.[8]

Thompson was under the impression that an advance on Port Stanley would await the arrival of the second brigade, 5 Infantry Brigade, and Moore's Headquarters. In the meanwhile he was to hold the beachhead, while probing out, and in particular pushing reconnaissance teams forward to find suitable helicopter landing zones on Mount Kent overlooking Port Stanley, place observation posts on the ground overlooking the route from San Carlos to Mount Kent, and provide reception parties at Teal Inlet (to which LSLs could unload). Once ashore, all these measures were put in train. The mission which Thompson gave his commanders in his orders was:

> To land at PORT SAN CARLOS/AJAX BAY complex and establish a beach-head from which to launch offensive operations.

As we shall see, an immediate advance would not have been possible for logistic reasons. The potential for friction and misunderstanding between Thompson and Task Force Headquarters was increased when the command was altered by the Northwood Headquarters to include Major General Moore, as divisional commander [9], before his arrival with the second brigade some nine days after the initial landings of 21 May 1982 (Annex B). This might have worked but for difficulties with the radios fitted in the ship in which he was travelling, which prevented him from communicating with Thompson or Northwood.

Despite this, for several days Northwood persisted in sending signals to Moore at sea for his action, and to Thompson ashore in the Falklands for information. When, during this critical period, Thompson came under pressure from Northwood, he had no means of checking that schemes hatched in the Task Force Headquarters bunker 8,000 miles away accorded with his divisional commander's intentions for the land campaign.

Thompson gave his orders for the landing verbally at a gathering of the commanding officers of the reinforced 3 Commando Brigade in the wardroom of HMS *Fearless*, the Headquarters ship in which he, Commodore Clapp and their staffs were travelling south. Such gatherings are called O (Orders) Groups. The operation order, which ran to 47 pages, had been issued the day before. Thompson did not read out the operation order at the O Group, but treated it as 'confirmatory notes' to what he and his staff had to say. The way in which an O Group is stage-managed depends upon the personality of the commander, the level of command and the circumstances. At platoon or company level the orders for a quick attack given face-to-face or over the radio do not require much if any stage management. But orders for this, the biggest all-British amphibious operation since the Second World War, needed careful stage management if all the information was to be got across clearly and concisely. By using the comprehensive operation order as confirmatory notes, much of the detail such as beach locations, the 49 artillery targets chosen to protect the beachhead, times of sunrise and sunset for a month ahead, and a mass of other instructions, could be digested later, so that commanding officers would come to the O Group with their minds uncluttered and able to absorb the essentials: how the landing was to be conducted, Thompson's design for battle should the Argentines attack the beachhead with ground troops, and some basic points of soldiering that he wanted everybody in the Brigade to assimilate.

Thompson impressed upon the commanding officers that the landing was not an end in itself, merely the beginning, and that this point was to be made clear to everyone. Every marine and soldier must know what the brigade task was in this phase, so that if leaders at any level became casualties, sub-units would press on to their objectives. Soldiers, and infantry especially, need to know the plan in the detail that, for example, the junior officers and ratings in a warship do not. Leaders at low level may be required to pick up the reins of command from dead or wounded superiors and carry on to the objective. They must know, among a host of things, what the objective is, how to get to it, what neighbouring units are supposed to be doing, what fire support is available and how to call for it, how to use the radios, and how to control their command.

Both the landings at Anzio on 23 January 1944 and in San Carlos Water on 21 May 1982 went well and without any serious opposition. At Anzio, VI Corps had suffered 13 dead and 87 wounded on the first day. Here the operation was on a vastly greater scale than at San Carlos. By midnight on D-Day, VI Corps had landed 36,000 troops and 3,100 vehicles, and captured the small port of Anzio.

The main enemy response in and around San Carlos consisted of wave after wave of air attacks against the ships, sinking HMS *Ardent* and damaging a number of other warships. Casualties to the *Ardent's* ship's company alone were 22 dead and 37 wounded. 3 Commando Brigade lost three dead and one wounded in two light helicopters shot down by enemy ground fire. By midnight some 3,000 troops, 24 guns, and a handful of vehicles were ashore. In both landings, the planned initial beachhead was secure before nightfall.

The principles of command and control during both landings were broadly similar. The land commander shared a headquarters ship with his naval opposite number. Here both were able to monitor progress, and amend the landing schedule where required. As the build-up in the beachhead progressed, the land commander transferred his headquarters ashore. At Anzio a far faster rate of build-up was possible thanks to some 241 purpose-built amphibious ships and craft, including some 84 Landing Ships Tank (LST), and numerous other landing ships and craft. This figure does not include the host of minor landing craft and DUKWs (the versatile 2 ton swimming truck). DUKWs enabled guns, ammunition and stores to be driven straight from LST tank decks, down the ramp into the sea, up the beach to the required destination, without laborious, time-consuming double-handling of loads. The logistic system for VI Corps was excellent. On D-Day, eighteen LSTs, three LCTs and four cargo ships sailed from Naples. The LCTs and LSTs carried a total of 1,500 trucks, each loaded with 5 tons of supplies, which drove straight ashore over the bow ramps either onto the beach at Anzio, or at the port. From then on a 'milk run' operated, as trucks emptied the previous day drove onto LSTs, for the return trip to Naples for reloading. In this way a continual shuttle was achieved, with the minimum of delays in the Anzio beachhead.

3 Commando Brigade at San Carlos was not so fortunate. The run-down of amphibious assets by successive governments between 1945 and 1982 had resulted in the proportion of purpose-built amphibious ships available to the British being far lower than that warranted by the size of the force to be landed. This proportion decreased further when 5 Infantry Brigade arrived. For the initial landings alone, at least twelve LSLs would have been appropriate, instead of the six that were all that the British possessed. Swimming trucks such as DUKWs and Terrapins[10] had long gone from the British amphibious inventory. To augment this sorry state of affairs, use was made of STUFT, merchant ships taken up from trade, but they lacked the necessary modifications, such as landing craft at the davits, that had converted numerous passenger ships in the Second World War to Landing Ships Infantry. Landing craft had to go alongside the

troop carriers such as the *Canberra* and *Norland*, and to embark heavily laden men who swung down on a rope from the galley loading port in the ships' sides, or climbed down scrambling nets. The landing and unloading of troops and stores at San Carlos was slow, and was not helped by being conducted under almost continuous air attack during daylight on five of the first six days of the operation. The one asset possessed by the British in 1982 which was not available in 1944 was helicopters. Of these there were pitifully few initially, and the number remained insufficient right up to the end of the land campaign. They did however allow some flexibility of movement of troops, guns, and ammunition, albeit at a painfully slow rate of build-up. They were invaluable for command, control and casualty evacuation, for in the Falklands, unlike Anzio, there were no roads inland from the beachhead. There was no port either, until Port Stanley was taken. The terrain was peat bog, and wheeled vehicles could make little or no progress, particularly if carrying the most modest load. Gun and trailer towers could go nowhere. Major movement of heavy stores out of the San Carlos beachhead had to be by sea to the nearest convenient landing place. From here helicopter lift was the only means of transport, augmented by the few tracked oversnow vehicles (bandwagons) taken south in the hope that their low ground pressure would enable them to move across the peat bog; an expectation that was fulfilled.

Command and control of the landing at San Carlos followed well-practised routines. As early as possible on D-Day, the Brigade Tactical Headquarters was established ashore at San Carlos Settlement. Thompson flew forward by helicopter from the *Fearless* to visit units as the landing progressed. By early evening, he made the decision to land his main headquarters and command from ashore by first light on D plus One. With most of his Brigade ashore, it was the right place to be, for control was easier, and the military radio sets worked far better than those in the *Fearless*. Flying forward from the *Fearless* was always more troublesome than from his own headquarters ashore. Flight deck space was limited, and his helicopter had to wait its turn. Often it was waved away if an air attack was imminent, causing further delay and frustration. The *Fearless* could have been sunk or damaged in the air attacks on shipping off the beachhead. The few, irreplaceable, radio-fitted bandwagons were safer ashore. Finally, there were suggestions that the *Fearless* might leave the beachhead at night to refuel, or for other reasons; and she did on a number of occasions. Thompson did not wish to be carted out to sea, leaving his Brigade bchind, leaderless.

At Anzio, Lucas did not go ashore until D plus Two. Both Alexander and Clark were able to visit the beachhead on D-Day. They expressed pleasure at the success of the operation. Before Clark left to return to his Headquarters in Naples, he said to Lucas; 'don't stick your neck out Johnny. I did at Salerno and got into trouble'.[11] Lucas had no intention of doing so, and dug in to consolidate the beachhead – his primary task. He did not intend advancing until his build-up was complete, including Combat Command A of 1st Armored Division. It is at this stage of the operation that criticism of Lucas starts. There are those who believe that he should have dashed forward to seize the Colli Laziali; and even some that had he pushed on to Rome, the German defences on the Gustav Line would have collapsed. This is cloud cuckoo land. There is little doubt that he could have established forces on the Colli Laziali, and perhaps even rushed a column to Rome. There is equally little doubt that the Germans would have dislodged and even cut off such a foolish enterprise, as they demonstrated by their reaction which was, as always, swift and violent. By D plus Two their build-up to contain the Anzio bridgehead was twice as fast as that predicted by Allied intelligence. By D plus 10 the Germans had moved nearly 34,000 more troops into the area than the Allies had predicted would be in place on D plus 16.[12] Eventually eight-and-a-half German divisions were moved in, of which a bare one-and-a-half came from the Cassino front opposing Fifth Army, making nonsense of Alexander's hopes that the enemy would denude this front, enabling Fifth Army to break out. After four years of war, it would seem that there were still those in the Allied camp who grossly underestimated the German ability to re-group and react. Lucas might have pushed on to take Campoleone and Cisterna, 14 and 15 miles respectively from the beach. Holding these might have delayed the German reaction. But he was not actually wrong to stay where he was. Although the navies expressed disappointment over lack of progress ashore, the senior soldiers and Eaker disagreed.[13]

In the Falklands, the Argentine land forces were supine and made no attempt to attack, let alone dislodge the beachhead. The delay in moving out of the beachhead was not caused by Argentine ground forces, but by their air force. The logistic build-up would have been slow enough, because of the lack of sufficient specialised shipping, craft and helicopters, without the interference of the Argentine Skyhawks and Mirages. Their appearance on the first day had resulted in a number of key STUFT being sailed, bearing much of the equipment and other stores, including rations needed for the first few days of operations. Most of this was not seen until the end of the war. All helicopters and craft were employed on moving ammunition and supplies ashore, leaving only a handful of helicopters available at night for moving troops. There was little point in rushing off to Port Stanley until helicopters could be released for logistic tasks in support of units up to 50 miles from the beachhead, the distance to Port Stanley.[14] Until the logistic offload had been completed and more helicopters had arrived, advancing to the high ground overlooking Port Stanley would be foolhardy. The infantry could advance on foot, but major battles, or repelling counter-attacks on the key positions near Stanley, would require guns and mortars, and heavy ammunition expenditure, of shells and mortar bombs in particular. The only way to lift these was by helicopter, and there were insufficient helicopters to maintain a substantial force in contact with the enemy, over the distances involved. To move just one battery of light guns and ammunition would have taken the available Sea King helicopters two full days.[15] These problems were not appreciated by Task Force Headquarters.[16] Because the Task Force commander was not able to visit forward, and there was no in-theatre overall commander, misunderstandings were an increasing cause of friction between those at the rear and those at the front. There was a strong suspicion in Headquarters 3 Commando Brigade that Task Force Headquarters had very little idea of what was actually happening on the ground, and lacked the experience to understand why, for example, unloading took so long.

At Anzio Alexander visited frequently, on some occasions staying for two or three days. Clark, to Lucas's irritation, established an advanced Command Post near VI Corps Headquarters.[17] Both senior commanders were able to judge exactly what was happening. Attempts to expand the Anzio bridgehead against increasingly strong German opposition failed despite hard fighting by all formations of a much reinforced VI Corps. By now the initial two infantry divisions ashore had been joined by United States 1st Armored Division complete, United States 45th Infantry Division, and 168 Infantry Brigade detached from British 56th Infantry Division on the Garigliano front. By 2 February, VI Corps, anticipating German counter-attacks, dug in.

Lucas's command style became all too apparent to both Alexander and Clark. It was not his practice to visit forward, and he spent most of his time in a cellar in Nettuno. On 10 February, at a critical moment in the aftermath of one of the earlier German counter-attacks, he went forward to visit British 1st Infantry Division for the first time since D-Day, eighteen days before. Here he found Penney, the divisional commander, and Major General William W. Eagles, commanding United States 45th Infantry Division discussing a counter-attack to regain the village of Aprilia (known to the troops as 'The Factory'). Here was an opportunity for Lucas to grasp the reins and give orders for a co-ordinated attack, or at least find out how he as corps commander could assist, if only by allocating fire support, and having his staff tie up the details. After listening to Penney's appreciation of the situation and recommendation for a strong and immediate counter-attack, Lucas thought for a moment, and said to Eagles, 'OK Bill, you give 'em the works'. Soon after he returned to his cellar. There was no co-ordinated plan, and insufficient fire support. The outcome was an attack in too little strength, too late, which was thrown back.

It is clear that Lucas did not give orders at proper O Groups, but merely held conferences, which by accounts resembled debating societies.[18]

Conferences provide an opportunity for the commander to discuss forthcoming operations with his staff. He should retain firm control throughout and, on completion, issue unambiguous guidelines to his staff to enable them to prepare orders to the formations and units under his command. When giving orders, the commander should not confer with his subordinates – he tells them what he wants done.

Alexander now ordered the remainder of British 56th Division into the beachhead, and said that there was to be no retreat from the much reduced perimeter. The major German attack, operation FISCHFANG (Catching Fish), was, after an initial penetration, eventually hurled back with heavy losses on both sides, but not before Clark had to order Lucas to mount a full-blooded counter-attack. By this time Major General Truscott, the commander of United States 3rd Infantry Division, had moved into Lucas's Headquarters on Clark's orders, as deputy corps commander. Truscott, the *beau sabreur*, one of the outstanding generals of the war at the operational level, whose courage was a byword in his division, immediately made his presence felt in the dank cave in Nettuno, telling VI Corps' 'gloomy staff that nothing ever looked so bad on the ground as it did on a map at HQ' [excellent advice], before going forward to see for himself.[19] Clark congratulated Lucas on the success of the counter-attack, which had been made at Truscott's prompting. Three days later, Lucas was relieved of command.

In the Falklands, by 25 May 1982, pressure had built up from home for a move out of the beachhead. Thompson and his staff were putting the finishing touches to the plan which relied on the use of four Chinook heavy-lift helicopters and several medium-lift Wessex helicopters arriving in San Carlos in the STUFT *Atlantic Conveyor* the next morning, when a staff officer informed them that the ship had been sunk by an air-launched Exocet. Only one helicopter, a Chinook, survived.

At first Thompson's reaction was to sit tight until Moore arrived. However, the Task Force Commander at Northwood summoned him to the satellite telephone to order him to move out of the beachhead. In addition a raid on Goose Green, earlier cancelled by Thompson, was to be remounted and the place captured.

The orders for the necessary moves were passed by secure voice radio by the Brigade Major (the Chief of Staff in modern terminology), and confirmed by Thompson, who visited each commanding officer. The moves put in train by these orders started 3 Commando Brigade off in two widely separated directions: 2nd Battalion the Parachute Regiment (2 Para) to the south to Darwin and Goose Green; 45 Commando Royal Marines (45 Cdo), and 3 Para east towards the high ground overlooking Port Stanley. All moves were by foot. 40 and 42 Cdos remained behind to protect the beachhead and as reserves.

There is no doubt that Thompson made a command error in the battle for Goose Green. He should have taken his tactical headquarters and another battalion or commando and taken personal command of the battle. By not doing so, he asked more of 2 Para than he should have done; which is not to criticise the commanding officer of the Battalion, nor the second in command who took over when the former was killed. Instead he attached a battle-experienced major from his staff to the Battalion as a liaison officer with a radio on a one-to-one link with himself, who was able to 'read the battle', and keep Thompson in the picture.

The Goose Green battle was a pointer for the battles that followed. The only secure voice radio sets in the Brigade were heavy and needed constant battery charging. These were installed in command bandwagons, at Brigade Headquarters, and one each at battalion/commando main headquarters. When commandos and battalions were moving without their command bandwagons, on night approach marches and in battle, radio traffic on the brigade net was confined to man-pack radios, at that time insecure. Use of this net risked interception by the Argentines. So, radio traffic was confined to short conversations, using codewords and nicknames where possible, and restricted to events happening at the time, or such a short time ahead that the enemy would not have time to react. Orders for operations more than an hour or so ahead and lengthy situation reports were best passed face-to-face between the Brigade Commander and his commanding officers, or by using liaison officers. Long range patrols and observation posts, other than artillery and mortar observers, passed most of their traffic using a laborious one-time pad code.

Thompson also gave orders at O Groups whenever a new phase of the campaign was about to start. These were similar to the O Group described earlier, but simpler, in that the battles about to be fought were less complicated than the amphibious landing kicked off by the O Group in the *Fearless*. On each occasion commanding officers of commandos/battalions and supporting arms and services were assembled in a small briefing tent, or hollow in the ground, or building if available. The Brigade Intelligence staff officer would give the enemy picture in as much detail as was known. Thompson would give the Brigade mission, the general outline or design for battle, and each unit its task. Addressing each commanding officer by his first name, Thompson would say: 'I want you to,' followed by what was to be done, but not how (unless there were specific limitations he wished to impose). Further detail would be given by the Brigade Major and the Logistic staff officer. [20] Confirmatory notes would usually, although not always, have been issued beforehand, on which commanding officers could scribble additional information. The confirmatory notes for a Brigade night attack might run to perhaps ten pages, including co-ordinating instructions, administrative and communications details, and a comprehensive task organisation section. Confirmatory notes were, for example, dispensed with at the hurried O Group to which commanding officers were summoned in the darkened room of a captured house in Port Stanley, when the Argentine defences collapsed. It was altogether a less structured occasion.

The formal O Group procedure was useful for reasons other than the passing of orders. Much useful business could be conducted in a relaxed way both before and afterwards. Unit intelligence officers could be taken aside by the Brigade Intelligence staff and given detailed briefings, fire plans could be discussed by battery commanders attached to battalions and commandos with their own artillery commanding officer. On arrival commanding officers found a welcome mug of hot soup waiting for them; it was a business-like, but family occasion, stage-managed by a highly efficient Brigade staff controlled by a first class Brigade Major and DAA&QMG.

Thompson also operated a 'Rover' (R) Group system. He, his artillery regimental commander, and sometimes his engineer officer, together with the necessary radios, would move as a group when away from the headquarters. This allowed discussion of any points that arose on trips around the brigade. When viewing the ground from an observation post, tactical problems could be discussed. Much time was saved by obviating the need to brief each other, and making clear what was in the Brigade Commander's mind.

Visits forward by commander and staff were also made as frequently as possible. During battle, which in the Falklands was always at night, the latter stages of Goose Green excepted, command was by radio and liaison officer, followed, when possible, by visits during the day. Thompson commanded from his Main Headquarters during one Brigade night battle. During another night operation involving only one battalion, he commanded from his Tactical Headquarters, while Main moved location, having been bombed that afternoon. He planned to run the final night battle for Stanley itself from a tactical observation post overlooking the town. In the event, the battle was never fought, because the Argentines surrendered on the afternoon of 14 June. But the orders had been given and all was set.

The methods used by 3 Commando Brigade and later by Moore in the Falklands War of 1982, differed little from those followed by the British land forces at Anzio in 1944. Once ashore, and with the arrival of Moore, Divisional Headquarters[21,] and 5 Infantry Brigade, Thompson's command and control problems became the familiar ones of brigade command. He was spared further communication with Task Force Headquarters, for which he was truly thankful.[22] That the relief in Whitehall and Task Force Headquarters was mutual is clear:

Pressure from Fieldhouse at Northwood and Moore's belated arrival soon overcame the tactical hiatus, and the superbly trained and powerful

Commando Brigade then got underway with great style and physical toughness for its 'Yomp' across the island to Stanley. The heroic action of 2nd Parachute Battalion ... at Goose Green ... swung the fortunes of the land campaign in Britain's favour from the very start.[23]

Thompson's satisfaction at Moore's arrival in the Theatre of Operations echoed that of Whitehall. But, it must be said that while wholeheartedly agreeing with most of the passage above, especially 2 Para's contribution to eventual success, in fact the orders for the Goose Green battle and the move out of the beachhead were given on 26 May 1982, four days before Moore's arrival in the beachhead. The moves were well underway, with Goose Green in British hands, by the morning of 29 May, 24 hours before his arrival. During that time, as over the previous five days, for the reasons explained there had been no communication between Divisional Headquarters and Thompson. Although this should have been comprehended at Task Force Headquarters and in Whitehall, clearly it was not, demonstrating how out of touch they were with events on the ground. This comprehension gap might have been closed had there been an in-theatre overall commander.

The land campaign in the Falklands had a reasonable chance of success once the troops and the bulk of their guns, ammunition, fuel and supplies were ashore. They were not surrounded and overlooked in the beachhead by a superior enemy force. The delays to the move out were all logistical, caused by lack of sufficient amphibious shipping, craft and helicopters. Had the enemy attempted to interdict the line of communication between the beachhead and Port Stanley, either from the air, or by serious ground action, the logistic problem would have been immeasurably worse, leading perhaps to stalemate. That the Argentines failed to take these steps was the result of luck, not British cleverness. It must also be said that a major contributor to the slowness of the unloading, and hence the logistic difficulties, was the inability to achieve air superiority over the beachhead before a landing took place, a lesson which had been learned the hard way in places such as Crete in 1941. This was not a failure by anyone in the South Atlantic, least of all the Carrier Group and its commander. It was unfortunate that Task Force Headquarters had promised that air superiority would be achieved, knowing this to be an impossible goal. The emptiness of these promises became apparent to the commanders charged with executing the operation too late to alter the stow of logistic ships to take account of a hostile air situation.

The situation at Anzio was very different. The landing as planned never had a chance of achieving the objectives for which it was conceived. Lieutenant General Lemnitzer, deputy Chief of Staff to Alexander, is clear that if only an initial two divisions were to be landed, there was no hope of holding the Alban

Hills (Colli Laziali):

> Gen Alexander realised that we did not have the strength to hold the Hills
> even if we did take them. He thoroughly approved of the caution with which
> the Corps Commander was acting. Neither General Alexander nor Clark
> gave any sign that they thought Lucas had acted unwisely.[24]

So why was Lucas sacked? Both Alexander and Clark had ample opportunity
to see him at work, because they were on the spot a great deal of the time. As
one of his own divisional commanders, Truscott, said, 'I was not blind to the
fact that General Lucas lacked some of the qualities of positive leadership that
engender confidence.'[25] This is supported by Clark:

> Lucas was not relieved because he had done anything wrong, but because
> Alexander did not think he could stand up to the strain of further operations
> in the prolonged battle this promised to be.[26]

With one exception, the senior minister mentioned at the beginning was wrong
when he drew tactical and operational conclusions from Anzio and applied
them to the Falklands, presumably in a misguided attempt to galvanise his
ministerial colleagues into putting pressure on the commanders. Although he
might have been well informed on Anzio, he clearly knew little about the
amphibious and land campaign in the Falklands. There was one aspect common
to both operations, whose significance was probably lost on the minister: a
profound ignorance in Whitehall about the circumstances on the ground and
the reasons for them. In the case of the Falklands War, this is not surprising,
since the command structure militated against a clear picture being available at
Task Force Headquarters, and consequently in Whitehall. At Anzio, however,
the senior commanders knew exactly what was going on; they were there, or
thereabouts. In 1944, it was the most senior minister of all, Winston Churchill,
who did not understand why the Anzio landing failed to produce immediate
results, and never had a chance of achieving the strategic object as perceived in
Whitehall. Perhaps Alexander was at fault for not keeping the British Chiefs of
Staff, and hence the Prime Minister, fully in the picture. It was easier to offer
up a scapegoat, and a convenient one was to hand: Lucas. He was sacked, not
so much for what he did, but for the manner in which he conducted his command.

173

Notes

1. John P. Lucas Diary, Part III, p. 11, held in the United States Army Military History Institute (USAMHI), Carlisle, Pennsylvania, USA, quoted in Julian Thompson, 'John Lucas and Anzio' in Brian Bond (ed.), *Fallen Stars,* p. 191, Brassey's, London (1991).

2. Interview with Field Marshal Alexander, Dr Sydney Mathews, p. 8, USAMHI.

3. Mathews interview with General Mark W. Clark, Part V, p. 6.

4. Lucas Diary, Pt. III, pp. 17-18, quoted in Thompson, 'John Lucas and Anzio', p. 193.

5. Public Record Office, WO 170/375, Headquarters 1st Infantry Division War Diary, January 1944, Operation Order Number 1, dated 12 January 1944.

6. The *London Gazette* of Monday 13 December 1982, Despatch by Admiral Sir John Fieldhouse GCB GBE, Commander of the Task Force Operations in the South Atlantic, April to June 1982, p. 16110.

7. Ibid., p. 16115.

8. Julian Thompson, *No Picnic,* p. 65, Leo Cooper, London (1992).

9. Or Commander Land Forces Falkland Islands (CLFFI).

10. An inferior British version of the American DUKW.

11. Lucas Diary, Pt. III, p. 40, quoted in Thompson, 'John Lucas and Anzio', p. 197.

12. HQ 5th Army INTSUM dated 30 December 1943, p. 3, estimated 61,000 by D plus 16. By D plus 10 there were 95,000.

13. C.J.C. Molony, *The History of the Second World War, the Mediterranean and the Middle East,* V, p. 686, HMSO, London (1973).

14. See Julian Thompson, *Lifeblood of War: Logistics in Armed Conflict,* pp.

269-279, Brassey's, London (1991), for a full discussion of the logistic problems.

15. Ibid., pp. 373-374.

16. Neither was the problem appreciated at the time by the officer tasked with 'co-ordination' in the South Atlantic, the Carrier Battle Group commander, see *One Hundred Days*, by Admiral Sandy Woodward, p. 325, Harper Collins, London (1992).

17. Lucas Diary, Pt. III, p. 18.

18. Major General Lucien Truscott makes this clear in his book, *Command Missions, a Personal Story,* p. 329, Dutton, New York (1954).

19. Ibid., p. 320.

20. In 1982, known as the Deputy Assistant Adjutant & Quartermaster General (DAA&QMG).

21. It was not called this by Northwood, whose predilection for complication was demonstrated by giving it the unwieldy title Commander Land Forces Falkland Islands (CLFFI). Those in the field preferred the more familiar Divisional Headquarters.

22. Thompson, *No Picnic*, p. 92.

23. Bill Jackson and Dwin Bramall, *The Chiefs: The Story of the United Kingdom Chiefs of Staff*, p. 416, Brassey's, London (1992).

24. Smythe interview with General Lemnitzer, USAMHI, 14 January 1948, pp. 9-10, quoted in Thompson, 'John Lucas and Anzio', p. 204.

25. Truscott, *op. cit.,* p. 320.

26. Mathews interview with Clark, Part IV, pp. 9-10, quoted in Thompson, 'John Lucas and Anzio', p. 205.

Annex A

ASSAULT FORCE COMMAND FOR ANZIO
Overall Naval Commander
(all ships in the area of operations)
Vice-Admiral H. Kent Hewitt USN

Assault Force USN and

Overall Amphib Commander

Rear Admiral Lowry USN-
USS Biscayne (HQ ship)

VI Corps
Maj Gen Lucas

Force X (US)
R/Adm Lowry
USS Biscayne
16 Major Warships
154 Landing Ships & Craft
57 Minor Warships

Br 1st Inf Div
Maj Gen Penny

Force P (British)
R/Adm Troubridge
HMS Bulolo
14 Major Warships
87 Landing Ships & Craft
46 Minor Warships

US 3rd Inf Div
Maj Gen Truscott

KEY (above):

——— Naval Command Chain

. . . . . Army Command Chain

KEY (opposite):

CTI   Commander Task Force

CTG   Commander Task Group

CTU   Commander Task Unit (nautical terminology, Task unit is
hardly appropriate to describe either brigade. 3rd
Commando Brigade consisted of eight major *units* and
sixteen *sub-units;* total strength some 5,500 men, 24 guns,
light helicopters etc.)

Annex B
COMMAND CHAIN, FALKLANDS, 1982
Before 20 May 1982

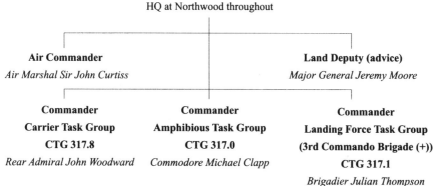

Commander Task Force (CTF) 317
Admiral Sir John Fieldhouse
HQ at Northwood throughout

Air Commander
Air Marshal Sir John Curtiss

Land Deputy (advice)
Major General Jeremy Moore

Commander Carrier Task Group CTG 317.8
Rear Admiral John Woodward

Commander Amphibious Task Group CTG 317.0
Commodore Michael Clapp

Commander Landing Force Task Group (3rd Commando Brigade (+)) CTG 317.1
Brigadier Julian Thompson

COMMAND CHAIN, FALKLANDS, 1982
After 20 May 1982

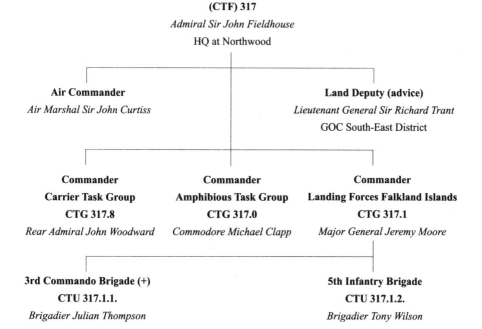

(CTF) 317
Admiral Sir John Fieldhouse
HQ at Northwood

Air Commander
Air Marshal Sir John Curtiss

Land Deputy (advice)
Lieutenant General Sir Richard Trant
GOC South-East District

Commander Carrier Task Group CTG 317.8
Rear Admiral John Woodward

Commander Amphibious Task Group CTG 317.0
Commodore Michael Clapp

Commander Landing Forces Falkland Islands CTG 317.1
Major General Jeremy Moore

3rd Commando Brigade (+) CTU 317.1.1.
Brigadier Julian Thompson

5th Infantry Brigade CTU 317.1.2.
Brigadier Tony Wilson

177

US AND ALLIED LEADERSHIP AND COMMAND IN THE KOREAN AND VIETNAM WARS

by Robert O'Neill

The Korean War (1950-53) and the Vietnam War (1965-73) are little studied or discussed in Europe. A set of superficial notions has been established in the public mind about the Vietnam War, as a result of episodic and simplistic media coverage, not to mention some of the products of the motion picture industry. But public and indeed professional academic knowledge of the Korean War is very scant.

As an Australian soldier and historian, both conflicts have made an impact on my life. As a cadet at the Royal Military College, Duntroon, in the mid-1950s my instructors were mostly senior NCOs and junior officers who had seen service in the Korean War. The atmosphere in which we were trained, the exercises, the 'enemy', the field dress, the defences we constructed, and the code of conduct to which we were expected to adhere if captured, were derived from the recent combat experience of those who taught us. The illustrations used in lectures and the anecdotes told around campfires in the field all gave us a vivid picture of war against an oriental enemy, heavily superior in numerical terms, and not lacking in initiative and fieldcraft, in a bitterly cold climate. We also heard interesting comparisons between the techniques, attitudes and styles of leadership then prevalent in the Australian Army, and its operating partners in Korea, the British, Canadian, New Zealand and United States armies.

In the mid-1960s it was my turn to go to war, in Vietnam, where I served initially as second in command of a rifle company, and for most of my year there as the intelligence officer of the 5th Battalion, The Royal Australian Regiment. That experience gave me views and insights not only on fighting the North Vietnamese and Viet Cong, but also on the methods and leadership styles of our principal allies, the Americans and the South Vietnamese. My first major task as a historian after entering academia was to write the official history of Australia's part in the Korean war, a task which occupied the greater part of my research and writing time for 12 years. This continuing involvement with both conflicts has given me a standpoint which may be somewhat different to those more frequently encountered in the northern hemisphere, as an Australian and as a soldier of those times.

THE NATURE OF THESE WARS

The Korean and Vietnam Wars were not total wars for the external powers that waged them, although they were for their servicemen and women who actually fought in them. Here is the special nature of the challenge they posed to leadership. Men, most of them not volunteers, were required to place their lives on the line, in quite bloody operations, for a year or more, for the sake of limited objectives. These were not crusades to destroy what were seen as all-threatening forces of evil such as Prussian-German militarism in the First World War or Nazism in the Second. They were prophylactic wars entered into by the United States and its allies to provide the ounce of prevention that would save a pound of cure at a later date.

Stalin, in the view of allied leaders of 1950, had to be shown that he could not make South Korea his Sudetenland. The North Vietnamese, and their Chinese and Soviet supporters in the 1960s, had to be taught that they could not hope to take control of mainland and archipelagic South-East Asia, and threaten the credibility of American guarantees to other, more vital parts of the world against Communist aggression. In terms of these aims, the commitments of the United States and its partners were reasonably successful, but these broader objectives did not determine the spirit in which the wars were conducted, or incline Western political leaders to accept significant risks of escalation from December 1950 onwards. Rather these wars had to be conducted within a framework of tight political constraints on the military operations undertaken. Their marginal, or corrective, strategic purpose was reflected in governmental resource allocations. Neither legislatures nor public opinion were inclined to press their governments to adopt a total war policy in terms of the men, money and other resources devoted to these conflicts.

Yet these were wars of appreciable duration. In terms of major combat operations the Korean War ran for three years and one month; the Vietnam War spanned thirteen years of intense action, during which the allies were engaged for eleven. US and allied service personnel served generally in both conflicts for a year at a time, although senior commanders such as Ridgway and Clark in Korea, and Westmoreland and Abrams in Vietnam, and some of their staff, served for much longer periods. Regular servicemen often returned for a second, or in the case of Vietnam, a third and even a fourth tour of duty. Much of the US Army was made up of draftees in both wars. So was much of the British contingent in Korea, but not the Australian, which was a specially-recruited force of volunteers. By contrast, the Australian Army in Vietnam was about half conscripts and half regulars.

Another feature of these wars is that the meatgrinder of operations was running virtually continuously. There were few pauses between major phases of actions. There were no lengthy periods of re-deployment of forces from one part of the front to another or from one theatre to another. When there were no major offensives, there was a constant stream of minor ones. Pressure on the enemy had to be sustained. Results were slow in coming and governments were impatient, under pressure from their backbenchers and public opinion.

For the average infantryman on a 52 weeks tour in either war, 50 were spent within range of the enemy's artillery or ambushing parties, and at least 26 were spent in close contact, mainly in patrol actions but not infrequently in brigade- or divisional-sized offensives. These were intensive wars, in which the enemy's heavy numerical superiority had to be offset by efficient use of the combined Western resources of manpower and technology. Hence the limited numbers of troops were used intensively, and they were made more effective by providing them with ample logistic support so that they did not have to cease fighting to be re-supplied, and with air and ground mobility so that they could be quickly re-deployed from mission to mission. In many cases men saw more action in one year in Korea or Vietnam than in the first three years of the Second World War.

But the soldiers of these two wars had the benefit of vastly better medical services, especially helicopter evacuation of wounded, followed rapidly by surgical attention by first class American specialists in operating theatres within an hour's flying time. The standard of army equipment provided was high, there were few serious supply shortages, and when soldiers were out of contact with the enemy and back in their base areas, they could shower, wash clothes and cease to contend with many of the privations which attend an infantryman's life in the field. Korea posed the special problems of a bitingly severe winter. Vietnam offered the challenges of a very hot, humid tropical environment, with all the insect and reptilian pests and skin diseases which thrive in such warmth.

As in all human experience, there was a long learning process, one which regrettably had to be re-started virtually *de novo* in the Vietnam war, in understanding the nature of limited warfare in the nuclear age. One of the chief problems for Western professional soldiers fighting in these wars was caused by the differing natures of the two unlimited wars of the 20th century and the two limited conflicts which then followed. Virtually everyone in a senior or mid-ranking position in the Korean War, on the UN Command side, had participated in the Second World War – political leaders, military commanders and staffs, combat troops. Also their national business communities, mass media and public opinion understood war, to the extent that they thought about it at all, in the context of 1939-45.

The standards that they all instinctively resorted to were those of unlimited warfare: politicians and public opinion in terms of seeking decisive outcomes; military commanders in terms of freedom to manoeuvre and to inflict damage on the strategic heart of the enemy; and the media in terms of looking for dramatic stories and charismatic leaders. They were all to be frustrated, and their frustrations were inflicted upon the frontline soldiers in different ways: constant political pressures for results; hence a need for continuous tactical offensives, but with little prospect of backing them with strategic attacks leading to victory; commanders who sought to make their periods in office memorable, but who were limited essentially to using infantry patrols and raids as regular means of operation; and journalists who, finding that the real stories were very complex and that the leaders were quiet professionals, either did not report much on the war or did so in a critical vein, thereby making their readers wonder why their soldiers were fighting at all.

Above all there was a tendency in public debate and military planning in both wars overly to emphasise military aspects at the expense of the political, despite the fact that these were fought as limited wars. Results, not surprisingly, were assessed all too often in terms which would have been more appropriate to the Second World War, for example where forces stood on the ground by comparison with their locations of three or six months ago, rather than the impact allied operations might have had on the political objectives of the enemy and his perceived ability to achieve them. Operations therefore tended to be conducted for military goals which were either meaningless or even counterproductive in terms of the overall objectives of the war. Who held Pork Chop Hill, that famous company outpost in Korea, did not matter in other than a purely tactical military sense. The operations launched in 1953 to wrest it from the Chinese were ultimately a disaster for the US Army, costing several battalions of infantry and in one day alone consuming 77,000 artillery shells. The Chinese raised the stake to a full division and finally were left in possession of the hill. More Chinese were killed than Americans, but what of the significance to each society of the losses in economic and, especially, political terms? For neither side were the gains worth the costs. In the United States such expensive actions produced an air of frustration and impatience with limited war which was to prove extremely damaging to the Democrats' cause in the US presidential elections of 1952, and to Eisenhower's room for manoeuvre in the final phase in 1953. There are all too many similar examples to be cited from the Vietnam War.

Another important general element of the natures of these wars is that they were fought by the United States and its partners to enable weak, developing, newly-independent states with authoritarian political systems to hold off totalitarian pressures and gain the breathing space to transform themselves into strong, prosperous democracies. Yet by driving the pace of both wars and treating the indigenous allies as very much inferior entities the United States reinforced those factors strengthening authoritarianism in South Korea and South Vietnam and undercut others which would have opened the way to more democratic reforms.

For these results the US military, particularly senior commanders, must shoulder much of the blame. But they received all too little instruction on these aspects of the war from their political masters who, for the most part, wanted quick military results so that the troops could be brought home. There were a few political and military advisers, both in the theatres of combat and in Washington, who recognised what was required for long term political success. Unfortunately they were unable to persuade their leaders until it was too late. The result was that both wars were conducted with too much emphasis on the military aspects of security and not enough on the political and social.

But given the relatively recent learning experience of 1939-45 through which political leaders, military commanders, the media and public opinion had passed, the reasons for this situation are not difficult to understand. The Korean and Vietnam Wars formed a very decided break with the established behavioural patterns and mindsets which had governed the conduct of war in the first half of the 20th century.

THE SPECIAL CHALLENGES POSED BY
THESE WARS TO ALLIED LEADERSHIP

American and allied success in Korea and Vietnam depended upon using, more efficiently, smaller numbers of men than those available to the enemy. Therefore the role of leadership was crucial in these conflicts. Morale had to be maintained, new operational methods had to be mastered, discipline had to be kept, and troops had to be led so that they would perform well, with fewer casualties than the enemy, in intensive engagements over a considerable period.

All this is reasonably obvious. What is not so obvious, especially from the perspective of experience of the two World Wars, is that it is difficult to sustain the enthusiasm of intelligent young Western men in the second half of the 20th century, when they do not understand the subtle policy objectives for which the war in which they happen to be involved is being fought. When their superiors can give them no satisfactory answers as to what would constitute victory or success, and even less explain to them in logical terms what real benefits their acceptance of the risks of war might bring, the challenges to morale and discipline are formidable.

These challenges are compounded by the inevitable presence in limited wars of enemy sanctuary areas immediately adjoining the combat zone – as in China for Korea and Cambodia and Laos for Vietnam. 'Why can't we go over there and finish the bastards off?', the troops asked. 'Why must we continue to tolerate Chinese fighters taking off from bases across the Yalu so that they can shoot us down and then return to safety?', allied airmen lamented in Korea. 'I can't believe that we have to accept major Viet Cong command posts, supply points and hospitals just across the Cambodian border, fed by the Ho Chi Minh and Sihanouk trails, which we cannot touch!' was a familiar complaint in Vietnam.

Troops who receive no satisfactory answers to points such as these will not be the easiest to motivate, and the longer such apparent contradictions to military commonsense are left without being addressed by leaders, the worse the situation tends to become. In Korea the sanctuary afforded by Chinese air bases proved ultimately tolerable because of the superiority achieved by US fighter aircraft. In Vietnam, by contrast, the inability of US and allied forces to control the territory west of the border with Laos and Cambodia, or north of the 17th parallel, had a severe effect on morale of both troops and commanders, and ultimately a telling impact on the course of the war.

This inability to control the approaches to South Vietnam has given rise to important books such as *On Strategy* by Colonel Harry Summers[1] or *The Key to Failure* by Norman Hannah,[2] which claim that victory could have been achieved by pursuing a more offensive strategy against North Vietnam and the Ho Chi Minh Trail. These theses are challengeable because the political weakness of the South Vietnamese Government in the populated areas was so acute that it could have been sapped by communists working from within, even had the American forces pushed well into the North Vietnamese 'panhandle' or cut the Ho Chi Minh Trail. To have been decisive those offensives would have had to have been sustained into the Red River Delta, the North Vietnamese heartland, a course which was ruled out for fear of provoking direct Chinese intervention, as in Korea. The Johnson Administration did not focus on improving the political basis of the South Vietnamese Government until it was too late.

Soldiers, especially when frustrated by their commanders and unconvinced as to why they are accepting the risks of death in battle, look forward to occasional visits by political leaders. But in both Korea and Vietnam they were rapidly disillusioned on detecting the small degree of contact which the politicians wanted to have with them, and by the simplistic, sloganeering answers which high-level visitors so often gave on the few occasions when they risked a discussion with the men implementing their policy. For the politicians, these wars were frustrating sideshows, so they were generally not eager to visit, and they had little by way of cheer or inspiration to impart once there.

When the rank-and-file soldiers turned, with their accustomed disdain for politicians, to seek consolation in the thought that they were fighting to protect their nearest and dearest, or in their absence, some grander objective such as freedom, democracy, or Western civilisation, little solace was to be found. Their nearest and dearest usually did not want them to be in Korea or Vietnam, and wrote frequently to say so. They sometimes added, in the case of Vietnam, that they were being harassed or hectored by their fellow citizens for consorting with a mass murderer.

When it came to the defence of freedom and democracy, where else should a conscientious young soldier turn for support but to the columns of a free, democratic press? But what did he find there for much of the Korean and Vietnam Wars? Little for comfort and few prominent, well written articles, describing the problems of the last few months of patrol actions or the appreciation of the indigenous peoples for the schools or dispensaries which the troops had built for them. What soldiers usually encountered when they read the newspapers was a boring, dishearteningly repetitive debate on the Government's management of the war, conducted largely in the context of the war's domestic political implications, and enlivened by exposés of the ineptitude of the senior commanders under whom they were fighting. In the case of men serving in Korea, they could hunt through the newspapers for weeks without encountering any coverage of the operations in which they had been participating. They felt truly forgotten while the journalists focused on the armistice talks at Pan Mun Jom. The men in Vietnam did not feel as forgotten, but they had to cope with the dispiriting effects of news of popular opposition to the war at home, expressed in numerous direct ways such as their colleagues being pelted with garbage or drenched in ox blood by opponents of the war on marching through their cities of origin at the end of their tours of duty. And, of course, many journalists who covered the Vietnam War did not venture out of Saigon to get to grips with its real nature as seen by the men who had to fight it.

In addition to these challenges of leadership at the individual level there were many others of a more systemic kind. Although the logistic system was good in both wars, supplies were not inexhaustible; ammunition, equipment, and accommodation and defence stores were expensive. Thus there was a premium to be gained by an army whose commanders could use resources more efficiently, such as firing ammunition only when there was a high chance of hitting a target whose value to the enemy was greater than the cost of its destruction to the attacker, or building and maintaining field defences which could render the enemy's artillery bombardments ineffective, yet which did not waste materials.

Another challenge was to make effective use of the indigenous people. The Americans and their allies were conducting these wars in the midst of millions of Koreans and Vietnamese. Most of them, theoretically at least, were of friendly disposition – but all too many of the local people with whom troops had contact when on leave were indifferent or downright exploitative and dishonest. Men who feel that they have been swindled by local merchants and bar girls are not likely to give much thought to the challenges of building a strong new political society among these people, unless they have a much deeper acquaintance with indigenous civilians or soldiers of better quality. Similarly, the indigenous people could not have been very favourably impressed by intervening foreigners who seemed to be interested in them largely as objects of pleasure, curiosity and denigration.

Yet the ways in which these two wars were conducted made mutual discovery of the real worth of interveners and indigenes extremely difficult to achieve. Hence it was all too easy for the soldiers to focus exclusively on the military side of the war and leave the social and political consequences of the conflict to someone else – but to whom? In most cases there were no others to tend to relationships with the local people. Despite their overriding importance, the development of a strong, mutually supportive partnership was all too often neglected. This was an aspect of the two wars which all too few bothered about. Racism and ignorance, particularly of culture, history and language, posed further significant obstacles. While all forces made some attempt to surmount them, the results achieved were far from notable. Mutual indifference and dislike resulted, which in Vietnam particularly had a very counterproductive effect on the course of the war, one which the communists were able to exploit to telling effect.

THE QUALITY OF ALLIED RESPONSES
TO THESE CHALLENGES

It is difficult to generalise about the nature of allied responses to the challenges to leadership in Korea and Vietnam. All armed forces taking part had their strong and weak units but there are a number of characteristics, positive and negative, which served to distinguish the leadership styles of the various nationalities from each other. Let me discuss three: those of the United States armed forces in both conflicts; those of the British Commonwealth in Korea; and those of the Australians and New Zealanders in Vietnam.

THE US RESPONSE

Although the United States armed forces in Vietnam were better educated and much more integrated racially than in Korea, their nature did not change a great deal from war to war. Their fighting spirit generally was high, and US soldiers were characterised by toughness and determination, bravery and effect-iveness in pitched battles, a high level of professionalism in the conduct of conventional operations and a readiness to accept significant casualty rates as the price of success. The norms of the American Civil War had not been entirely eroded by the experience of the two World Wars, and it was clearly understood that victory demanded a trade in human lives. American tolerance of casualties was not as high as that of the Chinese or the Japanese, but none the less it was what one would expect of a confident great power, well endowed with human and material resources, which had won all its wars and in which fierce competition was the normal way of conducting civil politics and business.

As a consequence American commanders were more aggressive than their allies and sought always to put their enemy on the defensive. The other side of this coin was a readiness to engage quickly and directly when a more considered, indirect approach might have been just as effective and not as costly. Not only did this tendency lead to a perception on the parts of political leaders, American and allied, that US generals lacked concern for the political consequences of losses, but it also undermined morale in the US armed forces in the later stages of both wars. The American way of war also tended to focus sharply on military aspects, as exemplified by the great weight placed on respective body-count figures in Vietnam. In an all-out conventional war against a similar enemy, relative loss statistics have great significance. In a protracted unconventional war, in which the political costs of casualties to the intervener are more obvious and more costly than they are to the insurgent force, body-count comparisons are a distraction. Yet the American tradition in war made this truth difficult to recognise. It took a long time before even parts of the US armed forces in Vietnam came to see the conflict primarily as a political competition with the communists for the votes of Vietnamese civilians, and for the continuing support of the American people at home. Even once the political nature of the war had been understood, many commanders gave it merely lip service and continued with the only style of warfare that they knew.

In parallel with this emphasis on the military sides of the Korean and Vietnam Wars, American commanders tended to prodigality in their use of firepower, particularly airpower. At least in Korea the air commanders came to recognise that the cost-benefit ratio in aerial bombardment was in the North Korean and Chinese favour, and in 1952 they adjusted their strategy. This lesson, however, appeared to have been forgotten in Vietnam, leading to persistence with a style of warfare which might have been supportable over four years had things been going well, but which proved politically self-defeating at home when continued over twice that period without decisive success in the field.

The size and firepower of the US armed forces in these two wars, and the natural disposition of their commanders to focus on military objectives, reinforced an American sense of indifference towards, or disregard for, both the indigenous people and their armed forces. In the Korean War, which after the Chinese intervention had become a highly manpower-intensive conflict, the South Korean Army had to be given large stretches of the front line to man. And for the most part they fought well, but they were in separate segments from the Americans and other allies and international co-operation was simpler than in Vietnam. There, the indigenous armed forces could not be put into separate areas and co-operation with them became both more important and more challenging. The South Koreans, even during their initial periods of defeat, always played a major part in the war, and in time came to be the dominant element in holding the front line. But in Vietnam the South Vietnamese Army was sidelined by the Americans in 1964 and relegated until the Nixon Administration tardily introduced Vietnamisation to cloak US withdrawal. As a result, the existing tendencies of the Americans to disregard their indigenous allies were strengthened, resulting in a more open field for the communists to exploit politically. Not until too late did the United States begin to prepare the South Vietnamese armed forces to withstand the communist ground offensives alone.

The combination of determined commanders pressing for measurable results, lack of caution, technological superiority and failure to make decisive progress led intelligent young soldiers increasingly to question the value of what they were doing. In the late 1960s, as drug usage became more common and racial tensions became particularly evident in a force which had a high proportion of black servicemen, discipline came under severe strain. While the US army can be criticised for allowing this situation to happen, it also deserves credit for taking stock of this new situation and attempting to counter it. The early 1970s were an acutely testing time for junior leaders, for they were the most direct representatives of official authority among potentially rebellious troops, and they were the first in line when hotheads began using violence to make their point, such as the 'fragging' of officers by lobbing hand grenades into their sleeping quarters.

The problems of leadership were eased by President Nixon's policy of handing the war over to the Vietnamese. Had the withdrawal of US forces been delayed by a year or two it is anybody's guess as to whether the US Army in Vietnam would have remained battle-worthy. The disciplinary problems of Vietnam had also begun to affect US forces in Europe. The crisis of military leadership in the United States had become profound by the end of the Vietnam War.

THE BRITISH COMMONWEALTH RESPONSE IN KOREA

The British, Canadian, Australian and New Zealand forces which made up the greater part of the First Commonwealth Division in Korea, were no less brave than the Americans, but they came from a very different military tradition.

Britain, as a seapower, normally maintained a relatively small army. The policing of its vast empire had to be done on an extremely economical basis, and therefore operational methods emphasised the avoidance of high casualty losses and the careful use of materiel. Britain also learned that effective control required the co-operation of the indigenous people, and developed ways of bringing them into a close working relationship, even against nationalists of their own countries. These attitudes and methods had naturally also conditioned the training of the Australian, Canadian and New Zealand armies.

Consequently within the Commonwealth contingents in Korea there was always a tendency to question whether the risks which senior American commanders were asking them to accept were really justified. On several occasions after protests had been made by Commonwealth subordinate commanders, senior US formation commanders modified their orders. They could have insisted that their allies obeyed them but they were aware that in the long run the political costs would not be worth the resulting military gains. The General Officer Commanding the Commonwealth Division was equipped with a directive from the British Government ordering him to protest through official channels to the British Government if a senior US commander required him to take action which would, in the judgement of the GOC, have unjustifiably imperilled his force. On the rare occasions when the GOC felt inclined to question orders he would initiate a practice which became known as 'waving the paper', i.e. making discreet, indirect reference to the directive while talking informally with his US corps commander. Occasionally American tolerance was stretched but the degree of independent judgement permitted by the directive enabled the several Commonwealth allies to work effectively with the Americans for three years of hard-fought and sometimes frustrating action. In this way Commonwealth commanders were able to preserve their forces from some of the more dire consequences of the US *modus operandi* and thereby reduce some of their leadership problems.

The Commonwealth Division's operational techniques, while being somewhat more cautious than those of the Americans, still demanded much of the men who had to implement them; not expending as much ammunition as the Americans in support of operations, more depended on the individual skills of the Commonwealth infantrymen. They had to be able to compete on better than even terms with their more numerous enemies. Given their tactical training, the quality of their personal weapons and the superiority of their field radio communications over those of their enemies, the Commonwealth infantrymen were able to meet the challenges of a war fought largely by patrols and raiding parties in its last two years. In so doing they adopted a more flexible approach to command and control than that of the Americans, delegating the initiative to company and platoon commanders because most operations were undertaken by sub-units of those sizes. Inevitably personal relations became less formal and more functional. A man's standing depended less on his rank than on his performance on patrol.

The degree of self reliance inculcated in Commonwealth servicemen in the Korean War was illustrated by their conduct in captivity. Of the 1,188 Commonwealth soldiers taken prisoner by the Chinese or North Koreans only a tiny number co-operated with their captors, whereas of the 7,100 US prisoners taken not a few became dispirited and were led into denouncing the UN cause and repudiating the authorities who had sent them to Korea. Commonwealth soldiers, even when separated from their officers and senior NCOs, proved somewhat more resistant to brainwashing and beating than some of their American fellow prisoners. It must also be said, however, that many Americans successfully withstood enormous psychological and physical pressures to co-operate with their captors.

Practising a different operational code and style of leadership, the Commonwealth contingents held their own and were well regarded by the Americans and South Koreans. For a protracted, limited war, where human and financial costs weighed heavily in the debates of legislatures on future strategy, the Commonwealth approach to leadership in the field was well suited for minimising the challenges faced by soldiers at all levels.

THE AUSTRALIAN AND NEW ZEALAND RESPONSE IN VIETNAM

The Australian and New Zealand armed forces, having developed in very close association with the British from the Boer War to Sukarno's confrontation of Malaysia in the 1960s, found themselves without British company for the first time in the Vietnam War. Although the ANZACs had become more specialised than the British in operations in South-East Asia, their general style of campaigning did not differ greatly from that of their original model. Most of the characteristics displayed by the Commonwealth forces in Korea were also shown by the ANZACs in Vietnam. Both sets of armed forces operated in a manner which was cost-conscious and placed a premium on the performance of lightly-equipped infantrymen relative to that of enemy infantry.

The ANZACs had the advantage *vis àvis* the Americans of several years of counter-insurgency fighting in Malaya/Malaysia, and the Australians had also had wide experience of jungle fighting in the South-West Pacific and South-East Asia during the Second World War. While the Malayan Emergency was a far less formidable problem than the conflict in Vietnam, experience in the former provided some useful guidelines for the latter. First was the primacy of politics, even at the grass roots level. Indigenous people would cease to support insurgents only when they felt genuinely persuaded that the government would in the long run give them a better deal than a revolutionary regime. Second was the overwhelming importance of developing an indigenous political system which functioned effectively at both the national and the local level. A corollary to this was the need to foster indigenous armed forces and police who could uphold the authority of the government in a manner acceptable to most of the people. Third was the importance of being able to outlast the insurgents as well as to contain them. Hence economical styles of operation had to be combined with effectiveness in the application of force.

The Malayan Emergency was not a perfectly conducted counter-insurgency operation. It was marked by poor command and control systems, inadequacies in intelligence and sometimes heavy-handed treatment of indigenous people. Yet it was successfully concluded, and those taking part learned a great deal about counter-insurgency warfare in the South-East Asian context during the 1950s.

The Australian involvement in Vietnam, like the American, developed slowly. A training team of junior officers and senior NCOs was built up from 30 in 1962 to over 100 in late 1964. In 1965 an infantry battalion group of over 1,000 men was sent and in the following year a small brigade was committed to Phuoc Tuy province in the southern central sector, and the training team was deployed in northern provinces. The escalation of forces had a political motivation, but it also facilitated an operational divorce from the Americans. The battalion group perforce had operated as part of a US brigade. A brigade could have its own independent area of operations. Thus from mid-1966, Australian, and supporting New Zealand, units were able to implement their own concepts and methods.

At this level of tactics they placed prime emphasis on stealthy, small-group, patrol operations to force the enemy out of areas close to South Vietnamese population centres. They did not seek then to follow deeper into the jungles and mountains to destroy the insurgents because they knew that unless there was political harmony in the populated areas, more guerrillas would be generated than were eliminated. They were also aware that pursuit of the enemy gave him the advantage of fighting on ground of his own choice, and therefore more chance of inflicting significant losses on his pursuers. So, having driven the insurgents back from the people, the Australians and New Zealanders then focused efforts on improving the indigenous infrastructure. They built dispensaries, schools, small hospitals, water purification and reticulation systems, roads and bridges. They came to know the local officials, civil and military, noting who were the most effective partners and who were the counter-productive ones. At the same time they maintained control over the approaches to the populated areas of their province, Phuoc Tuy.

Although this strategy brought demonstrable success in the course of the

191

first year of the ANZAC presence in Phuoc Tuy, it was clear to those with Malayan experience that the process of democratic state-building at the grass roots level in Vietnam would require many years of effort. Given the extreme political weakness of the Saigon Government, state-building had to proceed at a slower rate than in Malaya, yet the enemy was stronger, and the major ally, the United States, wanted ANZAC forces to take on wider responsibilities beyond the borders of Phuoc Tuy. As a result, after two very satisfactory years of progress, the situation in the province deteriorated as the ANZACs responded to the TET Offensive and other military pressures, losing sight of the principal political objective of the conflict – the building of support for a non-Communist government in the populated areas.

The challenges to Australian leadership in the field were formidable. Morale and willingness to work hard had to be sustained over a very long period. Some sense of continuity had to be built into operational policies, accompanied by a process of evaluation and readjustment of strategy as results required. Relations with the local people had to be fostered constantly, in the face of many difficulties and frustrations. Yet in this sphere there was a useful self-reinforcing process when operations were successful. The Viet Cong and North Vietnamese became less effective and less noticeable, and the South Vietnamese people became friendlier and more supportive, themselves helping to root out elements of communist infrastructure and to improve their own living standards. These changes in turn had a positive effect on the morale of the ANZAC troops.

Australian and New Zealand soldiers, like Americans, had become dependent on material standards far beyond those that could be offered in the field, and leave centres and amenities in base camps were important to both. But the ANZACs remained relatively free of drug problems, and their discipline and willingness to fight well were never as strained as those of the Americans. Nor were there the frictions between ANZAC conscripts and regulars which were to be found in US units.

The most serious challenge to leadership in the ANZAC forces was to keep each soldier sharp, proficient and focused on beating the enemy in patrol actions, despite the tedium of the many operations when the enemy avoided contact. It was not always easy to awaken in soldiers a sensitivity towards the needs and attitudes of the Vietnamese civilians for whom they were working and fighting, but the normal ANZAC friendly temperament tended to come to the fore when it was needed. Also ways had to be found to bridge the widening gap between what a young Australian or New Zealand male expected from life and what operational service was able to offer him. Discipline was best maintained within a relatively relaxed context of personal relations. As in Korea, ANZAC respect was conferred not according to rank but according to how effectively men did their jobs, and how reasonably they behaved to their fellows.

192

Thus unlike the American experience in Vietnam, the challenges to leadership in ANZAC units did not become unmanageable. Neither the Australian nor the New Zealand Armies were threatened with the kinds of serious disruption or disintegration which had begun to eat at the US Army like a cancer in the early 1970s.

THE DEVELOPMENT OF MILITARY LEADERSHIP AFTER THE VIETNAM WAR

The Korean War raised many of the challenges to leadership that were to become so acute in Vietnam: the problems of sustaining morale and willingness to think and fight intelligently in a protracted limited war which did not seem to the home population to have any immediate bearing on their security. The most effective ways of responding to these challenges were to apply force carefully and economically, to encourage the participation and support of the indigenous people, and to see that men were given achievable, significant tasks from which their own morale would be reinforced.

These were lessons which had been learned many times over by British forces, and Korea served to keep them at the forefront of military operational thinking. They were different to the main lessons derived from the two World Wars by the US armed forces, however, thus they were not embedded as deeply in US military culture and thinking as in the British and other Commonwealth states' doctrines. Consequently they had to be re-learned in the much less hospitable environment of Vietnam. As a result it took longer for the US armed forces to develop appropriate methods of operation and leadership in Vietnam than in Korea, or than was taken by their ANZAC allies in Vietnam. During this learning process the operational challenges and the political context in both the United States and South Vietnam deteriorated, with the result that in some parts of the US Army leadership could not cope and authority collapsed.

But, to their credit, US military authorities recognised these problems and grappled with them in the 1970s and 1980s, evolving new approaches to the conduct of limited war. Although the Gulf War was anything but a protracted struggle, it was clear from the way that the United States responded that much had been learned from Vietnam. A clear sense of political purpose, and hence of military priorities, was developed. Lives were not put in jeopardy until massive superiority had been achieved in the theatre of combat, the co-operation and support of indigenous allies was fostered assiduously, and domestic and international political support were ensured, not least through obtaining legitimation by the United Nations. As a result, the leadership challenges which arose in the field were far less formidable than in Vietnam, although of course not negligible. Painful and frustrating experience in Korea and Vietnam had finally been turned to useful effect in modifying US operational thinking and methods.

Notes

1.   Colonel Harry G. Summers, *On Strategy*, Presidio, Novato CA (1982).

2.   Norman B. Hannah, *The Key to Failure. Laos and the Vietnam War,* Madision, Lanham MD (1987).

COALITION
COMMAND IN THE
GULF WAR

by Stephen Badsey

On 6 August 1990 a delegation led by US Secretary of Defense Richard B. 'Dick' Cheney, and including the Commander-in-Chief (CINC) of US Armed Forces Central Command (CENTCOM) General H. Norman Schwarzkopf, flew to Riyadh to secure the agreement of HM King Fahd bin Abd al-Aziz of Saudi Arabia that CENTCOM forces could be sent to protect his country, under Operation DESERT SHIELD, in response to the Iraqi invasion of Kuwait four days earlier. British Prime Minister Margaret Thatcher, in the United States at the start of the crisis, had already pledged her country's support to the Americans, and troops from Egypt, Syria and the countries of the Gulf Co-operation Council (GCC) were also offered to Saudi Arabia as the start of one of the largest military coalitions in history. In mounting Operation DESERT STORM, the armed liberation of Kuwait which took place five months later, the coalition against Iraq received assistance from 46 countries, or nearly a quarter of the world's sovereign states. Of these, 29 countries provided armed forces which served within the Persian Gulf region, although the United States itself contributed almost two-thirds of the 800,000 troops involved. [1]

With its headquarters at MacDill Air Force Base near Tampa in Florida, CENTCOM was never intended to fight a war against Iraq. Created in 1979 as the Rapid Deployment Joint Task Force in response to the overthrow of the Shah of Iran, it was upgraded in January 1983 to become one of the nine US Armed Forces Commands. Its improbable function was to protect the oil-rich countries of the Persian Gulf by defending northern Iran against a Soviet attack, despite the United States having no troops based in this highly sensitive part of the world, and no formal military agreements with any of its governments. Throughout the 1980s, American sales and stockpiling of arms and equipment in the region, and tentative discussions with Saudi Arabia, helped make CENTCOM's mission a little more realistic; and on his appointment as CINCENT (pronounced 'sink-scent') in 1988 Schwarzkopf re-evaluated its plans in the face of a possible Iraqi threat. When the invasion came a CENTCOM plan, designated as Operations Plan 90-1002 *Defense of the Arabian Peninsula*, at least existed to give President George Bush his military option.

As General Colin L. Powell, Chairman of the Joint Chiefs of Staff (JCS) during the Gulf War, expressed it, 'Unleashing the American military leviathan is an awesome enterprise.'[2] Any action taken against Iraq would be a compromise between the needs of the specific crisis and the immense complexity of late-twentieth century industrialised warfare as practised by the United States. Like all the US Armed Forces Commands, CENTCOM was the military equivalent of a large late-capitalist American corporation: bureaucratic, impersonal, and heavily dependent upon institutional procedures and structures. The tradition of impersonal or indirect command was so well established that Schwarzkopf in his memoirs describes a personal pledge or commitment as something peculiar to Arab society. When he extracted such a pledge in writing from his logistics chief, Major General William 'Gus' Pagonis, that the critical ground forces movement of the campaign, the projection of both US VII and XVIII Corps into the desert to the west of the main Iraqi positions, could be accomplished in the allotted timescale of 30 days from the start of the coalition air offensive, this was by no means a friendly gesture.

Since the late 1940s, one of the more bizarre effects of the Cold War on the United States had been to freeze most of its institutional military thinking about warfare. Bigger and more expensive versions of the successful weapons of the Second World War, such as the tank, the heavy bomber and the aircraft carrier, remained central to ideas about war, with 'battle' envisaged very much as if that war had never ended. New technological developments, including thermonuclear weapons, were all absorbed into the old paradigm, to which the overwhelming majority of the world's wars bore increasingly little resemblance. When troubled to defend their thinking on this matter, commanders of the American-dominated North Atlantic Treaty Organisation (NATO) did so by the Strangelovian argument that they were preparing for a war against the Soviet Union which was made impossible by them preparing for it. Their critics dismissed the whole edifice as a dreamworld in which otherwise largely useless armed forces practiced 'make-believe war' for the benefit only of themselves and arms manufacturers.

In this sense, the Gulf War became the war that the US Armed Forces (and some of their NATO partners) had to fight. The Iraqi annexation of Kuwait, announced on 8 August just as DESERT SHIELD began, was the first occasion in history that a member country of the United Nations had sought to deprive a fellow member of its existence, and a clear case of international aggression almost unsullied by intra-state issues. The end of the Cold War also freed the United States and NATO to use against Iraq the armed forces and supplies which they had prepared and stockpiled for decades. The Gulf War would test – perhaps for the first and last time – how well the forces created and trained to fight the Third World War would have performed. The view of at least some British officers (and doubtless their American colleagues) was that:

> The Gulf War was just what the Army needed to show that it still had a vital role, and persuade politicians not to extract too large a 'peace dividend' from the changes in Europe.[3]

The era of 'make believe war' had also seen a vast expansion in military communications and a specialist vocabulary to go with them. By the Gulf War, military terminology had developed to the point that entire dictionaries were being published to list the acronyms and expressions in use, while reconciling the jargon of one service or country with that of another formed a considerable part of NATO's workload. Even the distinction between 'command' and 'control' had become the jargon term 'C3I' (command, control, communications, intelligence). During the Gulf War many American military commanders discovered that they scarcely had a language in common with their own people, and were ruthlessly satirised for the use of Orwellian 'briefingspeak'. [4] General Schwarzkopf's ability to speak recognisably normal American when required was a considerable factor in his favour as a commander, while his lapses into military jargon usually signalled a deliberate intent to obfuscate. Both traits were displayed by Schwarzkopf with consummate skill at his famous Riyadh press conference ('the mother of all briefings') on 27 February 1991 to announce the imminent and successful end of the war.

Although swollen almost beyond practical use by social and institutional pressures, this arcane military language still retained something of its original function. Ironically, this was the need to convey meaning as briefly as possible and without misunderstanding in the discussion and transmission of military orders. So a considerable part of command and staff training consisted of mastering the distinction between such terms as 'airborne' and 'airmobile', or between TACON (tactical control) and OPCON (operational control). These issues and distinctions, and the establishment of a common military language within the coalition, were of a critical importance to CENTCOM which outsiders found hard to grasp.

By the time of the Gulf War an American warfighting doctrine had been devised to make maximum possible use of communications technology and the jargon which went with it, while allowing for the inevitable problems and breakdowns. The CENTCOM commanders did not simply *use* communications, any more than a car just uses its engine. American forces and the means to command them were organised and constructed around communications systems developed since the Vietnam era, including some extremely sophisticated offshoots of the 'Star Wars' Strategic Defense Initiative (SDI) programme of the 1980s. Among the more successful were the electronics systems mounted in converted aircraft such as the E-3A/B Sentry AWACS (Airborne Warning and Control System) and the E-8 J-Stars (Joint Surveillance and Target Attack Radar System) which between them could 'see' and report on Iraqi forces on the ground or in the air hundreds of kilometres behind the front lines and control friendly forces against them. This was first demonstrated at what became known as the battle of al-Khafji, an attempted Iraqi incursion into Saudi territory on 29-31 January that was in fact only part of a much larger attack of at least divisional size, which was engaged and defeated before it could cross the Iraqi front line.

The principal American means of communication, other than at very short range, was by satellite relay. The US Defense Satellite Communications Systems provided three-quarters of the theatre-wide communications net, the rest coming largely from commercial satellites. In Washington the Military Intelligence Board convened to ensure co-ordination between the National Security Agency (NSA), the Defense Intelligence Agency, and the service intelligence organisations, and to act as the link with CENTCOM intelligence. In September the NSA compiled and distributed 'Joint Communications Electronics Operating Instructions' providing information required to operate over 10,000 different radio nets. Even so, with American forces using three generations of tactical communications systems, some of them incompatible with others, simply being able to talk to itself was both a major problem and a major achievement for the coalition.

The most important new communications invention in assisting coalition command and control was a relatively cheap and reliable system which, far from being secret, was available commercially. This was the NAVSTAR Global Positioning System, which by means of a small receiver linked to a signal from an orbiting satellite allowed commanders to know where they were to within a few hundred yards even in featureless desert. The single biggest difference in command between the Gulf War and all previous wars was that this was the first army in history whose commanders did not have to devote most of their time to working out where on earth they and their men actually were. [5]

The US Army doctrinal manual *FM 100-5 AirLand Battle* of 1982 (slightly revised in 1986 and also accepted by the US Air Force as part of its doctrine in 1984) emphasised 'depth, agility, initiative and synchronisation' as its key attributes, with similar ideas expressed in the equivalent US Marine Corps doctrine *Warfighting*. This included the adoption into *AirLand Battle* of a German command style known as *Auftragstaktik* under the name of 'Mission Oriented Command', the basis of which was that, given a common doctrine and an understanding of their overall mission, subordinate commanders would know what action to take without detailed orders being issued. This kind of warfare could not be, and was not meant to be, precisely controlled, and one of the skills of higher command was interpreting and assessing confused and contradictory reports. Although most commanders saw this confusion as part of the Clausewitzian friction of war, Schwarzkopf took a very firm line against what he saw as false reporting, and lower formation headquarters in the ground war were judged on their ability to avoid 'moonwalking' (from the contemporary dance step), meaning apparently moving backwards as they corrected their original reports of how far their forces had advanced.

By far the dominant reference for the United States as a country in the Gulf War was its own experience in the Vietnam War. An analysis of some 66,000 American national television, radio, newspaper and wire service stories on the war between August 1990 and February 1991 revealed that the word 'Vietnam' appeared 7,299 times, more than three times as often as the next most common term 'human shields'.[6] Two aspects of this preoccupation have made assessments of any aspect of American conduct of the Gulf War, and in particular the behaviour of its higher commanders, very problematical. One is the extreme care that the Americans took to create a false external image of their activities, based on the mistaken belief that open reporting would produce massive popular revulsion against the war. More than for any other war fought by the United States, historians have dealt from the start with tainted sources, to which the carefully written (or ghostwritten) memoirs of senior commanders do not add as much as might be hoped.

The second problem created by the legacy of Vietnam was that, having underestimated their enemy once, the Americans were determined not to do it again. There is evidence that the United States's command authorities disregarded advice from the Arab member countries of the coalition, and from Israel, on the likely performance of the Iraqi armed forces in favour of their own assessments. These in turn were not based on any real understanding of Iraq, but on a determination not to lose the war, and to minimise American casualties at all costs. The official Department of Defense assessment of its enemy, actually written a few months *after* the catastrophic defeat of Iraq, makes bizarre reading:

> Iraq possessed the fourth largest army in the world, an army hardened in long years of combat against Iran ... Saddam's forces possessed superb artillery, front-line T-72 tanks, modern MiG-29 aircraft, ballistic missiles, biological and chemical weapons and a vast and sophisticated air defense system. [7]

So politically important was victory to the Americans that, having spent decades planning to fight an enemy with the capabilities of the Soviet Union, that is

199

exactly what they did, disregarding the small point that the enemy was actually Iraq. It is a nice judgement whether this represents a major failure in American command, or a scrupulous following of political objectives by the military.

Two further lessons of Vietnam that the Americans brought to the Gulf War were potentially mutually incompatible. One was the need for unity of command. In the idealised structure taught in American (and other western) military academies, a clear political aim given by the command authority (in this case President Bush) should be translated by a military staff into a war plan, and then referred back for approval. Although this interaction has always been both complex and delicate, American views by the late 1980s were that politicians should avoid the temptation provided by communications technology to bypass their senior commanders and interfere directly with the actual fighting. There should be one hierarchy through which orders and reports were passed, from the front-line troops to the White House. The violation of this concept of 'unity of command' in the Vietnam War was something of which senior American officers were deeply critical, and President Bush promised repeatedly that it would not happen again.

So great were the problems of organising, controlling and commanding a late-twentieth century industrialised military bureaucracy that the Americans counted it as a major achievement to have largely achieved unity of command *among themselves*. Precise boundaries were drawn within the Persian Gulf region and designated as the CENTCOM AOR (area of responsibility). Once Schwarzkopf was installed as CINCENT, all American forces sent to the region automatically came under the control of his headquarters, although there was some friction between CENTCOM and intelligence gathering operations by organisations operating from the United States, particularly the Central Intelligence Agency. Later for the ground war, a second area was established as the KTO (Kuwaiti Theater of Operations – which actually included a large part of southern Iraq) outside which no major coalition land forces would venture.

The other major American lesson of Vietnam was the perceived need for the political support of a large alliance, based on their failure to attract more than a handful of allies in Vietnam compared to the large international alliance which had supported them in the Korean War. But while a coalition was seen as politically essential, the actual forces which it provided were judged as largely irrelevant in view of the massive American superiority in numbers and technology. In comparing ground forces with the Iraqis, most American accounts of the war counted only American (and sometimes French and British) formations. The political and military demands of coalition warfare were also potential threats both to the American command structure and to their approach to the war. General Douglas MacArthur, the first American commander of the

Korean War, on being reminded that his was a United Nations command, is supposed to have replied, 'That's entirely notional.' General Schwarzkopf could not afford to be so politically tactless.

Within the coalition as a whole, as one diplomatic American assessment put it, 'unity of effort' rather than 'unity of command' was achieved, reflecting the reality of compromise between the military textbook and the real world. [8] Co-operation between the NATO members of the coalition had developed for decades into a sophisticated balance of obligation and trust which largely made unity of command a reality. In comparison, the Saudi Arabian attitude as host country was almost a caricature of the idea (also taught in western military academies) that military force is an extension of state politics, and that states are governed by self-interest alone.

On 10 August the Saudis established a Joint Forces Command (JFC), headed by Lieutenant General HRH Prince Khaled bin Sultan, Commander of the Royal Saudi Air Defence Forces, with Major General Abd al-Aziz al-Shaikh as his deputy and Major General Talal al-Otaibi as his Chief of Staff. Although not the most senior member of the Saudi Higher Officers' Committee, Prince Khaled was the eldest son of the Saudi Minister for Defence and Aviation and Second Prime Minister, HRH Prince Sultan bin Abd al-Aziz, and also the brother of HRH Prince Bandur bin Sultan, the Saudi ambassador to Washington and principal link between President Bush and King Fahd. Prince Khaled was determined that the Saudi military forces should not be subordinated to purely American interests and the names of their leaders forgotten, like the South Koreans who had fought under MacArthur or the South Vietnamese under Westmoreland. 'My main concern, therefore,' he wrote, 'was to make sure that, in this conflict, there would be no supreme commander'.[9] To this end, Khaled insisted on the title of 'Commander of Joint Forces and Theater of Operations' (including command of land forces) for himself, in order to prevent the Americans claiming either title for Schwarzkopf. In American military terminology and command structure it was impossible for one individual to hold both posts. Only a personal intervention by Prince Sultan as late as 27 November got Khaled's position accepted even by other Saudi commanders, and Washington did not officially acknowledge his title until after the war was over, even blocking a Christmas message to American troops in which he made use of it.

While the Saudis were intent on not being dominated by the Americans, the idea that American forces should come under Saudi command was politically unrealistic as well as illegal in US law. The solution insisted upon by the Saudis was a 'parallel command' between CENTCOM and the JFC, whereby neither had command over the other, and each commanded its own troops side by side. To those who had seen the results of a disputed command structure in Vietnam, everything about 'parallel command' spoke of disaster. This was an important factor in the caution shown by the Americans. In a sense, they were more afraid of their coalition friends than of their Iraqi enemies.

TABLE 1: THE COALITION AGAINST IRAQ 1990 – 1991

	G	Gk	Gs	A	Ak	As	N	Ns	Na	T	Nr	M	F
(see key to symbols overleaf)													
USA	x			x			x	x	x	x	x	x	x
Saudi Arabia		x				x		x	x			x	x
OTHER NATO COUNTRIES													
Belgium								x	x	x	x	x	x
Canada			x	x				x	x			x	
Denmark								x					x
France	x			x				x	x			x	
Germany								x	x	x			x
Greece								x			x		
Italy				x				x	x	x	x	x	x
Luxembourg													x
Netherlands								x	x	x	x		x
Norway									x	x	x		
Portugal								x			x	x	
Spain								x		x	x	x	
Turkey										x	x		
UK	x			x			x	x	x		x	x	
OTHER GCC COUNTRIES													
Bahrain		x											x
Kuwait		x				x		x	x				x
Oman		x				x		x					x
Qatar		x											x
UAE		x				x		x					x
OTHER ARAB LEAGUE COUNTRIES													
Egypt		x							x				
Morocco			x										
Syria		x											
WARSAW PACT COUNTRIES													
Bulgaria													x
Czechoslovakia													x
Hungary													x
Poland									x				x
Romania												x	

	G	Gk	Gs	A	Ak	As	N	Ns	Na	T	Nr	M	F
(see key to symbols below)													

OTHER COUNTRIES

	G	Gk	Gs	A	Ak	As	N	Ns	Na	T	Nr	M	F
Afghanistan			X										
Argentina			X					X					
Australia								X				X	
Bangladesh			X									X	
Eire												X	
Finland													X
Hong Kong													X
Japan									X			X	X
New Zealand			X									X	
Niger			X										
Pakistan			X						X				
Philippines												X	
Senegal			X										
Sierra Leone												X	
Singapore												X	
South Korea												X	X
Sweden												X	

KEY TO SYMBOLS

G   Countries providing ground forces which entered Iraq and Kuwait during Operation DESERT STORM.

Gk Countries providing ground forces which entered Kuwait only during Operation DESERT STORM

Gs Countries providing ground forces which carried out defensive tasks in the CENTCOM AOR during Operations DESERT SHIELD and DESERT STORM

A   Countries providing air forces which attacked Iraq during Operation DESERT STORM.

Ak Countries providing air forces which attacked only Iraqi forces within Kuwait during Operation DESERT STORM.

As Countries providing air forces which carried out defensive tasks in the CENTCOM AOR during Operations DESERT SHIELD and DESERT STORM.

N   Countries providing naval forces which fought in direct support of Operation DESERT STORM.

Ns Countries providing naval forces within the CENTCOM AOR for Operations DESERT SHIELD and DESERT STORM for activities such as sanctions enforcement.

Na Countries providing naval forces (particularly minesweepers) within the CENTCOM AOR after the end of the Gulf War

T   NATO countries providing forces to guard Ireirlik airbase in Turkey during the Gulf War.

NR NATO countries providing forces for security within the NATO area during the Gulf War.

M Countries providing medical, humanitarian, practical or logistic aid within the CENTCOM AOR during or immediately after the Gulf War.

F Countries providing major financial assistance to the coalition forces either before, during or immediately after the Gulf War.

Notes to Table 1

1. The United States was also a member of NATO, and Saudi Arabia a member of GCC. France was strictly speaking not a member of NATO but of the North Atlantic Alliance.

2. Eire, which usually maintains a policy of neutrality, allowed American aircraft on the way to the Gulf to refuel at Shannon airport.

3. During the Gulf War Japan provided five C-130 Hercules transport aircraft to Jordan for humanitarian purposes. This was the first Japanese armed forces deployment (other than naval forces) outside Japan since the Second World War. Japan also provided minesweepers to help clear the Gulf after the war.

4. During the Gulf War US Air Force aircraft flew bombing raids against Iraq from Incirlik airbase in southern Turkey. In the first evr NATO operational deployment, as part of the NATA Allied Command Europe (ACE) Mobile Force or AMF, other NATO countries provided ground troops, missiles and aircraft to defend Incirlik against posssibe Iraqi counter-attack. Such an attack on Turkey as a NATO member would have, under the terms of the North Atlantic Alliance, brought the remaining members of NATO into the war against Iraq. This was also the first German armed forces deployment (other than naval forces within the NATO area) outside Germany since the Second World War.

In early August, Prince Khaled established his JFC headquarters in one of the sub-basements of the Saudi Ministry of Defence and Aviation (MODA) building in Riyadh. His two subordinate headquarters for DESERT SHIELD were Eastern Area Command (EAC) in King Fahd Military City at Dhahran, under Major General Salih al-Muhaya, and Northern Area Command (NAC) in King Khaled Military City at Hafr al-Batin, under Major General Abd al-Rahman al-Alkami. Of the two senior American commanders left behind when the Cheney mission departed, Lieutenant General Charles 'Chuck' Horner, commander of CENTAF (Central Command Air Force) established his own headquarters close to MODA in the nearby Royal Saudi Air Force HQ building. Horner was appointed Joint Forces Air Component Commander (JFACC) giving him authority over all coalition aircraft used in the region. The sensitive question of whether this placed Horner under Khaled was never probed to any depth, and certainly was not a factor in Horner's planning of the air campaign.

The other remaining senior American commander, Lieutenant General John Yeosock of ARCENT (Army Component Central Command, later also known as US Third Army) established CENTCOM Forward HQ one level down from Khaled's JFC HQ in the MODA building. Khaled and Yeosock also established the Coalition Coordination Communications and Integration Center, (which by a happy choice formed the acronym 'C3IC', both describing its function and disguising it from outsiders). Located both physically and organisationally between the JFC and CENTCOM headquarters in the MODA building, and managed for most of its existence by Major General Paul Schwarz and Brigadier General Abd al-Rahman al-Marshad, C3IC formed a clearing house for all liaison issues between the Americans and Khaled's forces.

On 26 August Schwarzkopf arrived in Riyadh, and with the transfer of authority from Yeosock the MODA sub-basement became CENTCOM Main HQ, run by its Chief of Staff, Major General Robert 'Bob' Johnston USMC. Schwarzkopf described the layout as consisting of:

> (An) intelligence center, a communications room, offices for the staff, a small auditorium that could seat forty for briefings, and most important, a war room that would be my command post if a war started. [10]

Schwarzkopf and Khaled both established their own offices and sleeping accommodation in the MODA building, and met daily on a regular basis. Yeosock moved to Third Army HQ in Eskan village, just outside Riyadh. The CENTCOM Rear HQ back at MacDill was left under Schwarzkopf's Deputy CINC, General Craven C. 'Buck' Rogers USAF.

Some American and British reports of the war portray JFC as a subordinate headquarters under CENTCOM. Although strictly speaking an error, this reflects both political and military reality, set against the constitutional fiction of the official command structure. The American solution to the problem of 'parallel command' was to exploit their own dominance of the coalition to ignore the issue whenever possible. Other than the original agreement to deploy American forces to Saudi Arabia, *all* critical command decisions pertaining to the war were taken unilaterally by the United States, within the American command system itself, including the decision in October 1990 to switch from a defensive to an offensive strategy requiring a doubling of American forces (which set the timetable for all subsequent events), the date and time for the air war to commence, the date and time of the ground war to liberate Kuwait, and the ceasefire decision to end the war. The general views of the more important coalition members might be canvassed beforehand, but unless there was a military reason (as with the British who took part in the first night's air attacks) they would be lucky to be told of a major military development in advance of the American media. As a small concession, in early December a 'Military Planning Group' of coalition officers was created in Riyadh to co-ordinate the final details of each country's role. CENTCOM's view of itself and its chain of command is well illustrated by an incident at the very start of the war in the early hours of 17 January, when Schwarzkopf called the war room staff together for a prayer by his chaplain, Colonel David Peterson, followed by a short speech from himself and the playing of a recording of the Lee Greenwood song 'God Bless the USA'. [11]

In constitutional theory the American chain of command ran from President Bush through Secretary Cheney directly to General Schwarzkopf as CINCENT. In practice the real command chain ran to Schwarzkopf from General Powell as Chairman of the JCS, who normally gave Schwarzkopf his orders. The position of the Chairman, and also of CINCs such as Schwarzkopf, had been strengthened by the 1986 Department of Defense Reorganisation Act (Goldwater-Nichols Act), which made Powell the principal military adviser to the President. Communications between Schwarzkopf and Powell in Washington took place several times a day by secure telephone and secure fax. 'Of course', Schwarzkopf added teasingly, 'it also meant there was no official record of many of our communications'. [12]

American political objectives during the crisis were set out by President Bush in a number of major speeches, together with twelve American-sponsored UN Security Council resolutions, culminating in the 'all necessary means' Resolution 678 of 29 November, setting a date of 15 January 1991 for Iraqi forces to withdraw unconditionally from Kuwait. Nevertheless, Schwarzkopf has criticised Bush and his advisers in Washington both for imposing too much direct political control at the wrong moments, and for failing to supply political leadership when required. In particular he complains in his memoirs of being forced to plan for the liberation of Kuwait from September to November in a political vacuum, and of being unable to secure a 'mission statement' from Washington. This document, a statement of the objectives which a higher command authority requires to be achieved by any military operation, was fundamental to the American command system. The mission statement issued by CENTCOM itself to its own lower formations could hardly have been faulted for clarity:

> Attack Iraqi political-military leadership and command-and-control; gain and maintain air superiority; sever Iraqi supply lines; destroy chemical, biological and nuclear capability; destroy Republican Guard forces in the Kuwaiti Theater; liberate Kuwait. [13]

General Powell has let it be known, diplomatically through an official biographer, that he regards Schwarzkopf's criticism of the Washington end of the command chain as inaccurate and unfair to himself. [14] But in a bureaucratised system, with a high political price to pay for failure, Schwarzkopf was not happy to proceed without a clear political context and written authority for his actions.

An important part of Schwarzkopf's command style was his ability to project an image of himself as a heroic leader. Reviving a tradition practised by many senior American generals in the Second World War, this cult of personality surrounding Schwarzkopf was useful in fostering a sense of common purpose between CENTCOM headquarters and the troops in the field. His frequent appearances in desert fatigues for his press conferences, crossing from an air-conditioned office far behind the front lines to the air-conditioned hotel ballroom that housed the Riyadh press centre, was an essential part of this process. Here – in media image – was a fighting man.

Particularly in the improvised conditions at the start of DESERT SHIELD, another critical function of the senior coalition commanders was that they possessed the authority to override their own military bureaucracy and take the necessary action. Not the least important of these actions was the authorisation of payment. Prince Khaled in his memoirs takes mild offence at Schwarzkopf for the American's description of his own position:

> (Khaled's) military credentials were nowhere near as important as his princely blood, since almost all power in Saudi Arabia resides in an inner circle of the royal family. Simply put, unlike the other generals, Khalid (sic) had the authority to write checks. [15]

Yet Khaled's own account opens with an episode in August when, faced with the unpreparedness of his country's northern defenses, he was able to beg his father for the equivalent of $5 million for the troops, saying that 'I did not want to have to go through military channels. There was no time for that.' [16]

Prince Khaled's memoirs are full of such well-bred but irritated corrections to Schwarzkopf or other American accounts of the war, claiming that sufficient credit has not been given to himself, his King or his countrymen in achieving victory by maintaining the coalition. His own view was unequivocal:

> Without Saudi Arabia, the Coalition could not have existed, Saudi Arabia was the host country for the Coalition, its pivot, its cement – and, by virtue of the powers conferred on me by Prince Sultan, who in turn received these powers from King Fahd, I was the man on the spot responsible for holding it together.[17]

Accounts based on American sources have Schwarzkopf displaying almost superhuman patience with Khaled, listening for hours while a man that he secretly despised as a pompous and arrogant amateur expounded on his grand theories of war, and managing to present the plan for DESERT STORM so skilfully that Khaled came away believing that it was his own idea. If so, then Schwarzkopf was only doing his job, and perhaps its most important part, in holding together a coalition that the Americans believed and the Iraqis hoped was in constant danger of fragmenting. 'Your Arab allies will desert you', Iraqi Foreign Minister Tariq Aziz had told US Secretary of State James Baker at their meeting in Geneva on 9 January, 'They will not kill other Arabs. Your alliance will crumble and you will be left lost in the desert.' [18] Given the massive disparity of force deployed against it, this was actually Iraq's best hope of avoiding defeat.

The one group against which Schwarzkopf could vent his anger and frustration was his own staff and subordinate commanders. It is claimed that he threatened to replace every one of his immediate subordinates at least once between August 1990 and March 1991. Given the pressure that Schwarzkopf faced this behaviour was understandable, but caused a strain as even senior officers became unwilling to voice disagreements or discuss problems with him. 'Nobody over there', General Powell was told after the fighting had started, 'is going to tell Norm Schwarzkopf he made a mistake.' [19] In November 1990 Lieutenant General Calvin Waller, an old colleague who had served with Schwarzkopf on several occasions, was sent out to CENTCOM headquarters with the position of Schwarzkopf's deputy (apparently with some reluctance and at Powell's insistence) to ease the situation between Schwarzkopf and his subordinates.

Other than the United States, the coalition against Iraq in its final form consisted of three main groups of countries: NATO members, Arab countries including Egypt and Syria, and a large number of other countries whose contributions were either indirect or militarily much less significant. Within the broad framework provided by the UN Security Council resolutions, countries were able to 'pick-and-mix' their exact contribution to the war against Iraq depending on their own political objectives, usually by means of bilateral agreements with Saudi Arabia. Roughly, naval forces represented the lowest political profile, followed by air forces and ground forces, but many countries contented themselves with supplying financial assistance, military assistance outside the region, or medical (or other specialist non-combatant) assistance. This help was by no means unimportant: the movement of US VII Corps from Germany to the Gulf would have been impossible within the allotted timescale without assistance within the NATO area from Germany, the Netherlands and Britain. For the war itself, including the United States, nineteen countries contributed naval forces, nine contributed air forces (five from NATO and four from the GCC) and eleven took some part in the ground war. The previous experience of the NATO countries in training together, standardisation of equipment and 'interoperability', particularly of communications systems, gave their forces much greater fighting value to the Americans than would otherwise have been the case.

Even so, given the extent, cost and sophistication of American technology there was real doubt that even Britain, anxious to prove itself as the United States' most loyal ally in the war, could match the same standard. Uniquely and with considerable effort, the British under Lieutenant General Sir Peter de la Billière had by January 1991 integrated themselves completely into the American command structure. As a former commander of the Special Air Service, de la Billière was also able to establish a particular niche for himself and his old regiment in supplementing the work of SOCCENT (Special Operations Component Central Command) commanded by Colonel Jesse Johnson.

Other than de la Billière, about a hundred British officers held positions within CENTCOM and the American command system. At least one of these officers was present in the CENTCOM war room round the clock, and de la Billière himself attended Schwarzkopf's daily briefings, sitting next to Schwarzkopf. One British officer, Lieutenant Colonel T. J. 'Tim' Sulivan, joined the elite team of four American majors and colonels from the School of Advanced Military Studies (SAMS) headed by Colonel Joseph H. Purvis and known to all as the 'Jedi Knights', requested by Schwarzkopf in October and responsible for the actual planning of the ground war. To aid his assimilation, Sulivan even abandoned his British uniform in favour of CENTCOM fatigues.[20]

Throughout both DESERT SHIELD and DESERT STORM, command and control of naval forces posed the least problem for the Americans. On 5 August, Vice Admiral Henry Mauz USN, commander of the already existing US Joint Task Force Middle East, was appointed to command NAVCENT (Navy Component Central Command) under Schwarzkopf, being superseded in October by Vice Admiral Stanley Arthur, commander of the US Seventh Fleet, who ran NAVCENT from his specialist command flagship USS *Blue Ridge*. NATO and Australian naval forces used standard NATO operating and signaling systems and found no difficulty in co-operation. During the war itself only American ships moved into the fighting zone, together with the British who provided minesweepers (known as mine countermeasures vessels or MCMVs). All coalition naval forces in the northern sector of the Gulf came under NAVCENT, while from 25 August until the end of the war of the southern sector came under the Western European Union, of which France held the rotating presidency. Naval and air forces from several NATO countries also provided security within the Mediterranean during the war in Operation SOUTHERN GUARD.

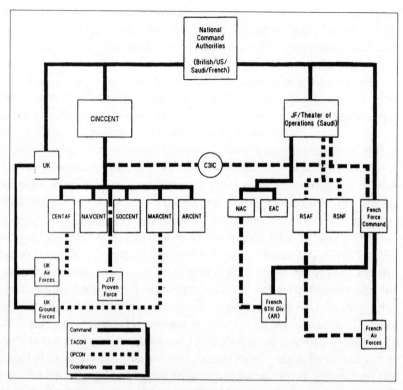

Figure 1: Coalition Command Relationships in Operation DESERT SHIELD.

The Americans also exercised virtually complete dominance over command of coalition air operations, partly in consequence of their superior technology, partly because of the political restrictions placed by some coalition governments on their use of air power, and partly through sheer numbers. US Navy aircraft alone numbered more than twice those of all other coalition national contingents put together. The plan for the air campaign, known to the US Air Force as Operation INSTANT THUNDER (a term disliked by Lieutenant General Horner), was drawn up by a team known as the Checkmate Committee under Colonel John A. Warden USAF, which first briefed Schwarzkopf at MacDill on 10 August.[21] While Warden directed the Washington end of INSTANT THUNDER, other Checkmate officers worked in Riyadh under his deputy, Lieutenant Colonel David Deptula USAF, who became CENTAF chief targeting planner under Brigadier General Buster C. Glosson USAF, the chief targeter. In November Prince Khaled, as an air defence specialist, was instrumental in instituting procedures to prevent coalition anti-aircraft defences attacking friendly aircraft by mistake, including a coalition 'Combat Reporting Center'. Together with plans to avoid coalition mid-air engagements or collisions

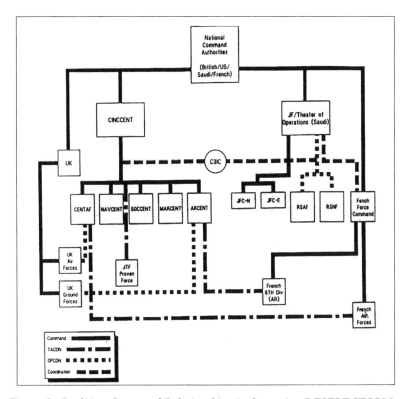

Figure 1: Coalition Command Relationships in Operation DESERT STORM.

this worked successfully, but the related problem of preventing coalition aircraft from attacking friendly ground forces was never completely solved, resulting in a number of deaths during the ground war.

The basis of the American air plan was the daily Air Tasking Order (ATO), each of which was a document the size of a telephone directory. Taking over a day to compile and about two hours to transmit, these were issued to units three days in advance, and obviously deprived the coalition of some flexibility in its use of airpower, although small changes even after the aircraft had taken off were possible. Lack of compatible communications between CENTCOM and the US Navy led to the ATOs being flown nightly from Riyadh to the command aircraft carries in the Red Sea and Persian Gulf on computer floppy disk, and then distributed among the ships by helicopter. Generally, both the US Navy and Marines preferred operating in areas designated by the ATOs as 'kill zones' open to all, and in direct tactical support of their own forces.

The main coalition problem was the command and control of ground forces, an area in which the United States could not exercise the same kind of absolute dominance if it wanted forces from other countries to take part. In the early stages of DESERT SHIELD, Prince Khaled's strategy in facing the threat of Iraqi attack was one of forward linear defence, motivated as much by political considerations as military ones. Khaled sought to avoid the problems of integrating into the JFC units of battalion size or less sent by GCC and other Islamic countries, by assigning them independent roles to protect locations close to the Saudi border with Kuwait and Iraq. Leaving weak and isolated positions as hostages to fortune in this manner was both contrary to American doctrine and anathema to Schwarzkopf, producing a dispute over strategy within the 'parallel command' which was never resolved, and which could have been very serious had the Iraqis attacked. After one last argument on 13 September, Schwarzkopf concluded that American forces were in themselves strong enough to stop an Iraqi attack, which itself appeared increasingly unlikely.

As the Americans moved to an offensive strategy they were particularly exercised by the role of the Arab contingents in DESERT STORM. At a CENTCOM 'Arab reaction seminar' on 2 October, Schwarzkopf concluded:

> Virtually *any* offensive would be acceptable as long as two conditions were met: first, Arab forces in significant numbers had to fight on our side; second, we had to win... (In) any ground war against Iraq, I told my staff, Arab forces must be the ones to liberate Kuwait City. [22]

The deployment of Third Army westwards once DESERT STORM began only served to expose further the problems of the 'parallel command'. The initial attack into Kuwait was to be mounted by MARCENT (Marine Component Central Command, under Lieutenant General Walter Boomer), which as Third Army moved out of the JFC area was left positioned between the forces of the two additional JFC operational headquarters created for DESERT STORM, JFC North under Saudi Major General Sulaiman al-Wuhayyib (including the strong Egyptian and Syrian contingents) and JFC East under Saudi Major General Sultan 'Adi al-Mutairi, so splitting Khaled's command in two. As with American political strategy, American operations only functioned by largely disregarding the presence of the JFC forces.

Understandably given their history, relations between the Americans and the Syrians were particularly poor, and a common American belief has persisted that Syrian troops refused to take part in the actual attack. Prince Khaled, whose own account rejects this, played no small part in acting as a cut-out between CENTCOM and the Syrians, and keeping them in the coalition. The French under Lieutenant General Michel Roquejoeffre also found it politically convenient to have their ground forces (chiefly the 6th Light Armoured Division *Daguet*) under JFC control during Operation DESERT SHIELD, transferring to CENTCOM for DESERT STORM.

For the ground war, which began on 24 February and ended four days later with a unilateral coalition ceasefire in the face of an Iraqi rout, Schwarzkopf and his CENTCOM staff are entitled to considerable credit for devising a plan which both played to the military strengths of each coalition member and fitted with its political position. The French were given a semi-independent role covering the western flank of the coalition attack into Iraq. The British, with compatible weapons and doctrines of manoeuvre war to the Americans, had their 1st Armoured Division fully integrated into US VII Corps, which would make the main assault. The two Egyptian and one Syrian divisions of JFC North were invited to perform a limited breakthrough of the Iraqi defences in support of the US Marines. Finally, had it been necessary to fight for Kuwait City, this would have been done by Arab troops, led by the Kuwaiti brigades of JFC North and JFC East themselves.

In conclusion, the greatest challenge faced by the American commanders in August 1990 was not the Iraqi enemy, but that of shaping their own forces and that of a growing coalition towards a victory that many who fought in the war five months later regarded as inevitable, once the more important battles within the coalition itself had been successfully managed and won. The American system was ill-suited to deal with allies who were not prepared to subordinate themselves (even temporarily) to American methods and interests, and seemed itself so bureaucratised as to be always on the verge of collapse under its own weight. Other alliance members faced the traditional difficulties of going to war as junior partners with a superpower. The 'parallel command' system, instituted by Saudi Arabia for political reasons, was later described by one critic as 'a jackass command organisation that would have earned any would-be senior officer a failing grade at any military staff course in the world'.[23] All this was made to work, and to fight a successful war, to the considerable credit of all those involved. As Prince Khaled told an American reporter, perhaps not entirely accurately, about the problems of the coalition command structure, 'The only two people who are not worried about it are General Schwarzkopf and me.'[24]

Notes

1. For general histories of the war see L. Freedman and E. Karsh, *The Gulf Conflict*, Faber and Faber, London (revised 1994); R. Atkinson, *Crusade*, HarperCollins, New York and London (1994); J. Pimlott and S. Badsey, *The Gulf War Assessed*, Arms and Armour, London (1992). See also Ghazi A. Algosaibi, *The Gulf Crisis, an Attempt to Understand*, Keegan Paul, London and New York (1993), for a careful, intelligent and diplomatic assessment from a Saudi perspective.

2. C. Powell with J. E. Persico, *A Soldier's Way*, p.467, Hutchinson, New York and London (1995) (US title, *My American Journey*); see also B. Woodward, *The Commanders*, pp. 273-277, Simon and Schuster, New York and London (1991).

3. M. A. Rice and A. J. Sammes, *Command and Control: Support Systems in the Gulf War*, p. 2, Brassey's, London (1994).

4. G. Black, Briefingspeak, editorial in *The Nation*, 11 March 1991, reprinted in M.L. Sifry and C. Cerf, *The Gulf War Reader*, pp. 389-391, Times Books/Random House, New York and Toronto (1991). See also N. Augustine, *Augustine's Laws*, pp. 29-36, AIAA. New York (1983).

5. *Conduct of the Persian Gulf Conflict, an Interim Report to Congress*, p. 15-3, Department of Defense, Washington (1991). A.D. Campen, *The First Information War*, passim, AFCEA, Fairfax VA (1992).

6. E. E. Dennis *et al.*, *The Media at War. The Press and the Persian Gulf Conflict*, pp. 41-42, Gannett Foundation, New York (1991).

7. *Conduct of the Persian Gulf Conflict, an Interim Report to Congress*, p. I-1.

8. J. McCausland, The Gulf Conflict: A Military Analysis, *Adelphi Papers* Number 282, p.56, IISS/Brassey's, London (1993).

9. HRH General Khaled bin Sultan with P. Seale, *Desert Warrior*, p. 37, HarperCollins, London (1995). Note that many other accounts give Prince Khaled's name, and that of locations such as King Khaled Military City, as 'Khalid'.

10. H. N. Schwarzkopf with P. Petrie, *It Doesn't Take a Hero*, p. 331, Bantam, London and New York (1992).

11. Atkinson, *Crusade*, p. 222; B. Brown and D, Shukman, *All Necessary Means*, p. 32, BBC Books, London (1991).

12. Schwarzkopf with Petrie, *It Doesn't Take a Hero*, p. 325; Powell with Persico, *A Soldier's Way*, pp. 483, 505.

13. Atkinson, *Crusade*, p. 21.

14. D, Roth, *Sacred Honor*, pp. 198-199, HarperCollins, New York and London (1993).

15. Schwarzkopf with Petrie, *It Doesn't Take a Hero*, p. 330; Khaled with Seale, *Desert Warrior*, pp. 31-32.

16. Khaled with Seale, *Desert Warrior*, p. 13.

17. Ibid. p. 217.

18. B. W. Watson *et al.*, *Military Lessons of the Gulf War,* p. 272, Praesidio/Greenhill, Novato CA and London (revised 1993).

19. Powell with Persico, *A Soldier's Way*, p. 510.

20. Atkinson, *Crusade*, p. 108; Brown and Shukman, *All Necessary Means*, pp. 81-85; P. de la Billière, The Gulf Conflict: Planning and Execution, in *Command in War: Gulf Operations*, p.13, Whitehall Papers Series, RUSI, London (1992); P. de la Billière, *Storm Command*, pp. 90-92, HarperCollins, London (1992).

21. For the conceptual basis or commanding and controlling the Gulf air campaign see J.A. Warden, *The Air Campaign: Planning for Combat*, Pergamon-Brassey, Washington (1989).

22. Schwarzkopf with Petrie, *It Doesn't Take a Hero*, p. 355.

23. Anonymous review of *Desert Warrior* in *The Economist*, 13 May 1995 p. 134.

24. Khaled with Seale, *Desert Warrior*, p. 194.

INDEX